CHARLIE 1/5 CAV

CHARLIE 1/5 CAV

An Airmobile Infantry Company's 67 Months in Vietnam

Steve Hassett

Deeds Publishing | Athens

Published by Deeds Publishing in Athens, GA
www.deedspublishing.com

Printed in The United States of America

Cover design by Mark Babcock.

ISBN 978-1-950794-79-9T

Books are available in quantity for promotional or premium use. For information, email info@deedspublishing.com.

First Edition, 2022

10 9 8 7 6 5 4 3 2 1

To the men who made the history: all those, alive and dead, who were assigned or attached to Charlie Company, 1/5th Cavalry in Vietnam. And to the other veterans of Vietnam: our wives, partners and best friends who nurtured and supported us for all the years since.

Contents

Foreword xi

Introduction xv

Part 1: The First Year — Securing the Central Highlands 1
Building A Base Camp 3
First Combat Operations 7
The 1st Cavalry Goes to Bong Son 15
To the Border and Back Again 25
Battle on Hill 534 33

Part 2: Rice Paddies and Mountains — Pacification in Bong Son 39
Operation Thayer 41
Dining in the Field 49
Operation Irving 55
Pinned Down on a Hillside 61
A Very Lost Patrol 67
Into the Ia Drang Valley 71
Standdown in Base Camp 89
LZ Bird 95
Operations Thayer II and Pershing 103
Battle on the Bong Son Plains 109
Side Trip to I Corps 117

Our Own Worst Enemy 125
Long Hot Days and Booby Traps 131
Firefight in the 506 Valley 139
Last Months in Binh Dinh Province 147
Battle on the Coast 153

Part 3: Operations in I Corps, 1968 **163**
North to the DMZ 165
The Battle for Quang Tri City 171
Rain, Cold and Short Rations 177
Utah Beach and the Street Without Joy 179
Operation Pegasus 187
Top Fowler's Last Patrol 195
Battle in the Sand 199
A New Normal 217
Grinding it Out 229

Part 4: Cavalry Screen on the Cambodian Border **239**
New War, New Mission 241
The New Area of Operations 245
Firefights Out of LZ Eleanor 249
Battle in the Rubber Plantation 257
LZ Dolly 261
Pinned Down at a Bunker Complex 267

Transitions   273
Buying Time   283
LZ Jerri   289
Meeting Engagement in the Jungle   297
Year Five and No End in Sight   303
Pacification in the Villages   309
Crisis and Opportunity in Cambodia   313
Into Cambodia   319
Winding Down   333

Photographs   **347**

Part 5: Charlie Company — A Day in The Life **365**

Afterword   **387**

Acknowledgements   **395**

Bibliography and Map References: **397**

Map References   **403**

About the Author   **409**

Charlie Company Areas of Operation 1965-1971

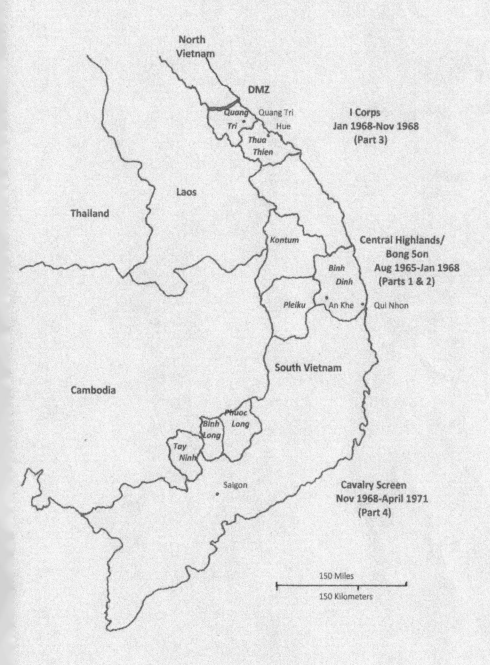

Foreword

This is the history of an infantry company in Vietnam, one of more than 300 Army and Marine infantry companies that served in that war. Charlie Company, 1st Battalion, 5th Cavalry, was a light infantry company, part of the Army's 1st Cavalry Division (Airmobile), the military's first unit specifically trained and equipped for helicopter warfare. Soldiers flying into battle and leaping from helicopters became one of the lasting images from Vietnam, but the reality was usually something quite different.

An infantry company usually had between 100 and 120 men, sometimes much less, sometimes a few more. Another 7 or 8 men were usually attached to a company as artillery forward observers and medics. There were four companies to a battalion and nine infantry battalions in the 1st Cavalry. To be light infantry meant to be in a battalion without tanks, armored personnel carriers, or heavy trucks, a unit where a soldier carried everything he needed to survive in the field on his waist and back, often seventy or eighty pounds of weapons, ammo, grenades, rations and other gear.

To be airmobile meant helicopters: different kinds and sizes, light scout choppers looking for trouble, rocket firing gunships and Aerial Rocket Artillery (ARA) choppers, 'dust-off' choppers with a large red cross darting into a landing zone to pick up wounded troopers, large choppers carrying artillery pieces to a mountaintop firebase. Most of all it meant 'Hueys', the workhorse of the war and the cavalry mount of the 1st Cavalry Division.

A Huey could carry six or seven fully equipped men on an air assault, fly in resupply and replacements to remote landing zones, and haul out dead soldiers wrapped in ponchos or body bags. But mainly it seemed Hueys would carry Charlie Company to a destination picked on a map by a battalion or brigade commander for reasons unknown to the men on the choppers. And once on the ground the men would walk, or "hump" as they called it, sometimes for days in mountains or triple-canopy jungle, through swamps or rice paddies, following a road or cutting a trail, just as infantrymen have done in wars since ancient despots raised their first armies.

Charlie Company was in Vietnam longer than all but about twenty other infantry companies and served in more areas of that country than most other companies, encountering different terrain and circumstances, and engaging in missions that reflected the changing nature and the larger political backdrop of the war. But its experience is no different than that of all the other companies that fought in Vietnam: stifling heat, mud, boredom, rain, mind-numbing exhaustion, more rain, comradeship, cold, fear, isolation, confusion, and too much death.

There are two aspects to this history. First is the overview and chronological history—the operations, troop movements, new missions, political maneuverings, and societal changes that provide the where and when and sometimes the what for Charlie Company's place in the war. I take full responsibility for this and any conclusions and speculations I've made in these pages. But this aspect is just a dry framework for what gives this history its true meaning: the stories shared by men who served in the company, sometimes in letters written the day after a firefight but more often in memories that have percolated and endured for half a century.

This history is theirs. They have kept their stories for many reasons, or rather their stories have kept them whether they wanted to hold on to them or not. In sharing them now, they do so largely so their children and grandchildren may understand what they once endured and did when they were young. But it is more than their personal experience. One former medic said that the value of the history to him will be to show his children "what the Company of heroes I served with did for several years."

It is an old cliché that a soldier in combat only sees and understands what is happening within a few feet of either side of him. Some of the recollections in this history may seem contradictory, but they are all true. They are what the men who relate them experienced, felt, and remembered. But for every story here, there are hundreds missing and untold.

It would be impossible to get a definitive count of how many men served in Charlie Company in Vietnam. Some were in the company only a week or two; one man died about two hours after arriving in the field as a replacement. Others—a relative handful—served their full twelve months in the field before rotating home. In between, men died, were wounded, caught malaria, got injured, got a job in the rear, or for scores of other reasons served less than a year with the company. A rough estimate is that as many as 1,700 men served in or with Charlie Company in its 67 months in Vietnam. The stories here come largely from Charlie Company veterans who attend yearly reunions or are on a contact list compiled over the years, a small portion of the men who passed through the company.

Hundreds of men who served with Charlie Company were African American. For the most part, they haven't joined veterans' organizations or attended company reunions and their voices and perspectives remain unknown and are missing here. Likewise, an unknown number were Hispanic and Native American and their voices too are mostly missing. Then there are men who want nothing to do with reunions or war stories or dwelling on long past events and feelings, who try not to remember with varying degrees of success. Above all, there are the men who died, in the war and in the decades since, whose stories will never be told. Hopefully the history and stories here are faithful to their experience.

Novelist Tim O'Brien, an infantry veteran himself, wrote this about the remembrance of war and the stories we tell:

And sometimes remembering will lead to a story, which makes it forever. That's what stories are for. Stories are for joining the past to the future. Stories are for those late hours in the night when you can't remember how you got from where you were to where you are. Stories are for eternity, when memory is erased, when there is nothing to remember except the story.

Introduction

By early 1965, the U.S. had been providing military support to the South Vietnamese government for years. Despite all the Special Forces teams, advisors to South Vietnamese army (ARVN) units, helicopter units, direct air support, and other assistance, the situation in Vietnam was deteriorating. The Saigon government was unstable, with frequent military coups. The Viet Cong were attacking ARVN units and outposts with battalion sized units, well equipped regiments of the North Vietnamese Army (NVA) were starting to infiltrate down the Ho Chi Minh Trail in Laos and Cambodia, and attacks on U.S. support units were gaining in intensity.

In March 1965, the first U.S. combat unit—a battalion of Marines—was ordered to Vietnam. They were followed over the next few months by the 173rd Airborne Brigade and a brigade each from the 101st Airborne Division and the 1st Infantry Division, seven battalions in all, as well as more battalions of Marines. But the next unit to be ordered to go was unique: the 1st Cavalry Division (Airmobile) was created specifically for the war in Vietnam and was the first full Army division to deploy to the war zone.

The Army had been working to develop an airmobile capability for almost two years, starting with the activation of the 11th Air Assault Division (Test) in early 1963. Initially training in the Carolinas and at Fort Benning, Georgia with three airborne battalions and newly created aviation units, the 11th Air Assault almost doubled in size in mid-1964 when three battalions from the 2nd Infantry Division were attached to it.

On June 16, 1965, Secretary of Defense Robert McNamara announced in a press conference that the Army was activating an airmobile division and that it would be "combat ready in eight weeks." He also said the new division would be called the 1st Cavalry Division, which at that time was an infantry division stationed on South Korea's DMZ.

On July 3, 1965, a change of colors ceremony was held at Fort Benning where the colors and regimental lineages of the 1st Cavalry Division were assigned to the newly formed airmobile division and the colors of the 2nd Infantry Division were transferred to the former 1st Cavalry in South Korea. On that day, Charlie Company of the 1st Battalion, 38th Infantry became Charlie Company of the 1st Battalion, 5th Cavalry (1/5th).[1]

The 5th Cavalry was first formed in 1855 as the U.S. Army's 2nd Cavalry Regiment. It's second commanding officer was Lieutenant Colonel Robert E. Lee. It was renamed the 5th Cavalry Regiment in 1861 and fought for the Union in the Civil War. Over the next 50 years, the 5th Cavalry fought in Indian

---

1. The 38th Infantry Regiment was first formed in the Civil War in 1864 as the 38th U.S. Colored Infantry Regiment. It was reactivated in 1917 and fought in France in World War I as part of the 3rd Infantry Division. There it got the nickname "Rock of the Marne" for its defense of positions on the Marne River during a major German offensive. In World War II, it again fought in France and Germany as part of the 2nd Infantry Division. Currently the 1/38th Infantry is part of the 1st Stryker Brigade Combat Team, part of the 4th Infantry Division at Fort Carson, Colorado.

Wars in the West, in Puerto Rico during the Spanish-America-ca War, against guerillas in the Philippine Islands from 1901 to 1903, and in the Mexican Punitive Expedition against Pancho Villa in 1917.

In 1922, the 5th Cavalry became one of the regiments of the newly formed 1st Cavalry Division. In World War II the division was converted to infantry and fought the Japanese Army in the Admiralty Islands and the Philippines. It remained in Asia after the war, first serving as part of the occupation forces in Japan and then in the Korean War from 1950 to 1953. In a reorganization in the late 1950's, the Army eliminated regiments as a specific type of unit. In the infantry, battalions retained their regimental names to preserve the lineage and heritage of those who served in their predecessor units.

The 1/5th, along with the newly designated 2/5th and 2/12th Cavalries, made up the new division's 2nd Brigade. The original three battalions of the 11th Air Assault were renamed the 1/8th, 2/8th and 1/12th Cavalries and became the 1st Brigade (Airborne) of the 1st Cavalry Division. The 3rd Brigade originally had only two battalions, the 1/7th and 2/7th Cavalries, but got a third battalion, the 5/7th Cavalry, in August 1966.

The new division was commanded by Major General Harry W. O. Kinnard, previously the Assistant Commander of the 101st Airborne Division. He had commanded a battalion of the 101st in World War II and jumped with it into Normandy on D-Day. Around Christmas of 1944, when the 101st was surrounded by German Panzer and Infantry divisions at Bastogne, it was his idea to respond to a German demand for surrender with one word: "Nuts". In 1963, Kinnard commanded the 11th Air Assault Division (Test) and was deeply involved in the development of airmobility doctrines and tactics. He wanted the entire 1st Cavalry to be airborne, but this was impossible with only a few weeks to go before deployment.

The ceremony over and their new 1st Cavalry patches hastily sewn on, the men returned to training for their imminent deployment. But hard training for combat sometimes has a price and Charlie Company had already paid it. A few weeks before the change of colors, members of the company were on four Hueys on a training mission. While flying over a swampy area in the rain, two of the choppers collided in mid-air and crashed, killing eighteen men, including both aircrews and much of the third platoon.

When Secretary of Defense McNamara made his announcement in mid-June, the division was ordered to achieve RED-CON-1 (Readiness Condition of highest priority) by July 28. On that date, President Lyndon Johnson told the nation, "I am today ordering the airmobile division to Vietnam." The 1st Cavalry's first mission would be to commence operations in the central highlands of South Vietnam, then considered the country's most vulnerable area.

In order to meet its readiness goals and deploy on schedule, the 1st Cavalry had to retain many men with only months left in their terms of enlistment. Some of them would begin rotating home after only a few months in the field. But this was a problem to be faced down the road and with the short-timers and men transferred to the division from other stateside units, the division was up to strength and ready for deployment by mid-August.

On August 14, 1965, an advance party of more than 1,000 officers and men left for Vietnam on C-130's, island hopping across the Pacific Ocean. The next day, the rest of the men and equipment of the division began loading on ships for the long journey by sea to Southeast Asia. Charlie Company was assigned to provide security for the advance party, making it the first infantry company of the 1st Cavalry Division (Airmobile) to put boots on the ground in Vietnam.

Part 1: The First Year — Securing the Central Highlands

Building A Base Camp

Charlie Company and the advance team landed in the coastal city of Nha Trang, once a resort for French colonial officials and plantation owners. They rested and drew equipment for a few days, and then flew by C-5 Caribous to a dirt air strip outside the village of An Khe, a small town on Highway 19 in the central highlands about halfway between the South China Sea and the Cambodian border. [Copies of the topographical maps used by the military in Vietnam can be found online. Coordinates and links for An Khe and many of the locations and events described in this history can be found at the back of this book.]

The company was led by Captain John Pope and First Sergeant Ralph Caveto and its callsign was "Roundcastle". One member of the company Command Post (CP) group was in Charlie Company for a second time. Sgt. Bob Parrish, the company's communications NCO, had previously been in Charlie 1/5th in the late 1950's on South Korea's DMZ.

An Khe would become the 1st Cavalry's base camp for almost two and a half years, but at the time it was an expanse of scrub brush, low jungle and tangled vines, thick clumps of bamboo, ant hills ten feet tall and patches of elephant grass six to eight feet high, with edges like a serrated knife. It was never officially stated by the Army but many of the men believed that the war would be won and they would be home in six months, a year at the most.

But first, the advance party set out to create a base for the Army's largest division from scratch. Just about everything was in short supply, even ammunition. Even while responsible for security, most of the men in Charlie Company had only a few rounds for each of their newly issued M-16's.

In addition to providing security and running short patrols, most of Charlie Company's time was spent clearing defensive perimeters for the base camp and developing the 'Golf Course', a large field that would hold over 400 helicopters from the division's aviation units—Chinooks, troop carrying Hueys, gunships and aerial rocket artillery choppers, and glass-domed observation and scout choppers. To preserve ground cover and keep the Golf Course from becoming a dustbowl in the dry season and a field of mud in the monsoon months, the work was done by hand with officers and men chopping brush with machetes and pulling grass and weeds on their hands and knees under the tropical sun.

The rest of the division, along with its choppers and equipment, began arriving by ship at the port of Qui Nhon in mid-September. After being flown by Chinooks over the coastal mountains, the other companies of the 1/5th Cav reunited with Charlie Company at it's An Khe base camp, now named Camp Radcliffe after a 1st Cavalry gunship pilot killed in August supporting a Marine operation.

Led by battalion commander Lieutenant Colonel (LTC) Frederick Ackerson, the companies set to work clearing brush and building bunkers for the 26 kilometer 'Green Line'—the perimeter around Camp Radcliffe—and setting up a battalion area on a small hill within the camp, soon known as 'Black Knight's Heights'. There was a large banyan tree on the hill which later was used to teach new replacements to rappel. In their spare time, Parrish, First Sergeant Caveto, and others built a club for the company at the foot of a dirt and mud company street, later named "Charlie's Hole". Caveto also started a contest with the platoon sergeant of the weapons platoon to see who could grow the largest handlebar mustache.

First Combat Operations

The following month, Charlie Company and the rest of the 1/5th Cav started their first combat operation in the field in the Vinh Thanh Valley, northeast of An Khe. It was a fertile rice growing area about twenty kilometers long and two to five kilometers wide under the total control of the Viet Cong. The operation was named 'Happy Valley' and that's what the area became known as for the rest of the division's time in the central highlands.

Contact was light and infrequent, mostly with local Viet Cong units, the "black pajama boys" as Bob Parrish called them. He recalls that the company had a few men wounded but no one killed on the operation. After clearing one village during the operation, Captain Pope told a reporter, "We learned a lot today—every man realized the importance of the mission." For a while at least, the main force Viet Cong units operating closer to the coast and the PAVN[2] units along the Cambodian and Laotian borders seemed to take a wait and see stance towards the division.

---

2. In 1965 and 66 North Vietnamese forces were generally called PAVN, short for People's Army of Vietnam. Between 1966 and 67 the Army also began referring to them as NVA or North Vietnamese Army.

Once in the field, the men adapted traditional cavalry terms to their role as airmobile infantry in Vietnam. To saddle up meant to put your own pack and gear on for an air assault or to hump in the hills. To mount up is to board a Huey and be one of six or seven men flying somewhere on a mission, maybe to a small clearing in the jungle or the edge of a village in one of the valleys. When they left their perimeters by foot or by chopper, the men called it "going into Indian county". This seemed especially true in the company's first year, when the battalions of the 1st Cavalry moved back and forth across the Central Highlands, trying to find and fight the VC and NVA in mountains and valleys where no U.S. unit had been before.

The 1/5th started November guarding positions and conducting patrols on Highway 19 around Deo Nang Pass, in the coastal mountains between An Khe and the port of Qui Nhon, as part of Operation Hitchhike. Qui Nhon was the main entry port for the hundreds of tons of supplies, munitions, and fuel the 1st Cavalry consumed every day. Supply convoys had been ambushed in the pass and the division had to secure the area. Charlie Company operated in the area for about two weeks until events across the country drew them in.

Operation Silver Bayonet in Pleiku Province marked the first large scale action against PAVN forces in the Vietnam War. In mid-October, the North Vietnamese B-3 Front opened a major dry-season offensive. Two regiments of the 1st PAVN Division crossed the border from Cambodia and attacked the Plei Me Special Forces Camp, about 45 kilometers southwest of Pleiku. The 1st Cavalry's 1st Brigade was sent to the area to assist ARVN forces trying to relieve Plei Me. After a few weeks, it was replaced by the 3rd Brigade, with its two battalions, the 1st and 2nd of the 7th Cavalry, joined by the 2/5th.

They were ordered to seek out and engage the PAVN regiments which had attacked Plei Me and which were thought to be regrouping a few kilometers from the Cambodian border in the remote and thickly forested Ia Drang valley. On November 14, 1965, three companies of the 1/7th air-assaulted into a football field sized clearing named LZ X-Ray where they were attacked by two battalions of PAVN, starting what would be one of the largest and deadliest battles of the Vietnam War.

The next day, the 1/5th was air-lifted on short notice to Pleiku Province to support the 3rd Brigade. Charlie Company secured LZ Falcon, an artillery firebase providing support to the 1/7th at LZ X-Ray and for the 2/7th and 2/5th, both of which were moving overland to relieve LZ X-Ray. By November 17, the fighting at X-Ray had died down and the battalions there dispersed: 1/7th, which had lost about half its force killed and wounded, was lifted out while the 2/5th was ordered to move overland to LZ Columbus, another artillery firebase, and the 2/7th to LZ Albany, a large clearing in the jungle about four kilometers away. LZ Falcon was to be shut down and Charlie Company would go to LZ Columbus to link up with the rest of the battalion and provide perimeter security.

That afternoon the 2/7th was ambushed by two battalions of PAVN as it approached LZ Albany and LZ Falcon remained open to provide fire support. Late the next day, November 18, the company was ordered to move to LZ Columbus but only the mortar platoon and a few men from the Company CP made it there that day. Sgt. Bob Parrish was directed to set up the CP while the rest of company loaded spent artillery casings onto Chinooks at LZ Falcon.

As scores of dead and wounded were being recovered from LZ Albany, another PAVN unit attacked LZ Columbus early in the evening with mortars and heavy machine guns raking the area. Parrish was stuck on the LZ hiding behind pallets with over a thousand rounds of 105 mm shells, not the safest place to be, when a Chinook approached for a landing. As he recalled:

> I tried to get him on the radio but didn't have the right frequency. The pilot was hit in the knee and managed to make a perfect landing but broke off the rear rotor. After dark, my company medic and I crawled over to the aircraft to render first aid, but they had already gotten out and we didn't know where they went until next morning.

That night some PAVN broke through the wire and in the firefight, Parrish and others had their M-16s jam, something that would be a recurring and often deadly problem for Charlie Company for the next two years. A cartridge would stick in the chamber and not eject—it could only be removed by ramming a cleaning rod down the barrel. When Charlie Company was issued their M-16s before deploying to Vietnam, the men were told the rifles didn't require much cleaning or maintenance. Only a few men had cleaning rods and they passed them back and forth during the fight. After LZ Columbus, Parrish sometimes carried a PAVN SKS carbine or AK-47 assault rifle when he could get ammo for it.

Eighteen men were killed at LZ Columbus, although none were from Charlie Company. Parrish remembers that the soldiers of the attacking force were professional, well trained, and well equipped. They were identified as the H15 VC Main Force Battalion, although they were mostly NVA, and they attacked the LZ in waves until about midnight when they withdrew, leaving behind twenty-seven dead. In the morning, the men on the

LZ thought some of the dead looked Chinese, not Vietnamese. A few bodies were sent back to the rear for examination, but they never heard anything about it.

A number of books and articles have been written about the battles at LZ X-Ray and LZ Albany, but there is rarely any mention of the attack on LZ Columbus. For some members of Charlie Company, it was their first fight—but not their last—with PAVN regulars.

The rest of the company got to LZ Columbus the next day. The major battles in the Ia Drang Valley had ended, but routine patrols went on. On November 20, Operation Silver Bayonet was replaced with Silver Bayonet 2 as the 3rd Brigade returned to An Khe and the 2nd Brigade took over. The next day, Charlie Company was sent on a company sized reconnaissance in force mission out of LZ Golf, looking for a PAVN radio transmitter. SP4 Oscar Cooper, 25 years old and from Bel Air, Maryland was killed on the mission, Charlie Company's first fatality in Vietnam.

Malaria was a major problem for the division in those early days. Mosquito nets and pills were in short supply and the Army had not yet started to spray infested areas with DDT. SP4 Charles Williams estimated that half of Charlie Company came down with malaria in its first months in-country. Like many men, Williams had only four months to go in the Army when he got to Vietnam. He was wounded by shrapnel from an air strike right after Cooper was killed. The wound was minor and he was sent back to the States for discharge, only to come down with a serious case of malaria a few weeks later. Another man, Sgt Robert Campbell, completed his term of service and returned to his wife and child in Philadelphia on November 25. Five days after returning home, he came down with a severe case of malaria he had most likely contacted in the Ia Drang Valley. Campbell died four days before Christmas.

The 1/5th returned to An Khe by convoy on November 26, coming through Mang Yang pass where a regimental sized unit of French troops had been ambushed and wiped out by the Viet Minh in 1954 in the last battle of the first Indochinese war. The battalion was assigned to the Green Line for two weeks, with Alpha, Bravo, and Charlie Companies rotating with two in the bunkers and towers of the line and one patrolling outside the wire.[3] The 1/5th, along with other battalions of the 1st Cavalry, received the Presidential Unit Citation (PUC) for its participation in Operation Silver Bayonet.

By now, Charlie company was already experiencing a manpower shortage. A number of men who had deployed with the company had started to rotate home for discharge even as the division took to the field. At one point in November, Charlie Company was down to about 35 men. Parrish felt the new replacements starting to arrive lacked the level of skill of the men leaving, many of whom had months of training in airmobile tactics in 1964 and 1965. PFC Joe Immler came to the company as a replacement in early December, never having been in a helicopter or seen or fired an M-16. Another new replacement was Corporal Butch Garner, one of a large group from the 82nd Airborne Division sent to the 1st Cavalry as replacements. A veteran of the Dominican Republic intervention, he became a squad leader and then a radio man.

On December 14, Charlie Company and the rest of the battalion left An Khe again for a short operation north of Highway 19 and west of the Kan Nak Special Forces Camp. After an initial air

---

3. When the 1 Cav deployed in 1965, each infantry battalion had 3 rifle companies (Alpha, Bravo, Charlie) and a support company (Delta). The 1/5 converted its Delta Company into a fourth rifle company in June 1966, the first battalion in the 1 Cavalry to do so.

assault, the company spent five days on the move through the jungle, setting up a new perimeter and getting resupply each evening. No contact was made in the operation and the company was back at 'Black Knight's Heights' by December 20 for a short stand-down.

The men of Charlie Company had their first Christmas dinner in Vietnam a day early as the 1/5th moved out again early on Christmas morning, back to the area of Deo Nang pass to provide security along Highway 19 between An Khe and Qui Nhon. The duty was uneventful and provided the battalion with a good chance to integrate new replacements into their platoons and squads. Air assaults and patrols conducted during the next week were as much training opportunities as combat operations.

A few days after New Year's, the company opened 1966 by being lifted back towards the Cambodian border for Operations Matador I and II. A Brigade of the 25th Infantry Division, newly arrived in Vietnam and based outside Pleiku, was starting an operation in the western highlands and the 1/5th would secure their base camp and be the standby Field Force reserve. On January 10, the battalion was released from reserve and flown to the Plei Djerang Special Forces Camp in northwestern Pleiku Province near where the Cambodian, Laotian, and Vietnamese borders meet in the remote Annamese Mountains.

The 1/5th secured the camp's airstrip for a few days and then air-assaulted into the Plei Trap Valley on the Cambodian border to conduct search and destroy missions with Special Forces CIDG units, recruited from local indigenous tribes.[4] Clearings in the area were small and sometimes obscured by the smoke from

---

4. Civilian Irregular Defense Group units were company sized or smaller units of paramilitary or militia soldiers equipped and led by US Army Special Forces Teams. Most were recruited from the indigenous hill tribes collectively known as 'Montagnards' and operated out of Special Forces camps along the Cambodian and Laotian borders.

artillery and rockets prepping the LZs. A number of men in the assault company were injured jumping from their choppers. Other than that, contact was light and after a week the battalion returned to An Khe to finish January manning the Green Line and running company sized sweeps outside the base camp's perimeter.

Captain Pope was a qualified helicopter pilot and, on some operations, he would somehow borrow an observation chopper and fly overhead to direct the company. Butch Garner and others would wear red bandanas folded and tied over the top of their helmets 'Mohawk' style so he could spot them from the air.

The 1st Cavalry Goes to Bong Son

In late January 1966, the 1st Cavalry opened Operation Masher in eastern Binh Dinh Province, the largest search and destroy mission of the Vietnam War at that time. Binh Dinh had a population of about 800,000 people, many of them concentrated in the highly productive coastal plains north of the coastal city and provincial capital of Qui Nhon. The province was considered a traditional Viet Cong stronghold and had been a base for the Vietminh in the war against the French from 1946 to 1954. In 1965, a CIA report concluded that Binh Dinh was "just about lost" to the communists and the South Vietnamese government had little presence outside of Qui Nhon and the surrounding area.

Over the next month, Charlie Company would be introduced to places they would return to repeatedly over the next two years. The Area of Operations for Operation Masher consisted of a narrow, heavily cultivated coastal plain with river valleys separated by ridges and low mountains reaching into the interior. The plain was bisected by the east-west Lai Giang River, with the rich rice fields north of it called the Bong Son Plains. The Lai Giang was in turn fed by two other rivers, the An Lao, flowing from the northwest through a long steep-sided valley of the same name, and the Kim Son, flowing from the southwest from the Suoi Ca Mountains.

In the mountains, the Kim Son River was fed by seven smaller streams, coming together in an area called the 'Crow's Foot' from its appearance on Army topographic maps. The Suoi Ca Mountains and An Lao Valley were mostly covered with triple canopy rain forest and fields of six to eight foot high elephant grass and provided excellent cover for VC and NVA base areas. There were also isolated outcrops of low mountains closer to the coast, some thickly overgrown and others bare and rocky with numerous caves. The whole area extended roughly thirty miles south to north and about twenty-five miles in from the South China Sea and came to be known to the men of the 1st Cavalry simply as 'Bong Son'.

For most of the next two years, the main opponent of the 1st Cavalry in eastern Binh Dinh would be the 3rd PAVN Division, also called the "Yellow Star" Division. It was formed around the 2nd VC Main Force regiment that had been fighting in the area since 1962, joined by the 12th and 22nd NVA regiments, recently infiltrated from the north, and supported by a network of regional and local self-defense units who fought as guerillas and provided support and replacements to the division.[5]

Even as the 1st Cavalry was ramping up to find and engage the VC and NVA, the Yellow Star division was preparing to go on the offensive. A Vietnamese history of the division written in 1989 summarized its mission:

---

5. In some reports the 12 NVA Regiment is identified as the 18 NVA Regiment. Its unclear if this was a mistake or if the regiment used both numbers to make it appear as if there were more NVA units in the area.

The Yellow Star Division and the 10th Regiment, in cooperation with local armed forces, would operate in northern Binh Dinh and Phu Yen, liberate the remaining district capitals, and district military headquarters, and stand ready to mount counterattacks to defeat the enemy's "search and destroy" operations. This meant that Military Region 5's 1966 Spring Campaign was targeted primarily against U.S. forces and that American troops were to be our principal battlefield opponents.[6]

Also participating in the operation were the ARVN 22nd Division, which had suffered heavy casualties from the 3rd PAVN in recent fighting, and the South Korean Capital Division, recently deployed to the Qui Nhon area. Ironically, Binh Dinh translates roughly in Vietnamese to 'pacified' or 'subjugated', something never quite achieved in operations there.

In the first two weeks of February, the 1/5th conducted search and destroy missions in and around the An Lao Valley, a Viet Cong stronghold since the French left in 1954. South Vietnamese forces had never operated there. In the weeks leading up to Operation Masher, several Special Forces Delta teams had been overrun and destroyed after being inserted into the valley on reconnaissance missions. Heavy monsoon rains delayed the start of operations, giving the VC and NVA time to move out of the valley. Charlie Company and other 2nd Brigade units made contact several times with small enemy units but mostly found abandoned campsites.

On February 14, 1966, the battalion closed on LZ Two Bits, an artillery firebase, for resupply before the next phase of the

---

6. *Grab Their Belts to Fight Them: The Viet Cong's Big Unit War Against the U.S.*, 1965-1966, Warren Wilkins, Naval Institute Press (2011).

operation. Operation Masher had been renamed White Wing by the Army after President Lyndon Johnson complained it sounded too aggressive, but this phase of the operation was designated Eagles Claw. Based on information developed during the interrogation of a captured VC battalion commander, the 1st Cavalry's 2nd Brigade was ordered to find and destroy VC and NVA base areas in the eastern Suoi Ca Mountains.

The target area, also called the Ho Son Mountains, was bordered by the Crow's Foot and Kim Son Valley to the west and northwest, the 506 Valley to the east, and the Suoi Ca Valley to the south. From these valleys, the mountains rose steeply from close to sea level to over 2000 feet in only a few miles and were densely jungled with limited clearings for landing zones. To the men who fought there, the area became known as the 'Iron Triangle' (not to be confused with the better known 'Iron Triangle' northwest of Saigon).

On February 16, after extensive preparatory fire from 105mm, 155mm, and 8" howitzers, 175mm cannon, and aerial rocket artillery and tactical airstrikes, the 1/5th air-assaulted into seven different LZs in the mountains. The 2/5th Cav set up blocking positions along the Crow's Foot and Kim Son Valley and on February 17, Charlie Company—along with Alpha and Bravo Companies—swept towards them, making heavy contact for the next four days. The fight was described by Shelby Stanton in his book *Anatomy of a Division: The 1st Cav in Vietnam*:

> Lieutenant Colonel Ackerson's battalion (1/5th Cav) led the attack but became deadlocked in combat against entrenched NVA defending the main camp. Frontal assaults against the formidable earthworks were mired in the thick tropical foliage as hidden machine gun bunkers built flush to the ground suddenly opened fire and cut apart

the advancing platoons. Casualties had to be left where they fell and fighting raged for days around the extensive jungle stronghold. The stalemate was punctuated by attacks and counterattacks on both sides. One of the most serious North Vietnamese sallies was defeated on 20 February after Company A's command post was nearly overrun by three separate assault waves. During this period, thirty-three separate battalion attacks, each supported by massive artillery and rocket expenditures, failed to breach the enemy bastion.

Rick Roy had joined the company in October 1965 and was now one of the company's RTOs. He recalls that the morning after they flew into the mountains, Charlie Company left their position on a knoll, passed through a small valley, and advanced up the next hill. As they moved up, the NVA opened fire from concealed positions and the company "caught hell." They pulled back and the firing died down, giving them the chance to carry out their wounded.

Roy and the company medic got word that one man was still missing, and they headed back up the hill to try to find him, covering each other as they moved from tree to tree. They found the wounded man far up the hill, close to the NVA bunkers—he had made it farther than anyone else in the company before being hit—and were able to carry him to safety. To their surprise, they weren't fired on by the NVA. It may be that the NVA were expecting an air strike and had moved deeper into their bunkers and tunnels.

As Roy and the medic moved to rejoin the company with the wounded man, air support did arrive in the form of 'Puff the Magic Dragon', an AC-47 gunship. Puffs were converted World War II cargo planes with 7.62mm 'mini-guns', each capable of firing 100 rounds per second, mounted to fire down from the side of the plane. Puff, also called 'Spooky' by troops, could fly in slow circles, and pour concentrated fire into enemy positions day or night. For men in a firefight, it was usually a welcome sight.

This time Puff overshot its target. Roy, the medic, and the wounded man were heading up a hill to rejoin the company when thousands of rounds hit the platoon on the trail ahead of them. Roy saw at least three or four men hit and thinks there may have been more. It was late in the day and the company wasn't able to get the casualties medevaced before night fell. Part of the company tried to take the wounded up a hill on litters improvised from ponchos and bamboo poles to a clearing but it was too dark and they had to pull back for fear of getting lost or running into an ambush.

After repeated assaults on the NVA positions, the battle wound down and Charlie Company had to account for everyone. Butch Garner found Sgt Freddie Green, another squad leader in his platoon:

> One of my sadder days. Not exactly sure how I got separated from the rest of the group at the time, but we were trying to account for wounded, MIAs, and equipment. I came across Freddie who was seated at the base of a tree, I thought he was taking a break. I nudged him with my foot and told him we needed to move out, that's when his head lopped off to the side and I saw a trickle of blood coming from a gunshot wound at the base of his throat. His eyes were still wide open, and I assume he never knew what hit him.
>
> Then I noticed his weapon and web gear with grenades were missing. Charlie had pretty much stripped him of anything useful. Being alone, I had no choice but to throw him over my shoulder in a fireman's carry and proceed up the side of the mountain to where choppers were coming in to take out the wounded. Freddie wasn't that big but he was solid and muscular. Luckily, other troopers saw

me struggling to get him up the side of the mountain and came down to my rescue. The incline was so steep we had to form a chain of two lines of troopers and drag poor Freddie by the wrists up to where the medics took over and eventually placed him in a body bag. Not even a week before he had shared a photo with me from his wallet of his wife and two little girls. He was so proud of his family.

Green was 23 years old and from Charlotte, NC. Three other members of Charlie Company killed in action between February 18th and 20th were SP4 Dominic Preira, 19, of Burlington, CT; PFC Ronald Kenny, 18, from Mount Airy, MD; and SSgt James Otis Allen, 27, of Indianapolis, IN.[7] Overall, the 2nd Brigade had 23 men killed and 106 wounded in the 'Iron Triangle'.

On February 21, 1966, all units were pulled out of the Kim Son Valley and two B-52 strikes hammered the area, but it appears the delay between the companies pulling out and the first B-52 strike gave the VC and NVA the chance to move to safer ground. On February 22, the 1/5th returned to the area with combat engineers to count bodies, recover weapons, and destroy VC/NVA bunkers and rice. Although 41 bodies were found, blood trails and discarded bandages and weapons indicated a much higher toll from the combat and air strikes. The 1st Cavalry estimated that between 300 and 400 VC/NVA were killed and as many as 900 wounded in that phase of Operation White Wing, most from the 2nd VC Main Force Regiment.

Few men in the field, from the newest PFC to company commanders, gave much credibility to casualty estimates after a major firefight. A lynchpin of the Army's tactics to win the war in 1966

---

7. Allen's death is listed as having occurred at Hon Cong Mountain, just outside of the Division's An Khe base camp, but this is likely a mistake.

was to beat the VC and NVA in a war of attrition—basically to kill more of them than they killed of us until they gave up. As a result, there was pressure at all levels of command to report high enemy casualty figures. Sometimes civilians killed in a crossfire were counted as dead VC. Other times the estimates seemed to be no more than wishful thinking. Clearly the VC and NVA suffered far more than the troopers of the 1st Cavalry in the Suoi Ca Mountains, but it remained a VC stronghold and the 2nd VC would go on the offensive again.

Charlie Company and the rest of the battalion rested for a few days and then on March 1, 1966, began the next segment of the operation, now renamed Operation Black Horse. Based on prisoner interrogations, the Army believed a NVA battalion was operating in the Cay Giap Mountains on the coast of the South China Sea. Bordered on the north by the Lai Giang River and Bong Son plains and on the south by the Dam Tra O lake and marshes, the Cay Giaps were rocky and densely overgrown. The 1/5th operated there for four days under the operational control of the 1st Brigade. There was no significant contact, and it appeared the intelligence was wrong or outdated and the operation was ended with the battalion returning to its base camp at An Khe on March 5.

During Operations Masher/White Wing and Black Horse, the Army relied on massive fire support to support the infantry units in the field. There were about 600 tactical air strikes called in—almost 20 a day—and another 171 B-52 strikes flown from bases in Guam and Thailand. About 132,000 artillery rounds were expended, roughly 100 rounds for each VC/NVA soldier claimed killed by the 1st Cavalry in the operations.

Over 27,000 Vietnamese civilians were driven from their

homes in the An Loa and Kim Son Valleys and other areas and relocated to refugee camps near Qui Nhon. The camps were run by the South Vietnamese government who were unprepared to deal with so many displaced civilians. Due to the combination of lack of resources, bureaucratic incompetence and indifference, and outright corruption, the conditions in the camps caused many people to lose faith in the government. When the operations ended, some drifted back to reclaim their ancestral homes and again provide support for the VC and NVA.

When Charlie Company wasn't searching for main force units in the mountains, it was sweeping through the villages and hamlets in the valleys and plains. It sometimes used a tactic that made some company members question whether they were really there to 'win the hearts and minds' of the Vietnamese people. Part of the company would move into an area and quietly set up outside a village without being detected. Later that day or the next morning, another platoon would noisily approach the village from the opposite side.

Upon seeing the Americans approaching, all the young men and teenage boys in the village would try to flee and would run right into the concealed unit where they would be taken prisoner. With their mothers and wives crying and protesting, they would be flown to the rear and turned over to the South Vietnamese for interrogation. If they weren't labeled as possible Viet Cong, they would be forcibly drafted into the South Vietnamese Army (ARVN). Butch Garner was a student of history and to him this seemed no different than the British forcibly impressing American sailors into their Navy in the early 1800's.

To the Border and Back Again

Upon their return to An Khe on March 5, 1966, Charlie Company and the rest of the battalion got a short standdown at base camp as well as a new battalion commander, LTC William Ray.[8] Sometime in March, Captain Pope completed his tour and was replaced by 1Lt Hansen, a Ranger trained officer who would be Charlie's acting CO for about two months.

After it's standdown, the battalion provided road security along Highway 19 in western Binh Dinh and eastern Pleiku Provinces for the remainder of March and the first part of April. Various stages of this mission were called Operations Lincoln, Hamilton II, and Buchanan II, but for the men of Charlie company it was mainly a boring routine of manning security checkpoints along the road, running short patrols during the day and setting up small ambushes at night.

In mid-April 1966, the 1st Cavalry developed intelligence that NVA units and a political headquarters had moved into an area east of Highway 14, which ran north from Pleiku to Kon-

---

8. An after-action report for Operation Eagles Claw states that LTC Ackerson was replaced by LTC Robert Lytle on 24 February. It is unclear why Lytle was replaced only two weeks later by LTC Ray.

tum, about twenty miles farther into the mountains. The 1/5th flew to Pleiku on April 21, 1966 to join operation Mosby II. The next day, elements of the battalion air-assaulted into LZ Ellwood to start a reconnaissance-in-force mission northeast of Pleiku. Charlie Company took small arms fire during the initial air assault with two men wounded but had no contact once it was on the ground. Platoon sized air-assaults were made over a wide area, in a tactic called 'fly-casting', hoping to draw the NVA out. Some of the platoons linked up with and conducted search and destroy sweeps with Special Forces CIDG units.

After a few days finding nothing and only encountering punji stakes, the battalion moved farther out, air-assaulting into an area called Plateau Gi, a relatively inaccessible region of high peaks and valleys on the border of Kontum and Binh Dinh Provinces, about thirty miles northeast of Pleiku. After a few days, the 1/5th was sent to the hamlet of Mang Buk, over twenty miles to the northwest to conduct company sized sweeps of the surrounding area while the rest of the 2nd Brigade continued to operate on the plateau. Aside from a small rice cache and some old weapons and gear, both phases of the operation turned up nothing and it was terminated on May 3, 1966. The 1/5th returned to An Khe and on May 5, 1966, was designated as the Division's reaction force.

The next day, Major General John Norton replaced MG Kinnard as division commander. Like Kinnard, he had led airborne units in World War II and was a qualified aviator, a requirement for all commanders of the 1st Cavalry. He had also been deeply involved in the development of airmobile tactics and doctrine in the years leading up to the formation of the division.

Charlie Company and the rest of the battalion were called up to return to Bong Son for Operation Davy Crockett. The 1st

Cavalry's 3rd Brigade had been deployed to the Bong Son plains after the division developed intelligence that the 12th and 22nd NVA Regiments were operating there, and the 1/5th was sent to join the 3rd Brigade for the operation. In one and a half hours, the entire battalion was assembled at the airstrip in An Khe, ready to move. The battalion flew to LZ Dog and on the morning of May 7, 1966, air-assaulted into four LZs on the northern edge of the Bong Son plains to cut off possible enemy escape routes through the mountains into Quang Ngai Province to the north.

No significant contact was made. It appeared the NVA had moved out of the area, so the focus of the operation turned back to the Kim Son Valley and Suoi Ca Mountains. Starting on May 11, 1966, the battalion conducted air-assaults and company sized sweeps in the Suoi Ca Valley, on the southern edge of the Iron Triangle, making only light contact. Joe Immler remembers the company going back into some of the same spots they had been to only a month or two before. One day they shot a sniper out of the same tree they had taken sniper fire from on an earlier operation.

On May 15, 1966, Operation Davy Crockett was terminated, and the battalion returned to An Khe by convoy. One man from Charlie Company was killed on the operation: PFC Ennis Scarbrough, 20 years old, of Birmingham, AL. He died on May 11, 1966, from wounds received the day before.

Around this time, Charlie Company got a new commanding officer as Captain Donald Sims replaced acting CO 1Lt Hansen. Sims' call sign became "Armored Vest" and he was one of the first African American officers to lead an infantry company in the 1st Cavalry.

Back in An Khe, the men barely had time to clean their weapons and gear and have a few beers at Charlie's Hole, the company's EM club, before moving out again, this time for Operation Crazy Horse. Charlie Company was going back into Happy Valley, a little more than six months after it had made its first air-assaults of the war there. A CIDG patrol from the Vinh Thanh Special Forces camp had captured a prisoner who indicated that the 2nd VC Main Force Regiment had moved into the valley and was planning to attack the camp on May 19, 1966, Ho Chi Minh's birthday. Despite reports that the 2nd VC had been crippled by heavy losses in February, it had rebuilt and was looking to draw the 1st Cavalry into another fight in the mountains.

The 1st Cavalry canceled other planned operations and ordered the 1st Brigade into the valley. When battalions of that Brigade came under heavy attack, the 1/5th joined the operation under its operational control. On May 17, 1966, the 1/5th flew into LZ Hereford, a one-ship clearing at the base of a hill where heavy fighting had taken place the day before and started climbing.

As the men moved up the trail, they were met by tired and dirty troopers of the 2/8th Cav bringing down their wounded and dead. Squads from Charlie Company fanned out to look for missing men. Rick Roy and the guys he was with heard movement in the bush and then a man stepped out, shot through both arms, and missing his weapon. About twenty feet farther on, Roy's group found the rest of the man's squad, six or seven more troopers lying dead and stripped of their weapons, gear, and personal items. The wounded man had survived by playing dead and said that at one point during the night, a NVA soldier sat on him while rifling through another man's gear.

Late in the day, Roy was walking point when his platoon ran into some NVA firing down on them from trees. It was a close-range fight with men firing on full auto. He was hit in the leg and foot, ending his tour in Vietnam. He spent about four and a half months in an Army hospital in Japan before making it back to the States.

Charlie and the other companies of the 1/5th started company sized sweeps in the Vinh Thanh and Suoi Ca Valleys and southern Suoi Ca Mountains. During the next week, the companies of the battalion made frequent contact, mostly with small units of VC using harassing and delaying tactics to allow the 2nd VC Regiment to move out of the area.

The Crazy Horse Area of Operations was a complex and thickly jungled morass, 3,000 feet from bottom to top and 20 kilometers square. LZs were so few and so small that only one or two choppers could land at a time and the VC were often able to target them. At times, platoons and companies had to be inserted by climbing down 'Jacob's Ladders' suspended from the rear ramps of Chinook helicopters.

The division pulled its companies to the outer edges of the AO to set up a double row of ambushes, while artillery began firing 12,000 to 13,000 rounds per day into suspected enemy locations and the Air Force provided both tactical strikes and daily B-52 raids. But the area was too big to be effectively cordoned off, and the 2nd VC Main Force Regiment evaded north into the An Lao Valley with much of its strength still intact.

Operation Crazy Horse continued into early June, but Charlie Company and the 1/5th flew back to An Khe on May 31 and returned to the control of the 2nd Brigade. Two men from the company died in the operation: PFC James Kennedy, age 21, from Seat Pleasant, MD, of a gunshot wound on 18 May, 1966, and PFC Walter Salley, age 20, of Philadelphia, on 29 May 1966, of friendly fire, hit by shrapnel from an artillery short round at LZ Hereford.

Once again, the company's standdown at An Khe was cut short. Due to increased NVA activity along the Cambodian and Laotian borders, the 1st Brigade of the 101st Airborne Division launched Operation Hawthorne in Kontum Province on June 2, 1966. The same day, the 1/5th was airlifted to Pleiku and from there into the field to provide security for combat engineer units building temporary airstrips to support the operation.

The battalion moved to Kontum early on June 9, 1966 and became the ready reaction force for the other units in the operation—the 1st Brigade of the 101st Airborne, the 3rd Brigade of the 25th Infantry Division, the 3rd Brigade of the 1st Cavalry and ARVN Ranger battalions. That evening, the battalion was placed under the operational control of the 101st Airborne, then heavily engaged with elements of two NVA regiments, and lifted to Dak To in support of its battalions.

Charlie Company spent the next week running search and destroy sweeps in the mountains northeast of Dak To and securing artillery firebases for the 101st. Joe Immler recalls crossing the border and going a few kilometers into Cambodia and Laos in search of NVA camps and supply caches. Casualties for the 1/5th on the operation were light, but one man who had deployed with Charlie Company the previous August would get his ticket home. Sgt. Bob Parris recently wrote:

> On June 15, 1966, Charlie Company was providing security for an Artillery Battery located on a very narrow and steep mountain in the vicinity of Dak To, Vietnam providing fire support to 101st Airborne Division. I helped the men of the artillery unit during the day with loading and firing their 105mm Howitzers. I had dug a foxhole about 50 feet from the gun and was trying to get some sleep when it started ed to pour down hard rain. SSgt. McKensie, Platoon Sergeant for

the third platoon, and I made a pup tent by snapping our ponchos together. Just before midnight the enemy started dropping mortars on our position and one landed near our tent, hitting us both. SSgt. McKensie had his left foot almost completely blown off and I had several pieces of shrapnel and parts of his ankle bones blown into my head. I had my radio operator call for a medevac helicopter for SSgt. McKensie but decided to wait for first light to evacuate myself due to the weather and dangerous LZ conditions. SSgt. McKensie and I were sleeping head to foot and if I had been on his side of the shelter I would have been killed instantly. The artillery gunner and loader that I had been helping all day were killed in the mortar attack.

Operation Hawthorne was terminated on June 20 and the battalion was released from the operational control of the 101st Airborne two days later. It remained in the Pleiku area for another two weeks providing road security on Highway 14 from Pleiku to Kontum and Dak To and serving as the ready reserve force for Field Force HQ.

Lt Jim Wolfe also joined the company at Dak To in late June 1966. One of the first things he did was write his father and ask him to buy some jungle boots from an Army surplus store and mail them to him in Vietnam as they were in short supply in An Khe. As a green platoon leader, he also got a few attitude adjustment lessons from men who had been there a while:

A company of the 101st had been involved in a terrific fight to the point that the Company Commander had called in napalm on his own position. The men of the 101st at Dak To had come up with a song they sang to the Johnny Cash tune "I Walk The Line". I don't remember any of the verses, but the chorus went "I call napalm on these men of mine; because they're mine, they burn so fine".

A few days later, he had to reprimand a man in his platoon for giving his squad leader a hard time. Later, he passed the soldier who said under his breath loud enough for Wolfe to hear, but no one else, "I'm gonna pop a cap on your ass, lieutenant." As long as he had that platoon, Wolfe never got in front of him.

On July 9, 1966, the 1/5th returned to its base camp at An Khe, once again traveling by convoy through Mang Yang pass. The battalion caught a welcome break, providing security on Camp Radcliffe's defensive perimeter, the 'Green Line' until July 31. This was time well spent as the last of the men who had deployed with Charlie Company in August 1965 were rotating home and there were new replacements to equip and break in.

Battle on Hill 534

Jim Wolfe remembers that by mid-summer, the 1/5th was being called a 'champagne' battalion by officers in other units because of its low rates of casualties. Other battalions had many more dead and wounded after the operations in the Ia Drang Valley and Bong Son in the previous fall and spring. That would soon change. On August 2, 1966, the battalion was air-lifted back to Pleiku for a new operation in response to intelligence reports that fresh NVA regiments were crossing the border to attack nearby Special Forces Camps or even Pleiku City. A few days later, it also got a new battalion commander, LTC Robert Siegrist.

On August 10, 1966, Charlie Company and the rest of the battalion joined Operation Paul Revere II, air-assaulting into an LZ in the Chu Pong Mountains in the Ia Drang Valley, close to where the battles of LZ X-Ray and LZ Albany had been fought the previous November. But while the 1st Cavalry had fought there before, this was the first battle for Siegrist and all of his company commanders.

On August 14, 1966, Alpha Company became heavily engaged with an NVA unit of unknown size and other companies of the 1/5th and 2/5th were fed into the growing fight. The ac-

tion was described in the Army's history of combat operations in
Vietnam:

The cavalry division had walked into a tempest. Although the size of
the enemy force was not known at the time, it seemed large enough by
the end of the day to justify a major American effort ... Siegrist's battalion reserve, Capt. Donald R. Sims' Company C, 1st of the 5th Cavalry, moved fifteen hundred meters northeast of Hill 534 ... Hopefully, firepower raining down on the North Vietnamese during the night
would keep them in place until the Americans could attack the next
day ...

When the fighting began the next day, 15 August, units under
Siegrist's control met the enemy three times. The first to fight was
Captain Taylor's Company B, 2d of the 5th. Moving from their overnight position to begin the hunt, the troops were pelted by mortar
rounds around 0800 and then assaulted from the north and west. Taylor pulled his men back and called for fire support. He was on the
radio when a mortar round burst nearby, killing him, his radio operator, and his first sergeant ... As the attack continued, the Americans
began to run dangerously low on ammunition. Responding to pleas
for more, two helicopters crisscrossed the jungle before finding the
company and delivering what was needed.

About an hour after Company B had started its fight, Captain
Shea's company [Alpha, 1/5th] was also hit. While operating about
five hundred meters northeast of Hill 534, his men began to receive
heavy automatic weapons fire. Over the next two hours the two sides
exchanged fire, but neither could gain an advantage over the other.
Later in the morning the enemy pulled back.

Fighting broke out at yet a third spot toward midafternoon. Colonel Siegrist had ordered Captain Sims' Company C to move southwest to relieve Company B. The platoons were closing in on the pe-

rimeter when machine gun fire forced them to take cover. With one platoon pinned down, Sims called in artillery fire and an air strike. Bombs landed between the two companies, forcing the enemy to withdraw, and allowing the Americans to link up.

— Stemming the Tide: Combat Operations in
Vietnam, May 1965 to October 1966
John M. Garland, Center of Military History, U.S. Army.

Charlie Company's role in the battle was described in more detail in a 1st Cavalry report from early 1967:

Sims began his march at nine o'clock in the morning [on 14 August 1966]. The terrain and vegetation made the march a slow and difficult one and by five o-clock in the afternoon he was still several hours march from the objective. Sims set up his company perimeter and planned to conclude the move the following day.

The next day's move remained uneventful though exhausting until 3:30 in the afternoon. Sims was moving in a column formation which often was forced into a file with his third platoon leading, followed by the second, CP, and first.

The third platoon point man, Private First Class Gregory A. Smith, noticed an enemy soldier, apparently dead, lying on a bunker. Smith turned around to warn the people behind him and the very much alive NVA fired a burst of automatic weapons fire which wounded Smith. The NVA had apparently been lying on top of his bunker when he was surprised by Smith. He waited for his chance to fire and get into the bunker, which opportunity came when Smith turned to warn his comrades. Lieutenant Earnest A. Torok, the platoon leader took a squad and attempted to maneuver left on the weapon position. The brush was too thick and he couldn't get through it. Torok pulled back, picked up the rest of his third platoon and tried to go around to the right. The platoon moved about 50 meters before coming under heavy fire. Torok called Sims and reported that he faced a large, well-dug in and well-concealed enemy force. His attempts to maneuver against them were repulsed. Sims sent the second platoon to reinforce. As they pulled up on the third platoon's left flank, they also became pinned down.

When Sims learned that both platoons were pinned down, he instructed them to pull back with their dead and wounded so he could soften the position with supporting fires. Coordinating between themselves and the forward air controller, the commanders of B 2/5 and C 1/5 were able to place an air strike on the bunkered enemy positions. Thus disengaged, C 1/5 moved around to their left, linking up with B 2/5 prior to darkness.

"Hill 534: 14-15 August 1966", Unit Historical Report No. 12, First Air Cavalry Division Office of Information and History, 1Lt William E. Kail (1967). Charlie Company was engaged with an estimated company sized NVA force in well camouflaged bunkers and called in napalm to within ten meters of its lines to destroy the bunkers, break the NVA's resistance and relieve Bravo Company, 2/5th.

By late afternoon, Siegrist had four companies on the slopes. The next morning, assuming that the enemy was still lurking around, the Americans launched a coordinated sweep of the area ... Siegrist's men moved methodically up Hill 534 from the south and then down the other side. They found nothing. Those North Vietnamese who had survived the fight had withdrawn in the night.

In policing the battlefield over the next two days, the troops uncovered living quarters, messing facilities, documents, graves, and scores of unburied bodies. The communications gear they found indicated the presence of at least a battalion and probably a regimental headquarters. Counting 126 enemy dead, they estimated that they had killed another 300, basing that judgment on "the volume of fire" U.S. forces had brought to bear. By comparison, 23 Americans died in the action and 27 more had been wounded.

Prisoner interrogations later revealed that Colonel Siegrist's force had fought all three battalions of the 32d NVA Regiment...Although there was no way to prove it at the time, Siegrist and the other American commanders believed that they had rendered the three units ineffective. Even so, Siegrist was convinced that no matter how much the Americans hurt the enemy, he would return to his old haunts as soon as they departed.

— Stemming the Tide: Combat Operations in
Vietnam, May 1965 to October 1966,
John M. Garland. Center of Military History, U.S. Army.

Six members of Charlie Company died in the battle on Hill 534: Sgt. Wayland Dunn, 39, of Raleigh, NC; SP4 Fred Brown, 23, Fort Worth, TX; SP4 Sanford Jackson, 30, from Buffalo, NY; SP4 James Langlois, 24, of Toledo, OH; PFC Donald Summers, 22, from Mayhill, NM; and PFC Fred Thomas, 23, of Athens, GA. Jackson was older than most SP4's in the company, but he had previously served both as a Marine and in the Air Force before joining the Army. He received a posthumous Silver Star for his role in the fight.

Lt Jim Wolfe had just moved from mortar platoon leader to XO for the company and his first job was to recover some of the bodies. Langlois's body was found in front of an NVA machine gun bunker and Wolfe and others had to tie a rope to his web gear and pull him down the trail to ensure the NVA had not booby trapped his body. Wolfe recalled:

Several weeks after his death, we received a letter from a jewelry store in California telling us his account was overdue. It was normal for a letter like this to go to the commanding officer of a soldier's company when he was behind on his bills. We wrote them back and told them he had been killed in action. Several weeks after that we got another letter from them asking for the address of his next of kin. We cursed them and threw the letter in the garbage.

The battalion continued operating west of Pleiku for another ten days, before being lifted back to An Khe on August 25. It remained on standdown for the next two weeks, getting new replacements for both the casualties from Operation Paul Revere II and the men lucky enough to be completing their tours and rotating back to the world.

During its first year in Vietnam, each operation taught the men of the 1st Cavalry new and valuable lessons. At the division's level, it meant better ways to use helicopters and artillery and to coordinate units in the field, but for the men of Charlie Company, the lessons were more practical: how to make a tent or hooch with two ponchos and some bamboo; how to burn leeches off your skin with the glowing tip of a cigarette; the best ways to set out claymore mines and trip flares each night; and to only put eighteen rounds in each M-16 magazine to keep the rifles from misfeeding and jamming in a firefight.

Part 2: Rice Paddies and Mountains — Pacification in Bong Son

Operation Thayer

By now, there was no one left in Charlie Company who had deployed with it in August 1965. For the rest of the war, every man who served in it was a replacement, filling the slot of someone who was killed or wounded, injured or sick, or who, with luck, completed their tour and made it "back to the world" more or less intact. There were four Army and two Marine Divisions now operating in Vietnam, plus a vast support network, with more combat and support units on the way. Planeloads of replacements flew into the country daily; the Pentagon chartered civilian airliners to ferry the men, with stewardesses to pass out food and soft drinks.

Some officers and NCOs knew they were coming to the 1st Cavalry, but most replacements were unassigned and first went to a replacement unit. There they stood in formation each morning as names were called and men parceled out to different divisions or brigades. Hundreds of men came to the 1st Cav in late August and early September 1966 and about thirty-five men were sent to Charlie Company, most just out of training. I was one of these replacements, coming to Charlie Company in late August 1966. Within the larger group, seven of us had trained together since the previous April, part of a platoon going through advanced infantry training and jump school. The rest were from other Stateside units or training bases.

Getting so many new replacements during a long standdown gave the company a chance to equip them, assign them to squads, and provide a little training. Even so, the company was short jungle boots, poncho liners, cleaning kits for M-16's, and other essentials for the new men. To the veterans in the company, it was a chance to clean up, get drunk, write letters, maybe get a pass to An Khe and Sin City, and talk about what they'd just been through. To us, it was stepping into a strange world, standing in the background in the barracks or Charlie's Hole, the company EM club, listening to them talk about what they did and saw on Hill 534.

Almost half of the company's replacements would by dead within ninety days. The first taste of what might be ahead for us came on September 3, 1966, when the VC mortared Camp Radcliff, hitting it with 119 mortar rounds over a five-minute period. While none fell close to the battalion's area, four men in the division were killed and seventy-six wounded. About one-fifth of the 1st Cavalry's 400-plus helicopters were damaged or destroyed.

Of my group of seven, four were dead by Thanksgiving and a fifth was seriously injured in a fall during operations in the mountains in January 1967. The sixth man tried to poison himself to get out of the field after only a month in the company. Supposedly he broke open cartridges from his M-16 and ate the gunpower to make himself urinate blood and mimic a kidney disorder. It may have worked—he was gone by mid-October. I spent a year with Charlie Company in the first and third platoons and rotated back to the States in August 1967.

The company moved out on September 7, 1966, back to Bong Son. This would start a new phase for Charlie Company, unlike the first months where it had bounced around the Central Highlands and Bong Son in response to NVA threats. The U.S. presence in the highlands had strengthened, with the 4th Infantry Division arriving in Pleiku in August 1966, and the South Korean Capital Division taking over road security functions on Highway 19 through the coastal mountains, freeing the Air Cavalry to launch operations in eastern Binh Dinh Province aimed to pacify the countryside and destroy or drive out the 3rd PAVN Division.

MACV and the 1st Cavalry had planned a major operation in Bong Son earlier in the dry season, but Operation Paul Revere II on the border forced a delay. This gave the 3rd PAVN the chance to step up attacks on ARVN units, threatening any progress made since Operation Masher/White Wing early in the year. On the night of September 7, 1966, they attacked five ARVN bases between Phu My and the Bong Son plains. The next day, two battalions of Main Force VC ambushed a large ARVN convoy moving north of Qui Nhon. In response, the 1st Cavalry launched Operation Thayer, the first phase of what the Army called the "Binh Dinh Province Pacification Campaign."

Charlie Company first flew in C-123's to a dirt strip by a Special Forces Camp near what would soon become LZ English, the 1st Cavalry's largest base in Bong Son. Charlie's first mission was to be a show of force to ensure the VC and NVA did not disrupt some national elections about to take place. The men set up on a hill overlooking one of the district's polling place with some of their M-60's aimed at the building.

The goal was to protect the election, but it may have looked like something else to the peasants coming to vote, caught between the VC they knew and the government that was new to them. It was the last month of the dry season, so the men could sit on the edges of their foxholes on the hill at dusk, smoking and softly talking until it was time for the first man to pull guard.

Operation Thayer's initial target were the VC and NVA bases in and around the Crow's Foot in the Suoi Ca Mountains, the same ground fought over so fiercely in February in Operation Masher/White Wing. On September 13, 1966, after two days of B-52 strikes in the area, Charlie Company air-assaulted onto a small hilltop covered with elephant grass so thick that the men jumping from the choppers became entangled in it trying to get out of the way as more choppers came in. The operation was the largest air assault undertaken up until that time in the Vietnam War, with five airmobile battalions assaulting into the mountains around the Crow's Foot and Kim Son Valley in less than two days.

For Charlie Company, it started on a sour note—that evening PFC Jerry Coffey, 22, of Palmyra, IL, was setting out trip flares at dusk outside the company's night perimeter and was accidentally shot and killed by his squad leader while coming back to his foxhole. Three days later, PFC John Cummins, from Roswell, NM, was killed by a booby trap set by the VC near a downed American plane his platoon was trying to find. Cummins, 19 and from Roswell, NM, was the first of the new batch of replacements to die in Vietnam.

A few days into the operation, Charlie air-assaulted onto another hilltop with Huey gunships on either side prepping the clearing with rockets and mini-gun fire. The rockets set some dry brush on the side of the hill on fire and it spread up to the LZ as choppers were still coming in. The last men to dismount joined the company running in full gear down a trail on the other side of the hill to wait while the fire burned itself out.

Operation Thayer was a bust. Any VC and NVA in the

Crow's Foot had moved out before it started. Once again, the hard humping on steep slopes and the hacking through elephant grass and bamboo turned up a few small supply caches and some bunkers rebuilt since the last operation there. Even without any contact, the operation took a toll on Charlie Company. There were heat casualties, especially among the new men. One morning, the company climbed a high steep hill at midday and had to evacuate eight men with heatstroke, some of them NCOs newly arrived in Vietnam after months or years of easy duty in the States. Most of them never returned to the field.

There was also malaria and injuries. On September 25, 1966, Charlie Company air-assaulted into an overgrown field that was covered with rocks obscured by heavy brush. The Huey pilots couldn't tell where the ground was so they hovered while the men jumped six to eight feet with seventy pounds and more of weapons and gear. Before the company even moved out, it lost about a squad's worth of men to ankle, leg, and back injuries.

That night, one of its platoons set up a night ambush on old colonial railroad tracks along the coast. It was an "L" shaped ambush set to catch any VC or NVA moving away from another 1st Cav company in the area. It might have worked, but about a company of them came from the other direction — there were too many to ambush so the platoon laid there, holding their breaths while the enemy passed through the ambush zone, oblivious to the men laying a few feet from them.

Charlie Company's only contact came at the tail end of Thayer and it seemed almost accidental. On September 29, 1966, first platoon was on a patrol by itself while the rest of Charlie Company set up for the night on a small hill overlooking some villages. Late in the afternoon, the platoon came down a hill through thick jungle and underbrush and went into a small village from the back, catching the people there by surprise. The platoon spotted two men running from the village over the rice paddy berms towards another village about 100 yards away. They were almost to the village and the platoon only got a few shots off before they were out of sight. Platoon leader Lt Tim McCarthy put the platoon in line and it started to sweep across the rice paddies to the next village.

Halfway there the platoon was hit by automatic weapons fire from the village and a flank and everyone dove for cover in the rice paddies. It was likely a squad of local guerillas, but they had one or two machine guns and first platoon was pinned down for about two hours with most of their weapons jammed or their ammo useless because of the mud and stagnant rice paddy water. It was my first firefight and wasn't anything like the war movies I watched as a teenager and I later wrote down my memories of that evening:

> The first burst of fire hit four or five men and we dove into the rice paddies and began crawling for the cover of the berms. There we were safe but we were stuck as it got dark, separated into little groups in different paddies. One of our wounded was our platoon sergeant, SFC Cristobal Melendez, who was the newest man in the platoon. He was a Korean War veteran who had come to Charlie Company about ten days earlier. He was hit by the first burst of fire and was now down in the stagnant water and buffalo shit of a Vietnamese rice paddy with leg and stomach wounds.
>
> Lt McCarthy told me to stay with him and I did, yelling for a medic. Other men in other paddies were also yelling for a medic but any movement drew fire from the village. His condition worsened and he began calling for Jesus and a woman, probably his wife or mother, and asking if he was going to die. I told him to hang on but a medic

never got to us and I couldn't tell where his wound was in the dark with both of us laying in a half foot of water. I don't remember but I probably held him most of this time as he likely would have drowned as he got weaker.

We finally got some mortar and artillery support and were able to pull back to dry ground to evacuate the wounded. Four of us carried Sergeant Melendez in a poncho—he was a big man, tensed and rigid with pain, and everything was wet and muddy, and he kept bumping on the ground. As we got close to where a medevac chopper could land, we could feel his body go limp and I knew he had died.

After the dead and wounded were evacuated, we moved back towards the village. There was no incoming fire by now but it felt good just to have something to fire at. After two hours in a rice paddy my M-16 was useless so I joined one of the platoon's veterans and began feeding ammo into his M-60. Men had worn the belts of machine gun ammo as bandoliers as they crawled through the rice paddies and they were soaked and caked with mud. Robbie's gun would jam every five or six rounds and in frustration he began to field strip it, pulling the bolt and other key parts out and laying them on the rice paddy berm.

Just then the VC gave us a parting shot of five or six 60mm mortar rounds, one of which exploded about fifteen feet in front of us. A piece of shrapnel ripped through Robbie's hand and another man grabbed him and lead him to the rear. I grabbed the M-60 and followed but in the darkness and confusion I left the bolt and other key parts behind. After his hand was bandaged and he got some morphine, the platoon moved in a slow file through the night to link up with the rest of the company on a nearby hill. I was towards the rear with a machine gun that couldn't fire and a .45 pistol that I later found out was rusted shut. I had no idea what happened to the M-16 I started the firefight with.

After Robbie was evacuated, I sheepishly told our acting platoon sergeant, SSG 'Sgt T' Tarkington, what had happened, and he was understanding. I lost most of my gear in the rice paddies, so I lay down on the ground next to someone's foxhole and fell asleep. The next day, after we swept through the village, we crossed the rice paddies and I found the bolt and other parts from the M-60 still laying on the rice paddy berm. I reassembled the gun and carried it for the next month.

First Platoon had two dead and four or five wounded. SFC Cristobal Melendez was 36 and from Rio Piedras, Puerto Rico. The other KIA was PFC Jack Campbell, 20, from Carterville, Il, another new replacement, killed a day before his 21st birthday.

The platoon rejoined the rest of the company in the middle of the night, soaking wet and with most of its weapons jammed with mud. The men cleaned up in the morning and then with the rest of the company, swept back through the village. It was abandoned by then, with only one old woman squatting at its edge as the company burned it to the ground. The company found an old Russian made light machine gun and two carbines dumped in a ditch and seven fresh graves. Later that day Charlie Company was lifted to LZ Hammond, a large support base, for hot showers and resupply. Operation Thayer was terminated and on October 1, the 1st Cavalry launched Operation Irving.

Dining in the Field

C Rations sustained the company in the field, sometimes for days at a time. Some were tolerable, a few were disgusting, and all got old pretty quick. Before a mission or when logs birds flew into a company's small LZ's with resupply, men would break open cases of rations and distribute them among each squad. There were twelve individual meals to a case, each in a cardboard box and always packed in the same order, and squad leaders would empty a case with the boxes' label sides down and shuffle them so nobody knew what meal they would get.

There were two types of meals in a case: eight meals each had a small can of meat, a little smaller than a tuna fish can, the choices being Beef Steak, Ham and Eggs Chopped, Ham Slices, Turkey Loaf, Boned Chicken, Chicken and Noodles, Meat Loaf, and Spiced Beef. These meals also either had a can of fruit –fruit cocktail, applesauce, or sliced pears or peaches in a heavy syrup — and a larger can with crackers, peanut butter, and chocolate, or a small can of white bread and a larger can with cookies, cocoa powder, and a tin of jam.

The other four meals had a larger can of Beans and Wieners, Spaghetti and Meatballs, Beefsteak with Potatoes and Gravy, Ham and Lima Beans, or Meatballs and Beans, along with two small cans, one with four crackers and a tin of cheese spread and the other with either Fruit Cake, Pecan Roll, or Pound Cake. Every meal included an accessory pack with a plastic spoon and small packets of salt and pepper, instant coffee, sugar, and non-dairy creamer, along with two pieces of gum, a pack of four ciga-rettes — usually so old and dry that they would flare up and burn to the end when they were lit — and some matches and toilet paper.

The most hated meal was Ham and Lima Beans, always called 'ham and motherf***ers' by the men. After the rations were distributed, guys would trade individual cans but no one wanted them. The best thing that could happen was to end up with both pound cake and sliced peaches. Most of the meals were pretty bland and guys had their family send them bottles of hot sauce to spice them up. When they found them, guys also 'liberated' small and extremely hot chili peppers growing in some of the villages they passed through.

The next worst was Ham and Eggs Chopped. Platoon Ser-geant Lester Tarkington, known to his men in the fall of 1966 as 'Sgt. T', would always trade better meals for ham and eggs. He claimed to like them, but most of the men in the first platoon believed he did to give them a break and keep up their morale.

Even empty C Ration cans came in handy, especially the large can of cookies and cocoa powder. Men would cut holes around each end of the can with their P-38 can opener to make a stove. With a piece of heat tab or C-4 lit and burning in the bottom of the can, and a can of meat or a canteen cup of powdered coffee or cocoa carefully balanced on top, it was possible to have a warm meal. The same can, with both ends cut off, could also be attached to the side of an M-60 machine gun to help belts of ammo feed more smoothly into the gun.

The VC found cans useful as well. A small can with both ends cut off was the perfect size to hold a grenade. It would be nailed or tied to a branch or a stake in the ground, with a grenade inside and a trip wire attached to the grenade stretched across a trail. The grenade's pin would be pulled but it wouldn't detonate until an unwary US soldier came along and hit the trip wire, pulling the grenade out of the can, and setting it off. It became standard practice to flatten or fly out used C Rations cans when leaving a position in the morning.

When rolling up their gear to move out, men would stuff their C-Rations cans in an old Army tube sock and tie it to the back of their rucksack, carrying enough for two or three days in the field. Rarely did anyone have to carry food for a longer stretch of time. Later in the war, men were sometimes issued dehydrated rations originally developed for Special Forces and long-range recon units. They were lightweight and tasted better than most C-Rations.

By the fall of 1966, the 1st Cavalry had built enough of a logistics infrastructure so that it could fly meals out to companies in the field once a week, sometimes more as time went on. As a company in the field set up its night defensive position, a resupply chopper would fly in a load of insulated containers with a meal, usually lukewarm and greasy, but better than Cs. The containers would be set out and some of the men could line up to get their meal on a paper plate while the others continued digging foxholes until their turn came. In the field, officers and NCOs always ate last. If there wasn't enough food to go around, they were stuck with C-Rations.

Sometimes there was too much. For Thanksgiving in 1966, the Army was going to try to bring turkey dinners to every unit in the field. Three days earlier, Charlie Company was ambushed in the Ia Drang Valley with about half the company killed or wounded. The head count for Charlie Company had been provided before the ambush and no one let its support units know that half the company was gone, and so it got twice as much food as it needed. The men sat in silence, staring at something only they saw, gorging themselves on turkey, stuffing, mashed potatoes, and ice cream.

There could be other problems as well. In mid-July 1967, the company was on a search and destroy mission with a Special Forces CIDG unit when it set up for the night in the Kim Son Valley. Hot food was flown in on the evening resupply run and the men lined up for BBQ chicken. As soon as they sat down to eat, three C-123s suddenly appeared flying down the valley at low attitude, spraying a thick sticky mist of Agent Orange over them. But BBQ chicken was a treat and men in the field knew nothing about the dangers of Agent Orange in those days, so they continued eating and spent the next day or two operating in the sprayed area.

Water was even more essential than food, especially when a man could sweat out a canteen worth of fluids in less than a half hour when humping in the mountains or jungles on a hot day. Between monsoon rains, rice paddies, and swamps, water was usually everywhere, but it was often undrinkable, at least without treatment. Most men carried at least four canteens of water, sometimes more, and refilled their canteens as often as possible. The Army flew in five-gallon jerry cans of water on resupply runs, but it always tasted of the purification chemicals used to treat it. Many men had their families send them pre-sweetened packets of Kool-aid on an ongoing basis to cover the taste.

Water from village wells was usually better, although a company passing through a village could deplete its wells in a matter of minutes. Men were supposed to add purification pills to their canteens, but they tasted bad too. Mountain streams looked good and the water was often cool, but looks could be deceiving. Third platoon was operating in the hills above the An Loa Valley in early 1967 when its men filled their canteens from a clear mountain stream flowing through a meadow. They drank some and then went another hundred meters upstream to find a dead and decomposing water buffalo in the middle of the stream.

Beer and soda were always a treat in the field. If the company was guarding a bridge or a firebase in a populated area, kids would gather outside the wire to sell individual cans or bottles for a few piasters or MPC. Often it was Vietnamese beer, called 'tiger piss' by the men, but sometimes it was US beer obtained through the black market. It wasn't unusual for the kids selling it to have a better selection than the men could find in the company club in base camp. Beer and soda bought this way was always warm, but it was a welcome change from treated water.

In 1967, First Sergeant Robert Fowler sometimes used his own money to get ice-cold beer and soda for the men in the field. There were few experiences better than to come through the wire after an all-day patrol in the dry season and be handed a can of cold beer. A man could roll the can on his forehead or the back of his neck for a few minutes before poking holes in the can with a bayonet and drinking it in one gulp.

Operation Irving

Charlie Company started its second October in Vietnam with a night air assault. On October 2, 1966, the company was on the perimeter of LZ Hammond when a Blue team reconnaissance platoon from the 1/9th noted unusual activity in the coastal village of Hoa Hoi. When they landed, they were immediately pinned down and two observation choppers were shot down. Companies from the 1/12th were fed into the firefight as it became apparent there was a main force Viet Cong battalion hiding in the village. As evening approached, the 1/12th had not been able to surround the village and Charlie and Alpha Companies were placed under its operational control and ordered to saddle up.

Shortly after dusk, Charlie air-assaulted onto a sandy beach outside Hoa Hoi, taking fire from the village as it approached. PFC Earle Mosely, 'Mose' to his buddies in the first platoon, remembers standing on the skids of the Huey as it approached the LZ, with green tracers arcing up from the village, ready to jump as it touched down. Night fell fast in Vietnam, and some of the choppers couldn't see the ground and the men had to jump from six to eight feet up.

Once on the ground, Charlie moved into a blocking position with Alpha Company on one side and a company of the 1/12th on the other. The line set up in the dark, curved with parts of the two companies facing each other across the dunes and low bushes. As small groups of Viet Cong tried to escape throughout the night, they triggered exchanges of fire between the two companies with red tracers crisscrossing in front of Charlie Company's line.

PFC Sonny Cowan had been with Charlie Company about a month and was a mortar FO (Forward Observer) in the 2nd platoon. He wrote his mother the next day and described what he had seen and experienced:

Well, I think I spent the most extraordinary Sunday evening of my life last night. It was about 6 o'clock. Our company commander gave us the word to saddle up and in about thirty minutes we were headed for the South China Sea where we had six hundred Viet Cong trapped. It was pitch dark when we got there, but not for long. Smokie started flying over and dropping flares which had one thousand candle power.

We started moving up to our objective which was to tie into A Company's right flank. You could see tracers flying every which way. We finally reached our position and started digging in. By nine o'clock we were dug in and ready for anything. There was heavy fighting until about two o'clock in the morning, then things quieted down quite a bit except for occasional sniper fire. Smokey kept the whole area lit up the whole night. About five thirty they (VC) tried to break through again.

At six o'clock we put on our gear and started sweeping through the village. I've never seen so many dead people in all my life. I don't know why but it didn't bother me at all. There was one thing that did bother me though. We were walking through the village and this Cong came running out of his hooch and surrendered. We weren't taking any chances; we got the prisoner and took him back to the rear. After we got him out of the way, someone threw a hand grenade into the hooch to make sure there weren't any more Cong in there. The grenade went off and out came a woman carrying a little baby. Neither one of them was hit very bad, just some cuts around the head. Then someone went into the hooch and found an old woman. She was in pretty bad shape.

We got lifted out around one o'clock, back to LZ Hammond. We just got our tents put up and had hot chow when our company commander told us to saddle up again. I don't know where we are going. I'll finish the letter when I get there if I get the chance.

A few weeks after the battle, an article in the military newspaper 'Pacific Stars and Stripes' reported that Charlie Company beat off repeated human wave assaults at Hoa Hoi. It may have happened to other companies, but in Charlie's section of the line, it was mainly small groups of VC trying to escape through the line and a cow, likely crazed by incoming artillery, that ran out of the smoke and between two foxholes of the 1st platoon before anyone could shoot.

Probably the biggest danger that night were the flares dropped by the Air Force and fired by a Navy destroyer offshore to illuminate the battlefield. Designed to slowly float down under a parachute, the burning magnesium of the flares sometimes burned through the parachute cords and they would plummet to the ground. Charlie Company's back was to the sea and the destroyer was firing over it and large chunks of burning metal fell around the company's positions during the night.

The next day, Charlie Company, and Charlie Company 1/12th lined up and swept the area, flushing out the remaining Viet Cong into blocking positions set up by the other companies there. All the companies at Hoa Hoi were awarded the Presidential Unit Citation for the action.

This was also one of Joe Immler's last missions. A few weeks later, he was medevaced to Japan with malaria and hepatitis. During his ten months in Vietnam, his father Joseph—a Bronze Star recipient with Patton's Third Army in World War II and a staunch Catholic—went to mass every day at 6 AM to pray for his son's safe return home.

The next ten days or so were spent guarding artillery bases. First was LZ Crystal, just off Highway 1 outside of the district capital of Phu My, one of the few places in that part of Binh Dinh Province where the ARVN and government still had a presence. Crystal was the largest firebase in the area with a battery of 155mm howitzers and another of self-propelled 8" howitzers and 175 mm cannon and was easy duty for an infantry company, with short patrols in the day and a few squad sized ambushes at night.

Charlie then flew to a small firebase in the coastal mountains, six 105 mm howitzers strung along a narrow ridge, treeless and rocky with a steep drop-off on each side and barely enough room for some small bunkers. Each morning men would shake out their boots in case scorpions crawled into them during the night. Each patrol meant a steep climb down into elephant grass and jungle and a steep climb back up at the hottest time of the day.

While the company was there, two men shot themselves in the foot on different days, one with a .45 and the other with his M-16. Both claimed it was an accident while cleaning their weapon, but most men in the company thought they were two men who had just reached their limit for whatever reason and could not take it anymore.

Other men were down too. SP4 Michael Kilpatrick had recently come in as the medic to the third platoon and became a close friend with Bill Stone, who was trying to connect him with his girlfriend's sister. While on the ridge, Stone came to Kilpatrick and calmly said, "Doc—I don't think I'd going to live." To Kilpatrick it didn't seem like a premonition so much as a simple statement of fact. He had been carrying a can of Vietnamese beer and he and Stone split it while they talked it out. They didn't know then what their next mission would be, only that it would be in the Suoi Ca Mountains.

Pinned Down on a Hillside

On the morning of October 15, 1966, the second and third platoons and the company CP air assaulted into a small clearing to start a search and destroy sweep. The first and mortar platoons stayed back to help secure an artillery battery and the battalion CP on top of a nearby hill. The third platoon moved out first. Late in the afternoon they came across a VC camp by a small stream. It looked abandoned but there were fresh footprints in the area.

As they moved up a trail with high ground on either side, they found some recently dug VC foxholes. Some men asked their platoon leader to call in artillery but he refused. It was getting late and he was under pressure to make it to the battalion's hilltop base before night fell. A few steps further on, the platoon walked into a 'U' shaped ambush—some men were able to take cover in the VC foxholes, but most were caught in the open. As the firefight developed, the men split into two groups, with one group and the platoon leader losing their radio but making it to a ridgeline. The other group, with an artillery forward observer and his radio, were pinned down on the slope but out of contact with the first group.

Second platoon and the company CP saddled up and moved

out as soon as they got the word third platoon was hit. Maps in the Suoi Ca Mountains weren't very accurate, and they didn't know the exact location of the platoon, so they approached the area along a ridgeline, figuring that if they were heading into a fight, it would be better to move downhill to the fight than uphill into it. Also along was the company XO, 1Lt Jim Wolfe, who recalls:

> It began to get dark quickly as we moved. I remember that we stopped at one point and when we moved out, two of our soldiers were left behind…Both men were picked up the next day by a helicopter they flagged down.
>
> We moved that night until we absolutely could not safely move any further. We did not dig in; we just stopped…you could literally not see your hand in front of your face. I remember sitting on the roots of a large tree under a poncho with a red lensed flashlight calling in the MIA report to battalion.

With them was PFC Dean Shultis, a third platoon trooper returning to the field after being sick, who flew in on a resupply chopper to find his platoon already moved out. So he grabbed his gear and went with the second platoon to try to get to them. Shultis remembers that as they moved that night, "it became so dark that we literally had to hold on to each other's shirt collar to keep from getting separated."

Second Platoon and the CP moved out again at first light and had not gone far when they drew fire. One of their squad leaders, Sgt John Wilson, 23, of Edmond, Oklahoma, was killed when his M-16 jammed on the first round. He had less than two months left in his tour. Shortly after that, they linked up with part of the third platoon spread on the slope of the hill. In

2002, Wolfe wrote a letter in support of another man who was there and described the action of the morning of October 16, 1966:

> I told several of the soldiers to watch the rear. They weren't there for what seemed like seconds when someone said, "Is that Johnson out there?". Someone else replied "No. Johnson is …" and then the world came apart. The North Vietnamese had come down off the hilltop where they had ambushed the 3rd Platoon and had come around to overrun us from the rear. I was on the left rear corner of the perimeter. A soldier by the name of Canady was killed laying flat on the ground ten feet behind me. He was shot down the throat while changing the magazines in his M16. One of the men at the point of the attack all of a sudden stood up and hollered, "Oh doc, I'm hit". He had a large hole in his left shoulder. We were also getting hand grenades in the middle of our position. Our artillery FO's RTO began to immediately call-in artillery. I remember seeing him not far at all behind me on one knee as he adjusted the fire … We took a number of friendly casualties from our own artillery.

The fight was at extremely close quarters. Wolfe could clearly hear the Vietnamese leader giving his people orders as they attacked. Harry Burke of the third platoon had been wounded twice the night before, the second time when a grenade exploded close to his face, blinding him in one eye. He was wounded again in the morning when a VC grabbed his leg and tried to pull him down an embankment. He kicked free but was shot in the butt as other men pulled him up.

With the artillery RTO bringing fire down almost on top of their position, the attack slackened, the VC withdrew, and second platoon was able to link up with and relieve the rest of the third platoon on the ridgeline. Burke heard later that his platoon was ambushed by two companies of VC.

Outnumbered, the platoon was also outgunned—the group trapped on the ridge was under heavy fire throughout the night from a VC 12.7mm heavy machine gun. SP4 Robert Marcavage had already been wounded twice crawling out to recover ammo for other men in his platoon. He now exposed himself to try to knock out the NVA machine gun with a LAW, a light shoulder fired rocket. Before he could fire, the machine gun hit his LAW, causing it to explode and kill him instantly. He was 19 years old, from Shamokin, Pennsylvania and, like Wilson, had less than two months to go in his tour. He had been wounded by a pungi stake about three months earlier. For his bravery he was posthumously awarded the Silver Star and Vietnamese Cross of Gallantry.

Dead on the trail from a head wound was SP4 Carlos Pirez-Berges of New York City, 22 years old and due to get out of the Army in less than a month. Just before the fight he told a couple of his buddies that he had written his mom that he was the mail clerk for the company and not to worry about him. William Stone of Denver, Colorado, 19 years old, was also killed. When the fire slackened and both parts of third platoon linked up, Doc Kilpatrick looked for Stone and asked if anyone had seen him. SP4 Sonny Cowan, the platoon's mortar FO, said, "Doc, haven't you heard?" Also killed in the fight was PFC Roy Canady of New York City, 19 years old. At least eight or nine men were wounded.

There were no clearings big enough to bring in a chopper, either for medevac or resupply. Both platoons were extremely thirsty and out of water. The battalion commander had cans of chocolate milk brought out and dropped to the men. The dead and wounded were lifted out in metal baskets lowered from a hovering Chinook. Wolfe saw one dead trooper almost fall out of the basket as he was being hoisted up and prayed, "Oh God, don't let him fall. He's been through enough," After the casualties were evacuated, the company moved out. As they were leaving, Wolfe noticed a couple of troopers taking a dead VC, leaning him against a tree, and sticking a bloody 1st Cavalry patch in his mouth.

No assessment of VC casualties was made as the second and third platoons pulled out of the area. A few days later, another unit swept through the area and counted fifty-nine dead VC, most from the 52nd company, 95th battalion, 2nd VC Regiment.

Late on October 16, 1966, all platoons of Charlie Company reunited on the hilltop LZ where the battalion CP was located. Also closing on the LZ was Alpha Company which had lifted into the area as backup earlier in the day. A few days later, Lt Tim McCarthy and his first platoon were ordered to go on a reconnaissance in force patrol with a platoon of Alpha Company, under the overall command of Charlie Company's XO Jim Wolfe. Many of the men in the platoon felt it was a mission ordered mainly because the battalion commander thought there were too many troops idling around his CP. They were told it would be an overnight mission and to travel light so most men only packed two or three cans of C-rations.

A Very Lost Patrol

The patrol left the hilltop about mid-morning on October 18 or 19, 1966 and descended into a narrow valley, passing first through fields of elephant grass and then into triple canopy jungle. By mid-afternoon, a monsoon storm rolled in from the South China Sea, bringing the heaviest rain the men experienced in their tours in Vietnam. By the next morning, all the streams in the area had risen so much the patrol was effectively cut off from the battalion's LZ. The maps were useless and neither artillery spotting fire nor choppers were available in the storm to help the patrol fix its position, and it was soon lost.

By the third evening out, the men had used up their rations. The patrol reached a small hill with a clearing big enough for a chopper and managed to establish radio contact with Captain Sims. The rain ceased and the clouds broke and the men of first platoon could see the battalion LZ across a wide valley and watched a chopper lift off with resupply for them. Before it could cross the valley, the rain and clouds blew in and the flight was aborted. As rain filled their foxholes, SP4 Lynwood Berry, a grenadier, and two other men shared a last meal of a tin of peanut butter and some crackers. It would be another day and a half before the weather cleared and rations could be dropped to the patrol.

The next morning it rained even harder. As the patrol came to a small stream, the platoon from Alpha Company began to ford it. While they were crossing, it rose rapidly and began to overflow its banks. By the time first platoon reached it, it was a torrent of muddy water and could not be forded. The men on the far side cut a long bamboo pole to reach across the deepest and swift-est part of the stream. Each man waded out as far as he could, grabbing the end of the pole, hanging on, and stepping into the current. Two men on the far side held the pole, swinging it like a gate as the current pushed the man across the stream where two more men would grab him and pull him out.

Men lining up to cross stood in water that was thigh deep and rising, holding onto a small sapling and each other's web gear as they waited their turn. About two squads made it across the stream and then four men went into the river—either the bank collapsed or the sapling uprooted or the current just got too strong for them to hold on. Two men were pulled out of the water but two were swept downstream.

SFC Elijah Daniels from Bessemer, Alabama, had been pla-toon sergeant for less than two weeks, having replaced the platoon sergeant killed in late September. His body was found four days later by the third platoon a few kilometers downstream, caught in a tree about ten or fifteen feet above the stream's normal lev-el. PFC Harold Lee Harris, a 19-year-old from Durham, North Carolina, was never found. He was married and was excited that his wife was expecting their first child, due any day.

Although it was hungry and exhausted, the platoon searched for them the rest of that day. One squad was forced to stay on the far side of the stream without a radio and eventually backtracked to the previous night's clearing where they were picked up the next day. The storm broke that night and the next morning a chopper dropped C-rations and dry socks to the patrol, and after that some saws, axes, and C-4. An LZ barely big enough for one chopper was hacked and blown out of the jungle and both platoons were lifted back to rejoin their companies at the battalion CP.

The rest of the month passed without incident. New replacements arrived and were assigned to squads. Rumors flew and some men hoped the battalion would go back to An Khe for a standdown and a few days of rest, cold beer, and maybe a pass to Sin City. Others were sure LTC Siegrist would keep them in Bong Son until he beat the division's record for most consecutive days in the field. As it turned out, no rumor predicted Charlie Company's next move.

Into the Ia Drang Valley

On October 31, 1966, Charlie Company was pulled out of the Suoi Ca Mountains, lifted to LZ Hammond, and flown from there by C-130's to Duc Co, a Special Forces camp southwest of Pleiku. A major operation—Paul Revere IV—was underway with the 4th Infantry Division and an attached brigade of the 25th Infantry Division in the Plei Trap Valley and the 1/5th was ordered back to the Cambodian border to cover their rear and block any infiltration through the Ia Drang Valley. When the men in the company found out where they were going, the older guys told the new replacements they'd be earning their Combat Infantry Badges soon.

The company spent the first few days set up near the Special Forces Camp. Dean Shultis shared his foxhole with a new man in his platoon, Carlito Dorsey. Dorsey was hoping to become a combat artist and drew Shultis' portrait on a back of a C-ration box, which Shultis sent home to his parents.

Dorsey was from the Philippines and hoped that serving in the Army would help him get citizenship and go to college in California, where his recently emigrated parents lived. His talent was known to the Army and he was offered an artist job with division headquarters but he turned it down as he felt he needed to see combat to be a real combat artist. Three weeks later he was killed in the Ia Drang Valley.

Charley Company then air assaulted into the Chu Pong Mountains, close to LZ X-Ray and Hill 534. The company operated there for a few days without contact, the only sign of the NVA a skull someone found on a patrol, a remnant from one of the earlier battles. The company then operated on the high plateau west of Pleiku for a few weeks. It was the dry season there and the days were fairly pleasant, at least as things went in Vietnam, and it was easier than operating in the coastal mountains, with their steaming humidity and daily rain, double and triple canopy rain forests, and fields of elephant grass.

In mid-November, Charlie Company was conducting search and destroy sweeps near a Montagnard village when it got a new CO, Captain Harold Wunsch. On the 16th or 17th, it went back into the Ia Drang Valley, this time air-assaulting onto LZ X-Ray. Although the men of Charlie Company were never told this, the 1st Cavalry had solid intelligence that fresh NVA regiments were poised just across the border in Cambodia, ready to infiltrate into South Vietnam. Captain James Taylor, then the CO of Bravo company, recalled that in terms of getting useful intelligence about NVA actions, intent, or capability, "Back in those days, down at our level, we were like mushrooms…kept in the dark with lots of BS." Still, it is reasonable to assume this intelligence was known at the battalion and brigade level.

On November 19, 1966, a scout chopper spotted about twenty NVA just inside the border. Charlie Company air-assaulted into a small clearing with each of its platoons fanning out in a different direction. They and Alpha Company, operating to the north, found fresh trails through the brush but no NVA. As night fell on the 20th, first platoon had not linked up with the rest of the company so it set up an ambush about 800 meters south of the second and third platoons, which were about 200 meters apart with third platoon along a wide and well used trail. All the positions were within a few hundred meters of the unmarked border with Cambodia.

During the night, the NVA probed third platoon and a few NVA penetrated the platoon's perimeter. One NVA soldier was shot and killed by SSgt Henry Brown and the others, probably three or four more, faded back into the bush with one NVA soldier yelling out "Tomorrow you die G.I." The dead NVA had new equipment and a fresh uniform.

SSgt Brown continued to hear movement outside their perimeter during the night, but Wunsch apparently dismissed it as the result of nerves. Sgt Edwin Cutler kept hearing a strange noise he couldn't identify. At first light he saw that the dead NVA had fallen on an ant hill and the noise had been hundreds of red army ants chewing on the corpse's exposed flesh.

First platoon started November 21, 1966, by moving south along the border to set up a blocking position for the rest of the company. By about 1000 hours, it was probably between 1,200 to 1,500 meters south of the other platoons. Third platoon remained at its ambush position where it was joined the by second platoon and company CP while resupply was dropped to them from a Huey. While they were together, third platoon's platoon sergeant and acting leader, a former member of the Army's Golden Knights parachute team, picked up the dead NVA's AK-47 and emptied the magazine into his head. He supposedly did this to show the new men the serious nature of war, but he was new himself, a replacement for a platoon sergeant wounded in mid-October.[9]

---

9. The men who were there all remember this happening, but decades later some differ on the details. One man remembers the platoon leader ordering a new man to shoot the dead NVA. Another man remembers Capt Wunsch as the shooter.

Third platoon had a man sick with severe abdominal pains with no nearby clearing for a medevac, so Wunsch ordered them to detach a squad to take him to LZ Hawk, about 1,500 meters to the northeast. SSgt Brown was picked to lead the squad—he considered it a suicide mission given the obvious signs of NVA presence, but handpicked some men for the task. In doing so he saved their lives.

Once Brown and his squad left with the sick man, thirteen men altogether, the remaining twenty-two men of third platoon stayed put while Wunsch and the second platoon began a wider sweep of the area with between thirty-five to forty men. The rest of the battalion was widely scattered. The closest troops were two platoons of Alpha Company about two kilometers to the north.

At about 0930 hours, second platoon spotted some NVA moving along the border and Wunsch ordered them to recon by fire and called in artillery. About a half hour later, the platoon spotted five or six more NVA standing on a small knoll with their backs to them. Despite having just hit the area with artillery and small arms fire, Wunsch thought the NVA were unaware of the platoon's presence and ordered it to sweep towards the knoll. It soon became clear that the NVA were intentionally exposing themselves to draw the platoon into a prepared ambush. As it neared the knoll, the company's artillery forward observer, SP4 Bill Tuey of the 1/77th Artillery, told Wunsch he was heading into an ambush.

Second platoon advanced towards the knoll and fired on the NVA, killing some of them. As they reached its base, the NVA opened up with machine gun and AK fire, hitting a number of men. At approximately 1005 hours, Wunsch radioed LTC Siegrist to report they had killed about six or eight NVA. He added, "I think we're holding our own." But the platoon was already pinned down in the high grass and the NVA on the higher ground simply fired wherever they saw grass move.

About ten or fifteen minutes into the fight, Wunsch radioed third platoon, about 200 meters away, to come to their aid. As they moved out, they were attacked on all sides by at least a company of NVA, who crawled undetected through the high grass until they were in hand grenade range. By then, both Wunsch and Lt Richeson, second platoon's leader, had most likely been wounded and gotten morphine from a medic. As third platoon got hit, the volume of fire against it was so great that Wunsch told his RTO to contact third platoon and, "Tell them to quit their damn firing." Shortly after that, the second platoon medic, SP4 Louis Castillo, 23, from Chicago, was killed and the company medic severely wounded.

Second platoon's fight devolved into small battles for survival led by the platoon sergeant and squad leaders, Sergeants Logan, Lee, Workman, and Giordano. After the platoon sergeant was hit, SSgt Henry Lee took charge of the platoon. Other leadership was provided by FO SP4 Tuey, who began to call in artillery support from a battery of 105 mm howitzers. Tuey, still a few weeks short of his nineteenth birthday, effectively handled all supporting fire and communication with the other platoons from that point on. Both Lee and Tuey were awarded Silver Stars. Lee's citation stated:

Sergeant Lee's squad and elements of another platoon engaged a large enemy force near a small hill as they searched for several North Vietnamese Army soldiers who had been spotted earlier. When one of his men was wounded, Sergeant Lee immediately moved from his secure position and exposed himself to the intense enemy fire to move the wounded soldier to safety. As the battle continued, both the platoon leader and the platoon sergeant were wounded. Sergeant Lee immediately took charge and continued to direct effective fire on the enemy positions. His gallant action contributed significantly to the defeat of the enemy force and prevented his platoon from being overrun.

The ambush of the third platoon probably lasted no more than fifteen or twenty minutes before the platoon was overrun. Tuey was in contact with the platoon's RTO, PFC John Godfrey, who said they were surrounded and asked that artillery be fired directly on their position. Tuey tried to raise Godfrey again on the radio but got no response so told Godfrey to press the talk button on his radio handset if he was still alive and unable to talk. Godfrey apparently did so as Tuey could hear gunshots and people speaking Vietnamese before the radio went dead for good. Godfrey was 22 and from Ligonier, IN.

A few men continued to fight after radio contact was lost and the two survivors of the ambush each recall being the last man firing. Sgt Julius Durham was hit in the arm trying to lead his squad to break the ambush. PFC Anthony Gray, an ammo bearer for a machine gun, kept firing and throwing grenades after the gunner and assistant gunner were hit. After his M-16 jammed, he was hit in the eye and jaw by rifle fire and grenade shrapnel. The NVA moved through the area killing any wounded men still alive and taking their weapons and Godfrey's radio. Durham and Gray played dead as they heard the NVA walking among them, talking, and laughing and shooting the wounded as they came upon them. Durham believes five or six wounded men were executed in this fashion.

The NVA who ambushed third platoon, estimated to be at least a company, then moved to join the fight against second platoon, still pinned down at the base of the knoll about 200 meters away. They hit the flank of second platoon with automatic weapons and B-40 rocket grenades, killing everyone except machine gunner PFC John Dalton. Although wounded twice, he stayed at his gun and repelled the attacking North Vietnamese until he lost consciousness. His position was overrun and his M-60 taken by the NVA, but he held them off long enough for the air strikes to arrive. He also received a posthumous Silver Star for bravery.

Shortly after the fight started, both the first platoon and two platoons of Alpha Company were ordered to move to support the company. Both groups had just started when third platoon was ambushed. At the same time, SSgt Brown's squad with the sick man was heading away from the ambush site. They had gone a few hundred meters when they heard gunfire and the calls from Godfrey saying that their platoon was surrounded. While they could hear Godrey and Tuey, they were unable to make radio contact with the rest of the company. They were taking sporadic fire and it was clear that some NVA were following them, so they continued on, while men at LZ Hawk fired shots to guide them in.

First platoon reached second platoon just after an air strike hit the NVA on the knoll with napalm and cannon fire, about two hours after the NVA first sprung their trap. No one at battalion or brigade requested air strikes until at least 1130 and the first strike did not arrive until after noon. By then over half the platoon were killed or wounded, both its machine guns knocked out, and some men had rifles that were hopelessly jammed. There were probably ten to twelve men holding off at least two companies of NVA, with some of them having to toss working M-16s back and forth during the fight. Everyone on the platoon's right flank was dead except for machine gunner John Dalton, and he was unconscious and died before he could be medevaced. He was 19 years old and from Chicago.

To this day, Ed McCoin wonders why second platoon wasn't overrun as well. He was the company's RTO and after Captain Wunsch was wounded, McCoin found himself on the edge of the platoon, with all the men to his right dead. His M-16 jammed early in the fight, and he tried to eject the spent round with a knife, but it wouldn't budge so he crawled over to the dead men and grabbed more rifles and ammo. The next M-16 he tried also jammed but after he found one that worked, he thinks he killed about six or seven NVA near his position.

I was a rifleman in the first platoon that day. It took us almost two hours of hard humping, sometimes trying to run in full gear, before we reached the second platoon, finally locating them by the noise and smoke from the air strike. I later wrote about my experiences that day:

My platoon reached the 2nd platoon just minutes after the air strike. Hit hard by the napalm, the NVA broke off their attack and were retreating to Cambodia as we approached from the other direction. A few shots were fired in our direction, but for the most part silence was settling back into the valley. One of the first men I saw had a jammed rifle and no way to clear it. The early model M-16's we carried were prone to seriously malfunction in combat—a cartridge would get stuck in the rifle's chamber and the only way to get it out was to break open the weapon, take the bolt out, and run a cleaning rod down through the barrel to knock the cartridge out. To do this while being attacked by NVA on higher ground and armed with AK-47's, a much more durable and lethal weapon, was difficult enough under any circumstances, but some of the men in the 2nd platoon did not even have cleaning rods. I don't know how many men had jammed M-16s on that day but there is no doubt in my mind that some of them died holding a rifle that couldn't fire.[10]

I gave my cleaning rod to the man with the jammed M-16. When he finished clearing his rifle, I took it to the next position where another man also had a jammed weapon. Then our platoon medic waved me over to help him with some wounded men so I told the man with the jammed rifle to pass the cleaning rod down the line when he was done. Our medic was treating the company medic who had been shot through both legs and the chest so I tried to stabilize another man with an arm wound until the medic could get to him.

Then Lt McCarthy told me to go and collect the dog tags from the casualties on the right flank. I didn't know then how many men were dead, so I was stunned when I got there. Most of the dead GI's were about eight to ten feet apart, but I found two friends of mine from training lying within a few feet of each other—PFCs Joe Scicutella from the Bronx and Joe Rabon from South Carolina. Some of the dead weren't wearing their dog tags around their neck so I had to search their bodies, cursing them under my breath as I did so. I came back to McCarthy's position with the dog tags I could find and gave them one of the 2nd platoon NCO's and then joined other men trying to cut down some trees to make a clearing big enough for a medevac chopper to land.

All we had were some machetes and we hacked away with them, but the trees were a type of tropical ironwood, and we barely scratched the bark. We continued for a while as much out of frustration as anything else, but we soon had to give up. The only way to get the wound-

10. The Army denied that the M-16 had a tendency to jam and blamed any problems on poor maintenance by troops in the field. It failed to take any steps to remedy the defects of the rifle until forced to do so by Congress, which conducted hearings in late 1967 after receiving complaints about the M-16 from the parents of soldiers and marines who had received letters from their sons telling how comrades had died with jammed weapons.

ed out was by a medevac chopper specially equipped with a hoist and it could only take one wounded man at a time. The first man lifted up through the canopy was the company medic — in addition to his chest wound he had been shot through both legs just below his genitals and our medic had to cut his clothes away to dress his wounds. His crotch was exposed and soaked in blood as he was strapped to the stretcher and hauled up and some of us thought he had been shot through his balls. Years later I heard he survived his wounds.

About a week after the battle, I got a letter from home saying that one of my closest friends from high school had been killed in action on November 19th. I sat on the edge of a foxhole and wrote a letter to his parents saying that he died fighting for a good cause, that we were in Vietnam to defend freedom, and more in that vein, words that I was rapidly coming to believe were empty and meaningless. Only decades later did I find out that he was killed, along with seventeen others in his battalion, part of the 25th Infantry Division, about 30 kilometers north of us as part of the same operation we were in.

Around the same time first platoon reached second platoon, Alpha Company arrived at the site of third platoon's ambush where they found nineteen men dead and three wounded — Durham, Gray, and a third man who died without regaining consciousness. When Gray realized they had been rescued by Alpha company, he asked for a friend of his, PFC John Dickerson. They had become friends in base camp after finding out they were both from Philadelphia. Alpha's medics treated Gray's wounds and Dickerson stayed with him until he was medevaced to keep him from going into shock. Gray was the first man medevaced and was back in the States and medically discharged within a month. With that and the loss of the rest of his squad in the ambush, he was overlooked by many of the men in the company who were there on November 21st. For decades, many of us thought Durham was the only survivor from the third platoon.

With no clearings nearby, the wounded from both platoons had to be lifted out by a medevac chopper equipped with a hoist. There was only one chopper available with a hoist and it could only take one casualty at a time so it would fly each man to a secure LZ to transfer him to another chopper and then fly back for the next casualty. Each wounded man would be strapped to a stretcher and held upright until he was slowly winched up through the canopy and hauled into the chopper. As more of second platoon's wounded were hoisted up, blood dripped down on the men steadying the stretchers.

It was late afternoon before the dead could be taken out by Chinooks who dropped cargo nets to the men below. The dead were wrapped in ponchos and stacked two and three deep on the nets with their equipment thrown on top of them. The nets were secured, hooked to a cable, and hoisted up through the trees by the hovering Chinooks, which flew away with the nets dangling beneath them, taking the dead to the rear and an early return home.

Charlie Company had thirty-four men killed that day, with another eleven to fourteen wounded, out of about fifty-five to sixty men from the second and third platoons and company CP. Thirteen of them had been in Vietnam a month or less and died in their first battle. Another eleven men had come to Charlie Company as replacements in late August. In addition to Lee, Tuey and Dalton, Sgt Durham, PFC Gray, and Captain Wunsch were also awarded Silver Stars after the battle.

Two of the men killed—PFCs Gary Byford and Larry Naasz,

21 and 24 years old—were from Roundup, Montana, a ranching and mining town of about 2,000 people in the middle of the state. They joined the Army together under the buddy system so they would be assigned to the same unit and were the only men from Roundup killed in the war.

Another pair of friends killed that day were PFCs Joe Scicutella, 20, from New York City, and Joe Rabon, 19, of Charleston Heights, SC. They became close friends in infantry training and jump school and came to Charlie Company together as replacements in late August. They were opposites in many ways and the men in their squad called them "Mutt & Jeff". They died next to each other on second platoon's right flank. Months later, after rotating home and spending an evening in an NCO club, their former squad leader, SSgt Frank Giordano, wrote Scicutella's sister Carol:

> This might not mean a lot to someone back home, but these kind of men in Vietnam were few. Joe & Rabon were different from the day they got there. Asking questions & wanting to learn. Never once did they show fear. I know it was there but they kept it in …
>
> Joe & Rabon were smart & brave. Maybe if they would have been like some of the guys who you had to kick in the rear to move out & make sure they didn't fall asleep. Maybe they would have come home. Never one time did I have to turn & go back and get them. When I moved they moved.
>
> The day of the fight, they were not in my squad. So if you're wondering why I came home. Well 15 men owe their lives to Joe & Rabon & the rest of the men of the 1st squad … You see we got hit & then they hit us in the rear & the 1st squad moved into the grass to meet them. We were busy on our side & no one knows what happened until it was over & I went to check the men & didn't find them on our right.

I moved to the rear & found them. Joe & Rabon were out the farthest with Sgt. Woodsmall. Their actions along with the other members of the 1st squad held them back & saved us until help reached.

Carol, there are a lot of guys in the army who play sick & more so in Vietnam. Now a lot of those guys are back, & the ones who do their job & know why they were there, either come home hurt or dead … In my feeling, it was a honor to know him & Rabon & it will be a long time before I forget them.

The other members of Charlie Company killed on 21 November were: SFC Bobbie Letbetter (32, Goldthwaite, TX); SSG Charles "Pops" Malone (40, Danville, PA); SSG Max Woodsmall (32, Elnora, IN); SGT Theodore Alkire (32, Rigedley, WV); SP4 Norman Farris (25, Springfield, MA); SP4 Eugene Mitchell (32, Scottsboro, AL); SP4 James Smythe (21, Reeds Springs, MO); SP4 Wilbert Stewart Jr. (20, Baltimore, ML); SP4 Donald Vernon (20, Ocala, FL); PFC Eduardo Chavez (20, Santa Paula, CA); PFC Carlito Dorsey (21, Seaside, CA); PFC Ralls Hawkins (19, Macon, GA); PFC Charles Hicks (19, Hazard, KN); PFC Harvey Johnson III (19, Madison Heights, VA); PFC Marion Johnson (21, Milledgeville, GA); PFC Carroll Jones (20, Richmond, VA); PFC Arnold Krasnoff (21, New York, NY); PFC Gamaliel Marcano-Diaz (20, Bayamon, PR); PFC Jerry Sabens (20, Salem, IN); PFC Edward Scahill (19, Randolph, MA); PFC Samuel Smith (19, Baltimore, ML); PFC Andrew Stephens (22, Livingston, TX); PFC Clifford Stout (20, Trenton, NJ); PFC Alvin Tucker (20, Nashville, NC); PFC George Turner (1/77th Artillery, 19, Mulga, AL); PFC Lester Unger (22, Centerville, OH); and PFC John Waden (21, Malden, MA).

A day after the battle, PFC Sonny Cowan, a mortar platoon RTO with the third platoon, wrote his mother (in part):

Dear Mom,

I can tell you right now this isn't going to be the most pleasant letter you have ever received, but I have to have someone to take my problems to. If a person can't take them to his mother, I don't know who he can take them to.

Yesterday was the biggest catastrophe that has ever happened to Charlie Company since it has been in Viet Nam. I guess I had better start from the beginning.

On November 20, the third platoon found a well-used trail leading into Cambodia... We had our positions set by 2:00 pm and settled down for the long wait. At seven o'clock we heard firing at our rear. I got on the radio and found out that five North Vietnamese Regulars had walked into our ambush from the rear. We killed one of them and the others got away.

The next morning the regular Forward Observer, Humble, was having pains in his side from where he had got his ribs banged up the day before.

We couldn't get a medicine ship in so a squad for the third platoon had to take him back to LZ Hawk which was 1200 meters away. I was in that squad and was I ever griping because they weren't sending any more than a squad back. Especially since I knew there were four NVA out there, but there wasn't anything I could do about it. Before we left, the second platoon joined up with the third. My squad's mission was to get Humble back to LZ Hawk then return to the third platoon.

My squad had gone about four hundred meters when we heard all kinds of automatic weapons fire. I picked up my handset and began monitoring my radio.

I can still hear Godfrey right now. He was the third platoon R.T.O. He was hollering over the handset to get A.R.A and artillery in there. He was telling them to shoot it anywhere, that the Cong were all around them. They needed an F.O. I begged and pleaded to Sergeant Brown to let me go back and see if I could help them out. I can call in Artillery and A.R.A both. About ten minutes after the shooting started, Godfrey came over the radio and said Sergeant Leadbetter had been hit in the back.

The Last time I heard Godfrey he was still yelling for A.R.A. then a burst of automatic weapons came over the radio and we couldn't hear them anymore. We could see some Cong moving up right behind us. Every now and then we could hear bullets fly through the trees.

We made it to L.Z. Hawk by 12:00. In the meantime, Bravo [sic] company was coming up on the third platoons rear to give them some help. When they got there all they found was 23 dead GIs. My platoon had been over run and wiped out.

Those were 23 of the best men in this world. Its kinda hard for me to understand how something like that could happen. I'll never forget those men as long as I live. They were the kind of people that would give you the shirt off their back if you asked them for it. I've never prayed so much in my life as I did on my way back to LZ Hawk. I guess God just meant for things to turn out the way they did. I don't even think I'm going to try to make any more friends over here. It just doesn't seem to do any good. It sure is a funny feeling to know I was one of the ten men that was spared out of the third platoon.

Before the day was over second platoon had 12 KIA's and 14 WIA's.

Well, I feel better now that I've talked to someone. I am still at L.Z. Hawk. We are supposed to be here for one more day, then I don't know where we are going.

—With All My Love Sonny

P.S. Please don't worry, mom. I know God is with me ever where I go, besides I've done enough worrying in the last two days for the both of us.

Charlie Company was lifted out of the valley the next day and spent the next two or three days at a large firebase. LTC Siegrist called the company together and told the men he didn't expect to see any prisoners taken by Charlie Company for some time.

Within days of the battle, the Army declared victory. The 1st Cav's in-house newspaper the "Cavalair" said Charlie Company mauled the NVA and won a fierce fight against a much larger force, identified as a battalion of the NVA 101C Regiment, recently infiltrated down the Ho Chi Mind trail to join the war in the south. Estimates of their casualties grew in the days after the battle. On November 22, the 1/5th operations log reported that the 'final' body count was 119 NVA KIA and 75 WIA. Then it was 145 enemy dead and then LTC Siegrist, the battalion commander, estimated total enemy loses, killed and wounded, as "near the 300 mark."

The Ia Drang Valley had little value to the Army except as a place to find and fight the NVA. But in the valley, the NVA revealed themselves and fought only when it was to their advantage. While Charlie Company may have been the last ones standing on a remote patch of ground in the valley on the evening of November 21, the Army abandoned it the next day as it did so many other remote clearings, hilltops, and valleys in the borderlands of Vietnam. As for the North Vietnamese infantrymen who also fought and died for the same remote patch of jungle, Bill Tuey summed it up years later in something he wrote for his children and grandchildren:

When checking the bodies of the dead NVA, I discovered a wallet on one of the soldiers. He was one of the NVA I had shot and had seen him fall when I shot him. Inside was a picture of what appeared to be his wife and young son. This was the first time I was able to humanize the NVA soldiers and understand they were fighting for a cause and were no different than us, only on the other side.

Charlie Company operated for a few more weeks west of Pleiku but stayed away from the border. It got a few replacements and a new company commander, Captain Robert Lowry, but basically worked as a two-platoon company until it returned to base camp in An Khe on December 6, 1966 via convoy through Mang Yang pass. Charlie Company and the 1/5th had been in the field for ninety straight days, its longest operation to date. Over the next few months, Lowry would do much to restore both the morale and combat effectiveness of the company.

Standdown in Base Camp

There was always a routine to the company's return to "Black Knight Heights" after an operation, even as the returns became less frequent. The first task was always to thoroughly clean each weapon with gasoline at a cleaning station at the end of the company street. Only then could a man shed what was left of his uniform from weeks in the jungle and head for the showers, a shed with a few 55-gallon drums on top holding water, warmed by the sun, for a company of men. Machine gunners often lost out as the water would be used up by the time they finished cleaning their M-60s. Men would throw their old jungle fatigues in a burn barrel by the showers, sometimes forgetting there were loose rounds in the pockets, and the rounds would cook off in the fire.

After cleaning their weapons and themselves and getting new fatigues, men would square away their gear in the company barracks. One for each platoon, they were wood sided with a tin roof, and on a concrete slab with sandbags piled on the sides. Men would lean their rucksacks off the end of their cots and hang their M-16s and M-79s on hooks on the wall. M-60s would lean against the wall or rest on their bipods under a gunner's cot with belts of ammo draped over them.

Then it was time to kick back. If a company got in early

enough in the day, some men might still get a pass to go into the Vietnamese town of An Khe. If not, "Charlie's Hole", the company's EM club, would open up and start serving beer and soon be smoke-filled and crowded. Poker games would start and guys would recap the last operation. Guys got drunk but their buddies looked after them. Still, there was some kind of incident at every standdown — either a man had to be disarmed or someone threw a tear gas grenade into another platoon or company's area.

The company got new replacements just about every standdown, but now about half the company needed to be replaced and Charlie Company used the time to outfit and absorb the influx, including most of what had been the 2nd Brigade's recon and security platoon.

The company also got a new first sergeant, Master Sergeant Robert Fowler, a decorated Korean War veteran who liked walking point better than the traditional duties of a company top sergeant. Once in Charlie Company, he kept extending his tour to stay with it and reportedly turned down a promotion to Sergeant-Major as it would require him to stay in the rear.

A few days after it returned, the battalion held a memorial service for the men lost in the past three months. Sonny Cowan wrote home about it:

Dear Mom,

We finally had the memorial services for the men we lost on our last operation. It was really a wonderful service and the 68 men that lost their lives out of our battalion really deserved such a fine service. They had 68 rifles with steel pots on them in a shape of a cross. It was centered around the flagpole. The flag was flying at half-mast. They read off all the names of the men that got killed, there were forty-eight from Charlie Company. The rest were from the other three companies in our battalion. Then they gave them a 21-gun salute and played taps. By the time it was all over with I had a knot in my throat so big I could hardly swallow. I hope I never have to go to another one of those things as long as I live.

Love always, Sonny

This standdown lasted over ten days, one of Charlie Company's longest. The 1st Cavalry had not yet established a training course for new replacements, so the company and battalion did training exercises outside of base camp, some with live fire. New men learned to rappel from a large banyan tree up the hill from the battalion mess hall. Between training and time off, there were always details, with the worst one burning shit from the latrines.

There was a crude outdoor movie theater by the banyan tree, a plywood screen painted white and some benches, but there was rarely anything worth watching. Most good movies went to units in the rear and Charlie Company usually got reruns of old TV shows. One of the most frequent was "Combat", about a squad of infantry men in World War II, and it was good for a lot of laughs and cynical jokes. The guys in the company didn't take it seriously but at one standdown in early 1967, some Montagnard soldiers did. They were members of a Special Forces CIDG unit and apparently were seeing people on a screen for the first time. When the men in the TV show got ambushed by Germans, one of them stood up and emptied his carbine into the plywood screen.

For the first two days of a standdown, about half the men in the company got day passes for An Khe at a time. An Khe had been little more than a village on the road between the coast and Pleiku before the 1st Cav set up there and now it was a garrison town serving the division's base camp. Men with a pass could be in town between 0900 and 1800 and for those hours at least, it resembled a town from the old west. Vietnamese with carts pulled by ponies were the only taxi service and troops with too much to drink would sometimes commandeer the carts for a race on the main street, paying off their owners in MPC. Other times the carts had to dodge large convoys rumbling through the town on the way to Pleiku, Kontum, and Dak To.

A man could do a lot in An Khe—get tailored jungle fatigues or have a Zippo lighter engraved—but the big draw was 'Sin City', located just outside of town. New replacements flying into base camp for the first time could see it on the approach and sometimes thought it was a military compound. It was in a way—the Army had set it up as a result of the high rate of venereal disease suffered by the division in its first six months around An Khe. Of course, the rate of VD was much higher among the service and support units permanently working out of base camp than among the infantry companies in the field.

'Sin City' was a square compound surrounded by barbed wire with one entrance guarded by Army MPs, who checked men's passes and made sure no one was carrying a weapon. All prostitutes were required to work inside the compound and be checked for VD once a week by Army doctors. Inside the compound were rows of small establishments, with bars and black-market beer in the front and small cubicles in back, each run by an older ma-ma-san who collected money and kept business moving. At 1700 hours each afternoon, the MPs would sweep the compound and order any men there to head back to base camp.

'Sin City' was a depressing place, with nothing exotic about it. The women who worked there were mostly peasant girls forced into prostitution to support their families after they ended up in a refugee camp. Still, when the company was on a standdown and a lot of men got passes at the same time, 'Sin City' was the only place off base where men could go and drink and hang out together. On those occasions, the comradery of the men was worth far more than anything 'Sin City' could sell. In late 1967, a magazine or newspaper printed a story about 'Sin City' in the States and the political uproar forced the Army to shut it down.

Around December 18, Charlie Company was placed under the control of 3rd Brigade for a small search and destroy mission four miles northwest of An Khe called Operation Santa Claus. While the battalion may have thought the operation would be a 'walk in the sun' to break in the new men, the company received sporadic sniper fire as it moved through the jungle. On December 20, first platoon leader 1Lt Timothy McCarthy, 25, of Ossining, NY, was killed and several of his men were wounded. The next day, several men in second platoon were wounded in a short firefight.

The company returned to An Khe on December 24, 1966, hoping for a few days rest over the Christmas truce. Instead, it was back to the field. At 1000 hours on Christmas Day, the battalion was ordered to return to Bong Son to join Operation Thayer II in response to intelligence reports that the PAVN Yellow Star Division was planning major attacks on 1st Cavalry firebases in the Kim Son Valley. The men squared away their gear and replenished their ammo and rushed through a hastily prepared turkey dinner. They were flown in C-130's to LZ Hammond southeast of the Suoi Ca Mountains. Once there, Charlie Company spent the night sleeping in the open by the side of the airstrip, waiting for further orders.

LZ Bird

Around mid-day on December 26, Charlie Company was lifted to LZ Uplift and put on the perimeter. As it took up positions that evening, two battalions of the 22nd NVA Regiment were closing in on LZ Bird, an artillery firebase where the Crow's Foot opened up to the larger Kim Son valley. Bird was on a small hill with a tributary of the Kim Son River winding around it. Despite there being higher hills on two or three sides, it had been used as a firebase off and on for the past ten months.

Now it held two batteries of artillery and was unprepared for an assault despite clear intelligence that the 3rd PAVN Division was planning to attack a US firebase around Christmas. It was secured by Charlie Company of the 1/12th, strung out in two-man positions, without barbed wire on much of the perimeter. The company was assigned to LZ Bird because of the heavy casualties it had taken in the past month and was understrength with about a third of its men new replacements.

The attack started around 0105 with mortar, recoilless rifle, and heavy machine gun fire, followed closely by a two-battalion assault. On one side of the perimeter the NVA had crawled under their own mortar fire to within four or five meters of the bunkers on the line before assaulting them. At 0125 Charlie Company was ordered to be ready to move. By then, much of the perimeter of Bird had been penetrated.

Radio contact with the LZ was lost for half an hour as the battle there broke down to close quarters fights in the gun pits. Charlie was ready for pickup at 0155, the men carrying just weapons and ammo. The company was picked up in three lifts but the first two were diverted to LZ Pony where the men stayed on the choppers, their rotors turning, while the third stayed at LZ Uplift, until contact was restored with LZ Bird.

On Bird, the survivors of Charlie Company, 1/12th and the two artillery units were pressed into one corner of the LZ. Most of the perimeter and a battery of 155mm howitzers had been overrun and some were being destroyed with satchel charges. On parts of the LZ, men survived by playing dead. When the NVA massed for a final attack, a 105mm howitzer lowered its barrel and fired two beehive rounds directly at them. This was the second time beehive was used in combat and it shattered the attack.

As the NVA started to pull back and radio contact was restored, reinforcements began to arrive. First in was a Blue Troop of the 1/9th Cav at 0224, followed by Charlie Company in three waves, landing one chopper at a time just outside the wire and climbing into the perimeter. When one of the first choppers touched down, a panic-stricken survivor of the assault ran by the men jumping off and leapt onto the chopper as it was lifting off.

The company was on the ground and spreading out by 0300 but the NVA had already pulled out, except for a few who didn't get the word. At 0400, Captain Lowry reported to the Division that the LZ was secure. For one Charlie Company man, it was his introduction to the war. PFC Joe Oleszkiewicz was a brand-new replacement:

When I reported to An Khe, I was assigned to Charlie Company, 1st Battalion, 5th Cav. I was told that the Company was out "in the field" and that they were on their way back to base camp. They came back on Dec 24, 1966. Christmas was the next day and after breakfast, we were told that we were moving out. (Merry Christmas!) The company had been back less than 24 hours and they were moving out again. We went to LZ Hammond and spent the night there. The next day we went to LZ Uplift. On Dec 27 at 1:20am they woke us up and told us that LZ Bird was over run and that we were going in as rein-forcements. They told us to only bring "guns and ammo". I remember someone saying that it must be pretty bad if we had to leave every-thing behind and only bring "guns and ammo". I was the new guy and it must have showed. One sergeant said to me "stick with me and you'll be OK". We landed at the base of the hill and made our way up as the NVA were retreating. I had been in the field less than 48 hours, and this was the first combat experience.

When PFC Dean Shultis reached the LZ, someone directed him to a position on the perimeter near a large fuel bladder:

The bladder had been penetrated by mortar fragments and was leak-ing fluid. The flares that illuminated the night were floating down by their parachutes. I saw a flare headed for the bladder. I didn't know what kind of fuel was in the bladder so took off with just my rifle and ammo, expecting a huge explosion. It didn't actually explode but it did catch on fire and burn. It burned for hours. At daylight I went back to find my gear melted in a puddle.

The day after the battle, PFC Sonny Cowan wrote a letter to his mother, saying in part:

In my last letter I told you we were a reactionary force. At five o'clock on the twenty-sixth we moved to LZ Uplift, where we figured we would probably spend a couple of days. At one thirty in the morning, we got a call from our battalion commander to roll up our gear and get ready to move. Landing Zone Bird was getting overrun by the Viet Cong. It was quite chilly out and a steady drizzle was falling. In thirty minutes after we got the call, we were in Huey helicopters heading for Bird. There were so many choppers in the air, it looked like a sky full of green and red flashing stars. When we reached Bird, they were still receiving some sniper fire, but nothing compared to what they had just gone through. Talk about some people glad to see Charlie Company come in. They said when Charlie saw the Hueys coming in he took off. When we set down, all you could see were dead and wounded laying around. It must have been some battle … Nobody from my company was hurt, which I'm sure must have disappointed our battalion commander. Everywhere I turned there was a puddle of blood.

Spencer Matteson was a mortarman with Charlie Company, 1/12th that night and recalled that "When you guys from the 1st of the 5th showed up, I thought I just might survive the night. You were a sight for sore eyes." Decades later, he wrote about his night at LZ Bird and described the scene that Charlie Company flew into:

Dawn is a long time coming. Sometime during the night, elements from the 1st Bn., 5th Cav. showed up to reinforce us. We've taken a terrible beating—especially my company and especially my platoon. Out of 26 men in my platoon, only six emerge without a scratch. I am one of them. We count about 15 dead and five wounded. The hilltop smolders and dead bodies sprawl everywhere. A strange silence envelopes the hill (though I'm half deaf from the battle) and the scene is surreally like living in a Bosch painting. Demolition experts arrive to disarm the satchel charges that failed to explode. We carefully reconnoiter our old positions, wary of booby traps, searching for wounded and assessing the damage in human terms.

The death toll at LZ Bird remains in dispute. Various Army sources put it at 27, 28, and 30 KIA with as many as 75 wounded, but many men who were there think it was much higher. A 1st Cavalry Unit Historical Report written just a few months after the battle by the Division's Office of Information and History puts the U.S. death toll at 58 KIA with 77 WIA. As Matteson noted, his small platoon alone had about 15 KIAs that morning.

His Platoon Sergeant, SSgt Delbert O. Jennings, received the Medal of Honor for leading the defense of the LZ. The NVA suffered greatly, especially from the surprise of the beehive rounds, and left around sixty bodies in the perimeter and more in the surrounding bush when they pulled out. For many men of Charlie Company, much of the next day was spend moving those bodies.

The Army wanted to assess the effect of the beehive rounds on live people, so they flew in waves of officers from battalion, brigade, and division levels who seemed to have no useful function, followed by a team of pathologists to conduct some on the spot autopsies. First, they ordered some men to drag all the NVA bodies inside the perimeter to a central spot on the LZ where the pathologists picked some out to cut up and examine. They draped a few ponchos on top of a low bunker and used that as their dissection table, helped by Charlie Company's senior medic, Doc Michael Kilpatrick.

A small bulldozer was lifted in to dig a mass grave for the

NVA outside the perimeter at the base of the hill. It was the height of the monsoon season and the ground was so saturated that the grave flooded as it was being dug. Men formed two-man teams to bury the dead NVA, with each team looping wire or a rope around a corpse's ankles and dragging it down the hill to be tossed into the shallow grave. The ground was wet, and a muddy trough formed as bodies were dragged down the same path, slick with blood and a few body parts. No officers or senior NCOs bothered to come down to check on the grave, so the men shoveled a thin layer of dirt over the dead NVA and went back up the hill to other duties.

Late in the day, the men's rucksacks and other gear that had been left at LZ Uplift caught up with them, dumped in a heap in the mud with many items missing or stolen. Charlie Company stayed at LZ Bird for two more days until the firebase was abandoned. The Army said it was no longer needed and by then the stench of rotting bodies was so bad that Bird was untenable.

On December 29, 1966, the company air-assaulted close to a small coastal village on the southern fringes of the Cay Giap Mountains where it set up overlooking the village and conducted day long patrols and night ambushes for the next few days. The NVA and VC had announced a twenty-four-hour truce for New Year's Day and the Army said it would suspend patrols so the men looked forward to a day of relaxing. The village was by a rocky cove with a sandy beach and on January 1 company members were told that half the men could go for a swim in the South China Sea at a time, with the other half guarding the perimeter on the hill.

The first group of men were enjoying themselves, many of them never having been in an ocean before, when the incoming tide created a dangerous undertow and men began being pulled under and swept away. A number were pulled out and saved by more experienced swimmers, but two men drowned. First and second platoon medics Bob Kastner and Pete VanTil gave CPR and mouth to mouth resuscitation to PFC Michael Cannady but were unable to revive him. Cannady was 21 and from Boones Mill, VA. PFC Larry Bullock's body was never recovered. He was from Somerset, KY and it was his twentieth birthday. A few weeks later, a Board of Officers declared him dead.

Operations Thayer II and Pershing

The next day the 1/5th was placed under the operational control of the 1st Brigade and all of its companies air-assaulted into rugged mountains west of the An Lao Valley, seeking the NVA units that had attacked LZ Bird. Charlie Company spent the night of January 2, 1967 on a high narrow ridge lashed by high wind and heavy rain from a storm blowing in from the ocean. It was too steep and windy for foxholes, hooches, or any semblance of a perimeter. The men huddled on the sheltered side of the ridge, but there was little chance the NVA would be anywhere near the higher elevations. The next day, Charlie Company air-assaulted into a small saddle closer to the valley, set up a perimeter and sent out ambushes and listening posts.

At about 2200 on January 3, 1967, the company was notified it was in the target area for a B-52 strike scheduled for 0800 the next morning and needed to be at least a kilometer away from its position by then. A few hours later, the LZ was hit by small arms fire and grenades with eight men wounded, two seriously. No medevac ships could land there during the night because of the terrain and weather and the wounded men weren't lifted out until about 0730 the next morning. The men moved rapidly down a wide trail, sometimes running in full gear, to clear the area and reach a deserted village on the valley floor before the B-52 strike. As the company got there, an OH-13 scout chopper flying overhead was hit by NVA fire and crashed and burned nearby.

On January 5, 1967, the battalion returned to the control of the 2nd Brigade and spent the rest of the month operating out of LZ Uplift and running air-assaults and search and destroy sweeps in the Suoi Ca Mountains and the highlands of the An Lao Valley. This set the pattern for most of the rest of 1967 in Binh Dinh Province: short and mostly uneventful search and destroy missions in the mountains, alternating with counterinsurgency and pacification sweeps of the villages on the Bong Son Plain and occasional stints guarding artillery firebases. Plus, the occasional firefight. At some point during the month, command of the 1/5th Cav passed from LTC Siegrist to LTC James Mapp.

In early February 1967, Operation Thayer II was terminated, and Operation Pershing began. A brigade of the 25th Infantry Division had moved from Pleiku and was operating in Bong Son south of the Lai Giang River. With Highway 1 and its rear secure, the 1st Cavalry established LZ English as a major combat support base near the district town of Bong Son, just north of the river. Its primary focus became the agriculturally rich Bong Son Plain, where the 22nd NVA Regiment was believed to be rebuilding from its losses at LZ Bird and other battles. Other rice growing areas where the company had operated were being systematically denied to the VC and NVA. Shelby Stanton described it in *Anatomy of a Division: The 1st Cav in Vietnam*:

> The 1st Cavalry Division instituted drastic clearing measures against the most troublesome VC base areas. The Kim Son (Crow's Foot), Soui Ca, and An Loa valleys were all written off as too remote and too hazardous to be effectively occupied. Classified as "denial areas",

the division made final sweeps of them and forcibly removed the remaining inhabitants. Once depopulated, the valleys were smothered with Agent Orange by the Vietnamese Air Force, which flew repeated crop-destruction missions. The division hoped that liberal application of this toxic chemical would poison all future rice production in the valleys, ruining their usefulness as enemy havens. The mass roundups also denuded the land of VC labor and military recruits but produced more than 93,000 refugees. The displacement problem became so acute that plans for other denial areas had to be dropped.

Most of the men of Charlie Company never knew they were now on a new operation as their daily routine barely changed, the main difference being a little less time in the mountains and more time sweeping through villages. For the most part, the units of the Yellow Star Division avoided combat unless they were cornered. The biggest threats to the men became hit and run attacks by small units and the growing number of booby traps found in and around the villages, many of them fashioned from dud U.S. bombs and shells repurposed by the VC and NVA.

One small attack came on the morning of February 7, 1967. A day or two before, the battalion started an operation in the An Loa Valley. Charlie Company air-assaulted onto a mountain ridgeline west of the valley and started to hump down to the valley floor. The terrain was thickly jungled, there were boulder fields on the valley slopes, and it was still the monsoon season. The company had to set up on the side of a hill when night fell.

The company rolled up and moved out by 0800 and within just a few minutes third platoon drew automatic weapons fire and its RTO, PFC William Hancock, was hit and killed walking behind his platoon leader, Lt Jim Wolfe. He was 19 and from

Fayette, WV. Wolfe described Hancock's death in a letter to his fiancée:

Mary, I lost a very good friend today, he was killed in action. He was my radio operator. I could tell you his name, but you would not know him. We were searching a hillside this morning and as my platoon was crossing an open area a couple of shots rang out. I hit the dirt and turned around to get the radio mic when I heard a groan from my radio operator, he was laying on his stomach. The medic came up just then and we turned him over and he died a minute later. I couldn't believe it, for he was just walking about two feet behind me and he was one hell of a fine kid. An infantry platoon leader usually only becomes friendly with three men in his platoon—the platoon sergeant, the medic, and the radio operator. I can't become friendly with any other of my men for a leader who is a nice guy gets people killed. Honey, my radio operator was a fine guy, I never heard him gripe once. If I told him to go do something, he did it with no questions asked. In fact, I guess I'd have to say the kid took care of me for we wouldn't have stopped for the night no more than 10 minutes and he'd come over and ask me if I wanted a cup of coffee. He knew how much I like coffee. I can't really believe he's dead, I was lying beside him when he died and I saw the men carry his body off but I can't believe he's gone. It's a lousy rotten war, Mary. I don't know now if I should have told you about this, but I had to get it off of my mind, so I told you.

Within a few more minutes, both second and third platoons were fully engaged with an estimated twenty VC. The company pulled back, taking one more man wounded, and called in an air strike. As four men struggled to carry Hancock's body down the rocky hillside, under fire and with no cover, Top Fowler yelled at them to carry him like a human being and not "a sack of shit."

Shortly after that, a new man was covering one of the company's flanks when a NVA soldier walked around a boulder and they had a face-to-face shootout with the NVA solider losing. Later in the day, Charlie Company pulled a few NVA out of a cave and captured a machine gun. Ed McCoin has always felt guilt over Hancock's death; they were from the same area of West Virginia and had become friends in the company. The week before Hancock died, McCoin had recommended him to Captain Lowry for an open RTO position.

Sometimes the danger came from our own side. PFC John Nowling, then a new replacement with third platoon, had a close call a few weeks later after setting up a defensive perimeter one evening:

Another soldier and I dug our foxhole for the night and set up our poncho hooch. He volunteered to take first watch and I stretched out on my air mattress in the hooch. I was soaking wet and cold and since it was still light out enough for me to have a fire I decided to get up and fix a can of hot chocolate. I made myself a heat tab cooking stove and prepared a can of hot chocolate. I stood up and started to take a drink when all of a sudden there was a loud noise right behind me like a shot went off. It startled me enough that I jerked and spilled the hot chocolate. All of us were puzzled at first as no one had fired a shot. Then someone noticed my hooch. It was ripped open and inside the hooch was splattered with mud. My air mattress had mostly disappeared in a large mudhole. Then someone figured out what had happened. In the process of getting artillery registered for the night, the artillery FO had called for a smoke marking round to be fired. The smoke markers had landed outside of our perimeter where they were wanted but the empty artillery casing had landed squarely on my air mattress. If I had not decided to drink a hot chocolate, I likely would have been torn apart by the heavy casing coming from high in the air.

In mid-February 1967, Top Fowler pulled off the rare feat of sinking a Huey. The company had set up by a river when a resupply chopper approached its LZ. It was about to touch down when the First Sergeant decided he wanted it to land closer to the CP so he waved it off. As it passed over the river, its propwash detonated a large booby trap buried in the sand, causing the pilot to lose control, and set down in about five feet of water. No one was hurt and the chopper was later salvaged. But first some of the men in the company borrowed a local villager's canoe and paddled out to rescue the hot meal the chopper was carrying.

Battle on the Bong Son Plains

On the evening of March 19, 1967, a company of the 1/8th Cavalry made contact with an estimated NVA battalion on the northern edge of the Bong Son Plain near the mountainous border with Quang Ngai Province. Four other battalions, including 1/5th, joined the fight over the next twenty-four hours. Just as this happened, Charlie Company's well-liked CO, Captain Robert Lowry, was relieved because of high blood pressure and replaced with an unknown staff officer, Captain Daniel Anderson. Alpha, Bravo, and Delta Companies of the 1/5th air assaulted into the fight on the afternoon of March 20 and Alpha Company was soon hit on three sides by the NVA.

Charlie Company had been held back but made a night air-assault at 2230 to come to Alpha's relief. After moving more than a kilometer through the darkness, it linked up with Alpha Company by a burning village that lit the area as bright as day. By then the NVA broke contact and there was only sporadic covering fire as they retreated, under fire from the AC-47 gunships called "Puff" or "Spooky" by the men. Charles Hagemeister, a medic with Alpha Company, was awarded the Medal of Honor for his actions that night.

At mid-morning the next day, part of Charlie Company got

online and assaulted a line of houses, firing from the hip as they moved. There was no return fire and John Nowling always felt that the assault was ordered to give an ABC news crew that was nearby something to film. Around that time, other units made contact with a second NVA battalion about three kilometers to the southwest. At about 1340 hours, Charlie Company was picked up and air assaulted into a field and began sweeping the closest village. The ABC news crew flew in with them and filmed part of the air assault and subsequent action.

First platoon medic Bob Kastner was in a Huey that hovered four or five feet off the ground as troopers jumped out. The last man out, part of Kastner's web gear caught on a piece of metal, leaving him hanging out the side of the chopper as it dipped its nose and started to lift off. A quick-thinking door gunner on the Huey pulled Kastner's gear loose and he fell about ten feet to the ground.

As the company moved toward the village, the NVA opened up, catching it in the open with first and second platoons hit hardest. Alpha, Bravo, and Delta Companies, along with a company from 1/8th, had been inserted into the same area and were also hit, but not as hard as Charlie Company. SSgt Bill Sharp was a squad leader in the second platoon and remembers the day:

> [CPT Anderson] had just taken over for CPT Lowry that morning. We had just airlifted to a blocking position. We were going to surround the village, the 3rd platoon was on my right, 1st platoon was on the left and 2nd platoon's first squad was on the left leading into the village. SGT Lee was in the first squad and they and the platoon leader went on down the trail. I had the 2nd squad in the middle of the rice paddy.
>
> SGT Finley was about 20 feet from the village and just as he

turned around and said, "Sarge, what did you say?" three rounds went through his rucksack and got his #3 B can. At that time, we all returned fire and dropped down behind the rice paddy dike.

We didn't have radios for every squad in the platoon. Weapons platoon and headquarters platoon were set up on a little hill returning fire and were getting fire from both sides—enemy as well as friendly. I figured if I was going to get shot, I had to do something, so I stood up and went up the trail looking for the command section.

When I got there, SP4 Richard Brewer and SP4 George Chiaramello were down in a fox hole and said that the "old man" was hiding in a fox hole behind them. That is when I got on the phone to the S3, CPT Taylor, and told him we needed them to knock out the tops of the trees because that is where the enemy was and we needed to get out of there. He told me to pop smoke and he sent in the gunships.

When the firing stopped, we found our platoon leader who had cracked up. We took him up on the hill and TOP Fowler came in and relieved him. We lost three that day from the 2nd Platoon. That is when TOP Fowler made me Platoon Leader, since I was the ranking person there.

John Nowling recalled how the day unfolded for the third platoon:

We moved south through a village area. The one thing I most remember about that was the strange quietness of the villagers as they stood in and near their doorways watching us pass by. I had the thought that they were terrified of us. Today I believe they were terrified—not of us but because they knew there were large numbers of the enemy in the immediate area and very soon all hell was going to break loose. An hour or so later, we were approaching the village of My Binh. Everything was quiet and peaceful.

We followed a well-worn path through an open field towards a grove of coconut palms. On our right was a stream lined by trees and bamboo thickets. We entered the grove and spread apart and formed a rough perimeter. Then without warning there was just this huge sudden eruption of dozens of rifles and automatic weapons from Charlie opening up on the whole company. Bullets were whining and ricocheting everywhere.

My heart sank as I realized—THE ENEMY IS HERE! I hugged the base of a palm tree, getting what cover I could. Suddenly, separate from all of the other firing, a loud shot rang out and Doc Seput lurched forward, landing on his back. He was still, lying there with his sad eyes staring upward. He did not try to speak. Sgt. Anders yelled out, "Doc! Doc!"

The men of third platoon dropped their packs and carrying only their weapons and ammo, retreated back through a deep drainage ditch, carrying their wounded medic with them. As they reached a new position, the platoon leader, Lt. Frank Olevitch, had Nowling and another man cover the direction they had just come from.

I happened to turn my head toward the firing in My Binh just in time to see two G.I.'s scrambling into the cover of a hedgerow. Just after that, Lt. O decided we needed to lay down a base of fire in that direction. I spoke up and told him about the two G.I.'s over there. He was surprised and then said that they must be Fourth Platoon.

He yelled "Hey, Fourth Platoon!" in that direction and someone answered him, so he ordered us to make our way over there and link up with them. We joined Fourth Platoon in a defensive perimeter in a medium size field surrounded on all four sides by hedgerows.

Lt. O thought we should be doing more to help the company and he asked for volunteers to go with him toward the village. About four or five got up to go with him and I joined them, although my squad leader just looked at me and shook his head as if he thought I was crazy. We didn't get far. The incoming fire grew heavier and we were targeted so we stopped and moved back to the perimeter.

When the firing started, first platoon was pinned down in the open. SP4 Jack Hanger was hit as he tried to move to a safer spot. Platoon medic Bob Kastner recalled the day: "I was pinned down in the open. Bobby (Robert Henderson) covered me with his machine gun fire. Jack got hit pulling back when he was trying to get up over the bank to higher ground. I was going to stop and help Jack but he told me to keep going because he said he wasn't going to make it. I got to higher ground and that is when I saw that Bobby was gone." Hanger was 19 and from Cypress, CA. PFC Robert Lee Henderson was 24 and from Fairfax, SC.

The fire grew intermittent as the afternoon wore on, but the platoons received no direction from the company level until Top Fowler showed up late in the afternoon. As Ed McCoin, one of the company's RTOs recalls the day, Fowler was back at An Khe appearing before a promotion board when he heard Charlie Company got hit. Fowler left the board and exerted his authority to convince a Huey pilot to fly him directly to Bong Son, where he got dropped off in the middle of the fight.

He walked through the battlefield alone until he got to second platoon and found the CO still in his hole and took effective command of the company. He got his RTO, SP4 George Chiaramello, and they walked through the area to reach the third platoon. Fowler was bulky and Chiaramello was tall and one man remembered their approach. William Fells, a SP4 and frequent point man in the third platoon, wrote in an email about forty years later: "If anyone saw him that day walking crouched over behind Top (you would have to be blind), they would have laughed. Then again that wasn't a laughing day. We were on pure adrenalin."

Nowling remembers Top Fowler was not happy about third platoon's inaction when he arrived:

> He told Lt. O he should get up and lead us over to the village where we were needed and that we should be helping bring out casualties. Lt. O had no sooner stood up when a single shot rang out and wounded him in both legs so the platoon remained in place.
>
> Soon there was a setting sun followed by a stream of troops coming from near the village and paddies into our relatively secure "rear area". Charlie Company established its perimeter for the night and medevaced its dead and wounded. There could not be a log bird that night so we who had dropped our packs had no rations to fall back on, nor any sleeping gear. Early in the evening, a couple of mortar rounds exploded nearby, a parting shot from the NVA.

Lt Jim Wolfe was with the third platoon medic, SP4 Fred Seput, as they waited for a medevac chopper and remembers, "I talked to him while we waited. He kept saying that he would not make it and I kept telling him he would. He knew better than I." When the first medevac chopper finally arrived, the ABC camera crew tried to board it and Wolfe had to threaten them with his M-16 to ensure the wounded would be taken out first. Seput died later that day. He was 19 and from Chicago.

Also killed was second platoon squad leader SSgt Henry Lee, who had been awarded the Silver Star for his actions in the Ia Drang Valley the previous November. Lee was 28 and from Kingsville, TX. Years later, Pete VanTil posted this memory on the Vietnam Wall of Faces:

Henry was my friend and brother-in-arms. He was a squad leader in 2nd Platoon. I was 2nd Platoon medic. On 3/21/1967 our company air assaulted into a hot LZ outside a small, remote village in Binh Dinh Province. We were pinned down by a much larger NVA force. A small group of eight men were surrounded in a small clearing. Three were KIA, including Henry Lee. He was wounded but still alive when I got to him but was hit again while I was treating him. He died in my arms. SSgt. Henry Lee was a true hero. Rest in Peace, my brother.

In addition to Hanger, Henderson, Seput, and Lee, two other Charlie Company men were killed in that action: SP4 Daniel Holcomb, 21, of Buena Park, CA; and SP4 Ray Anthony Rhodes, 20, of Moulton, AL.

Later that evening, the NVA broke contact and retreated into the mountains. The next morning, Charlie Company assaulted and burned the village. The men of third platoon found their packs ripped and burned by the NVA with items like entrenching tools, bayonets, and smoke grenades taken. Sweeps through both areas produced a count of over 120 enemy dead for the three-day struggle, compared to 34 Americans killed.

This was also 1Lt Jim Wolfe's last fight. Not long afterwards, he completed his tour and returned to the States to get married. He was one of the few officers to spend his entire twelve months with Charlie Company, having led the third and mortar platoons and been the company's XO. He would return to the 1st Cavalry in 1969, first as a divisional staff officer and then as CO of Charlie Company, 2/12th Cav.

Side Trip to I Corps

April 1967 brought a new division commander and the division's first deployment into I Corps. On the 1st, Major General John Tolson replaced MG John Norton. Like his predecessors, he had led paratroopers in World War II, was an experienced aviator, and had been heavily involved in developing air mobility doctrine and tactics before Vietnam. Less than a week into his command, the Army ordered him to send a brigade north to Quang Ngai Province to relieve Marine units that had been operating there since late 1965.

The 1/5th and 2/5th were ordered to move on short notice. At the time, Charlie Company was guarding the Bong Son bridge on Highway 1, the only bridge over the Lai Giang River, just about the easiest duty in Bong Son. The men could swim in the river, get haircuts, buy cokes and beer from the kids outside the wire, and more. Early on April 8, 1967, the company was ordered to saddle up and by 1300, it had been flown on Chinooks to LZ Montezuma, a Marine firebase outside the district town of Duc Pho.

The Marines were moving north due to increased NVA activity along the DMZ and in the hills surrounding Khe Sanh. They would be replaced by Task Force Oregon, built around a brigade of the 25th Infantry Division, which was being moved by sea from Qui Nhon to a beach near Duc Pho. In the meantime, the two Cavalry battalions would take over operations in the area, a longtime VC stronghold.

Every village showed signs of having been fought over before, but the VC in the area had not yet had to deal with airmobile units. For the next five days, Charlie Company crisscrossed the area, drawing frequent sniper fire, fighting a small firefight, and bringing in numerous VC suspects. Excerpts from the battalion operations log give a picture of the day-to-day actions of Operation Lejuene:

April 10, 1967

1005hrs Company C has 24 VC suspects prime age, will send back on back haul.

1332hrs Company C pick up 4 VC suspects while searching village.

1630hrs Company C has 5 VC Suspects ages 25-50, found in a rice paddy.

1635hrs Company C requested medevac for Vietnamese gunshot wound in stomach.

1830hrs From C Company: All villages searched today had trenches and well-constructed bunkers, supported with railroad ties, located about 10 feet from the houses location. Also on hill big bunker system and tunnels, some big enough to stand up in, 3-man size.

2015hrs C Company across railroad tracks saw a blinking light, the light stayed off 4 second and on for 2 in process repeated for about 3 minutes.

April 11, 1967

0525hrs Company C received 2 rounds sniper fire from 300 meters southwest of their position.

0950hrs C Company found about 1500 lbs rice laying out to dry. Company C six said they would dump the rice in a well, also put CS grenade into the rice.

1007hrs Company C requested medevac for one man who took some CS gas into his lungs

1745hrs 39 VC suspects evacuated to Bn2 from C Company.

April 12, 1967

0845hrs C Company touchdown LZ Chesty, gunships received fire.

1155hrs Company C medevac requested for 3 VC suspects, LZ secure, shrapnel wounds from grenade thrown into a bunker.

1730hrs C Company has 35 VCS at his location.

April 13, 1967

0950hrs C Company 49 VCS to Bn S2.

1000hrs C Company requested medevac, 1EM M79 round bounced off a log resulting in shrapnel wounds, LZ secure.

1535hrs C Company reports lot of rounds fired from location BS827420, ARA set one platoon, air strike in area, 1610hrs.

1624hrs C Company medevac for 2 WIA, also have 1 KIA.

2015hrs Company C Two men tripped a flare, were fired upon, no indication of any hits, 100 meters due east of their location, will check for results at first light, possible two VC wounded.

Dan Favreau, then a SP4 in the third platoon, remembered that day:

> The April fight when Sebastian was hit, I had my magazines around my waist and in claymore bags. I was sure when I was crawling, someone shot between my legs from behind me, from the trees in the ville. I thought I saw someone disappear so I grabbed a 45 and some matches. Away I go back there. Down the tunnel calling out Lai Day or whatever, I had never smoked so was not having a very easy time with the matches. Much less, what the heck was I supposed to do with the 45. I get to a turn in the tunnel, lit a match, it touches the nose of fella I was looking for. I do believe I was a hell of lot more scared than he was, at that instant. I crawled backwards a bit in record time. We got him out.

"Crazy George" Sebastian, a machine gunner and one of Favreau's closest friends, had been hit in the chest. He was an 'old man' by platoon standards, having already done a three-year stint in the Army, including a tour with the 1st Cav in Korea in 1964. He enlisted for a second time to avenge the death of his brother, killed early in the war. When he was carried on a stretcher to a medevac chopper, he was smoking a cigar and men swear they saw smoke coming out of the hole in his chest.

That evening or the next day, Favreau captured another VC. When his platoon came to a stream, he crossed first and saw a VC, probably fleeing from the firefight, pressed against the bank hiding in the reeds. "I went first, to see how deep it was, got about 10 feet and Tony said something from the bank, and I looked back and saw two big brown eyes staring at me through the reeds. If he would have had a weapon, that would have been the end of me."

April 14, 1967

0735hrs Company C spotted one VC swimming in black PJ and white T-shirt, took him under fire, he is either WIA or KIA, can see him lay across river approx 300 meters away.

1037hrs Company C spotted 4 VC trying to evade, took them under fire, negative results at this time.

1340hrs Company C--5 VC taken under fire wounded one, suspect that he is a VC officer, arm almost blown off, wearing pistol belt with grenades in it, also some documents on him, medevac requested.

When the men of the company spotted the VC across the river that morning, he was just coming out of the water—actually a tidal estuary just off the ocean—and slowly walking across the mudflats at low tide. He had likely been wounded in the previous day's firefight and was trying to make his way to safety. Men lined up and fired at him, trying to bring him down, but the range was too great for accurate M-16 fire. It looked like he was hit a few times, but he kept moving slowly forward until he was killed by an OH-13 observation chopper hovering over and machine-gunning him.

The company continued moving south on a narrow peninsula, burning hooches and blowing up bunkers. There were still civilians in the villages so a man would pause at a bunker's opening and shout, "Lai De, Lai De" (come out, come out) and wait a minute to see if anyone did before throwing a grenade into it.

Six or seven women and children came out of one bunker and were standing to the side when one man threw his grenade from about ten feet away. It bounced off the wood frame entrance to the bunker and exploded among the women and children, wounding most of them, some severely. Captain Anderson refused to call a medevac for them to the disgust and dismay of many company members.

Late in the day, the company forded the estuary, neck deep with the tide coming in and over 100 meters wide. As the men emerged on the far side, their file curved to pass close to the dead VC as though they wanted to see if he was truly dead and what kind of enemy could take such punishment. The wounded Vietnamese were left on the peninsula to fend for themselves. By then at least one woman had died. The next day, April 15, Charlie Company flew back to Bong Son to rejoin Operation

Pershing. The man killed on April 13 was PFC Dale Bishop, 19, from Dolton, IL. He had been in Vietnam less than a month. This would make him a veteran compared to the company's next fatality.

Our Own Worst Enemy

By now, I had four months to go on my tour and was the weapons squad leader in the third platoon, leading its two machine gun teams. I had long stopped believing many of the rationales for why we were in Vietnam, especially that we were there to 'win the hearts and minds' of the people. A series of events brought home to me that the reality of the war on the ground had little to do with anything we had been taught or told in training. It was a long while coming, but from then on cynicism and absurdity were about the only lens through which I could view what I was doing and experiencing in Vietnam.

One day in early April, we swept through a village somewhere in Bong Son and a platoon sergeant ordered us to destroy all its rice. The village was considered pacified and friendly, and the village headman had proper ID documents from the Saigon Government. But the sergeant saw large earthenware pots filled with rice outside each hooch and decided it was too much for the people living there and was likely being stored for the VC and NVA in the mountains. He was a career soldier on his first tour and had been in country maybe three weeks and was either oblivious or didn't care that the rice had been harvested only a few weeks prior. The headman tried to tell him the rice would need to feed the village until the next harvest six months away, as well as provide seed for another planting, but he was ignored.

We dumped the rice in the village's wells and went on our way, leaving the village facing months of hunger and ruined wells. It's possible some of the rice might have made its way to the VC, but it was clear to me that the sergeant knew nothing about the culture and life of the people we were supposedly trying to win over. It wasn't the first time our assumptions of superiority outweighed facts on the ground.

Then about a week later, when Charlie Company was operating near Duc Pho, we made two air assaults one day. It was around April 12, 1967 and the first assault was by a village that had already been worked over by the Marines. We drew some small arms fire on the approach but the village was abandoned and partially destroyed. It looked like it had once been fairly prosperous with hooches with concrete or stucco walls that were larger than those we usually saw in rural villages.

As we moved into the center of the village, I took cover behind the low round wall of a well. About fifteen feet in front of me were two piglets with similar markings—they looked like they could have been litter mates from earlier in the year. One was dead with his stomach sliced open by shrapnel or a round and the other had its snout pushed into the wound, eating the dead piglet's entrails. Nothing else was moving in the village and I couldn't stop watching them. I thought about shooting the piglet but then we were ordered to pull back to our LZ for another mission.

We then air-assaulted next to another village two or three kilometers away. This one was both occupied and poorer, with mud-walled hooches with thatch roofs. The first wave went in with gunships on each side firing rockets and some of the villagers were hit. As I entered the village I saw one of our medics working on a woman whose breast had been almost sliced off by shrapnel. Men fanned out and began burning the remaining hooches. As we stood around, two women ran to the well and back with small tin buckets but the thatch was dry and soon most of the village was burning. We operated around that village for the rest of the day, pulling people out of bunkers and sending them to the rear as VCS (Vietcong Suspects).

Ten days later, on April 21, 1967, Charlie Company was back in Bong Son conducting village sweeps in the Bong Son plain. We were told not to torch hooches unless they looked unoccupied, but this was generally ignored. If someone was working in the fields or gone to market in another village when we passed through, they often came back to a pile of ashes and caved in walls. I had reached a point where I wouldn't torch hooches anymore, at least not without a good reason, but earlier it had sometimes seemed empowering, especially in areas known for booby traps.

I was standing in front of a hooch when another man walked up behind it and lit the thatch with his Zippo. As it started to burn, I went in for a quick look. There was a bed and a small chest and in the corner was a small table set up as a Buddhist shrine, with a red cloth and a bowl for incense. On the table was an old photograph in a frame of a couple wearing formal Vietnamese clothes and staring stiffly at the camera. They were likely ancestors of the people living in the hooch and I assumed the photo was one of their most valuable possessions. I had learned enough about Vietnam by then to know that ancestor worship was central to beliefs, so I took the photograph outside and hid it under a straw mat on the ground, hoping the family would find it after we left.

We set up a perimeter in the area that night, rising early to continue our search and destroy mission the next day. As we rolled up our gear, a resupply chopper brought in ammo, rations, and a few new replacements, who were quickly assigned to platoons and squads. First platoon moved out first and as it approached a nearby village it was sniped at by a few guerillas, killing one of the replacements and wounding a few other men. He had been in the field about two hours and for years no one knew his name. Years later someone found it on one of the online data bases that are now available. PFC Ira Rice was 21 years old and from Cardwell, MO.

First platoon pulled back and third platoon was directed to swing around to the far side of the village to try to cut off the VC. The first platoon leader, a green 2nd lieutenant, called in an air strike without getting clearance from the CO or battalion. As third platoon neared the village, we began to cross a stretch of dry rice paddies when an Air Force Forward Air Controller (FAC) flying overhead mistook us for some VC.

FACs flying overhead in their small planes were a common occurrence and no one in the platoon paid it any attention until a Willy-Peter (White Phosphorus) marker rocket exploded about thirty feet in front of our point man. Some of us instinctively looked up to see the first of two Air Force jets rolling into their dives and opening up with their 20mm cannon, firing 100 explosive rounds per second. I thought "Oh shit" and then a wall of explosions rushed at us.

The jets were aiming at the Willy-Peter and by some fluke of luck, their strafing run missed most of the platoon, wounding a few men towards the front of our file. The only seriously wounded man was an assistant machine gunner named Smitty, whose arm was blown off by a direct hit near his shoulder. SP4 Tony

Martin, a grenadier with the third platoon, did two more tours in the infantry in Vietnam. He was in the 2/7th Cav in 1968-1969 and the 2/46th Infantry of the 196th Light Infantry Brigade in 1970-1971. For him, as for me and most of the men in the third platoon, it was probably the most terrifying five seconds he experienced in Vietnam.

For the rest of my tour, I felt that our side was as much of a threat to my survival as anything the VC or NVA had thrown at us. And if it wasn't one side or the other, some days it seemed like the land itself was out to kill us.

Long Hot Days and Booby Traps

Luckily, my remaining months were pretty quiet ones for Charlie Company. Operations went on in Bong Son as before. It was the height of the dry season and the war seemed to have slowed down, at least for our company with little contact other than sniper fire and booby traps. Sometimes the men would come back from a long hot patrol and be greeted by Top Fowler passing out cans of ice-cold beer or soda as they came through the wire.

From mid-May to mid-June 1967, 1/5th provided security around An Khe. The rifle platoons rotated, with one acting as a quick reaction force and the others manning outposts and running patrols outside the base camp's Green Line. In late May, the Army abruptly ordered that all airborne-qualified men under the rank of Sgt in the 1st Cavalry be involuntarily transferred to either the 173rd or the 101st Airborne. This impacted five or six Charlie Company men, all of whom had been with the company nine months or more. The company lost their experience and expertise, and they lost the comradeship and attachments developed over the months with their squad and platoon mates.

As Charlie Company returned to Bong Son later in June, it got a new CO, Captain Joseph Lyttle, and a new XO, 1Lt Dan

Terry, a former enlisted man. At battalion level, LTC Daniel Rickard replaced LTC Mapp. In mid-month, the company assembled at a firebase for a change of command ceremony where Captain Anderson was awarded a Bronze Star for dubious reasons, and everyone looked forward to different leadership. McCoin and other men always felt that discipline in the company went downhill under Anderson and that some men became too quick to rough up civilians or burn hooches or even villages without good reason when he was CO. Lyttle brought the company back to a better standard.

SP4 Gary Clayton, then in the 2nd platoon, described the nature and pace of operations in Bong Son that summer in a letter written in mid-July to his sister:

I got your letter a couple of weeks ago, but we've moved all over the place since then...we went to LZ English, and from there to LZ Ollie. We ran patrols from there for 3 or 4 days and picked up a few VC suspects. Then we went to LZ Laramie, it's up on top of a mountain and we could see the South China Sea about 10 miles to the east. We stayed there a few days, then went to LZ English again, stayed overnight—made an air assault right outside of a village (somewhere in South Vietnam). Ha! We captured a few VC and shot a few. Then some ARVN's came in and interrogated our prisoners. Talk about torture, those ARVN's really know how to hurt a guy and still keep him alive. The poor bastards would have been better off dead. Then we walked through a village where B Company got hit. Boy, did it stink from all the dead VC they left laying around.

Then we went to LZ Hamond, from there to LZ Two-Bits, that was a nice LZ. We even got to see movies at night and 3 hot meals a day. But we also had to go out on night patrols from there and I don't like them very well. We stayed there 8 days, that's the longest I've been

in one place since I've been here. Then we made an air assault out on
the beach to help the First Battalion, 9th Cav. We took almost 150
prisoners that day. Then we went to LZ Abbey, then we made an air
assault at the base of a mountain to help some ARVN's out. But after
we got there, all we found was one woman with a big chunk torn out
of the back of her head from shrapnel. She was VC, but I still don't
like to see a woman messed up like that. We stayed around the mountain a couple of days and checked out all the draws. All we found were
some bunkers which we destroyed. This morning we got up at 5:00
and rolled up and moved out before dawn. We walked about 5 miles
to LZ Pony. Then got on choppers and flew in here to Uplift. So you
see we're always moving.

While contact was scarce, booby traps of all kinds remained
a constant threat. On July 2, 1967, Charlie Company set out on
foot at 0350 to surround a village in the Phu My District. Its
mission was to set up a cordon around the village while the villagers slept. A unit of South Vietnamese National Police would
then go through the village interrogating villagers and searching for food and weapons caches. First Platoon was the point
platoon and at 0500 hours its new and green platoon leader, Lt
Curtis Clark, tripped a booby trap. Just prior to that, Clark and
point man Tom Kanawyer had disagreed about the best route to
take as they neared the village:

He wanted me to take us on the rice paddy dike and I told him that
it was too dark to see booby traps, so it was agreed that I would lead
the column through the center of the rice paddy. However, he and his
radio man took off across the dike. I hadn't gotten too far across the
paddy when behind me and a little to my right, Lt. Clark tripped a
"Bouncing Betty" booby trap. It shot up about two feet off the ground

and caught at least half a dozen of us with shrapnel. It really tore up the Lt. and his radio man, but neither was killed.[11]

In late July 1967, the company walked out of LZ Uplift for an all-day sweep when first and second platoons drew sniper fire from a village. As third platoon passed through a field, flanking the village from another direction, it lost eight men wounded to pungi stakes. Most returned within a few days, but for a few it was a 'million-dollar' wound. As the wounded were evacuated, a tank and a duster, with its twin 40mm cannon, linked up with the company for the rest of the day, one of the first times the men operated with armor.

Charlie Company lost two men KIA to booby traps in August while operating in the Crescent mountains. On August 11, 1967, PFC Gary Gatti was killed and three others wounded. Gatti was 20 and from Lynwood, CA. On a separate operation in the same area eleven days later, August 23, 1967, third platoon's RTO was killed and another new platoon leader, Lt Wheeler, was seriously wounded. Bill Pelton was in the fifth month of his tour and was also wounded:

> We started up the hill and broke into a flat area where we found a freshly used campsite with a fire still smoldering. We continued up following the well-used trail. About a quarter way up another slightly used trail went off to the right. Our RTO Carroll and I were told to

---

11. The battalion daily log described the booby trap as a "CBU pull type booby trap". CBU's or Cluster Bomb Units were small bomblets packed with shrapnel that were dropped by the millions by the Air Force in Vietnam, Cambodia and Laos. CBUs were packed in large canisters which opened in the air when dropped in a tactical air strike, scattering them over a wide area. Many failed to explode and the VC often put new fuses in and used them as booby traps against US soldiers.

check it out. About 100 feet down the trail we found what looked like a hand dug cave. Carroll radioed back and told our new Lt. what we found and he told us to have a look around and then rejoin the platoon.

We did and then the platoon continued up the hill still following the well-used trail. We came to a kink in the trail where I couldn't see the few men in front of me. We came to a stop and within few seconds an explosion knocked me down. I was hit in the left thigh with shrapnel and our medic Pete VanTil came running up and asked me how bad it was. I said, "Not Bad" and pointed to the front where the booby trap went off. It was a bad scene there. Carroll was hit bad and died within a minute and our new Lt. was badly wounded. We had to get him out NOW.

Although we had been getting sporadic sniper fire for the past few days, Dennis Grice climbed up a tree and began cutting away branches to clear a space so a chopper could drop a basket on a cable down for the Lt. Within 5 minutes or so a medevac chopper was hovering above us and a basket was coming down through the thick canopy. Doc VanTil strapped the Lt. in and he was almost up to the chopper when shots rang out and the chopper flew up and off with the Lt. still dangling in the basket.

Now I've got to walk down the hill to get to a chopper and my leg wasn't working very well. I saw a small amount of blood so I tied it off with a bandana and down I limped. Getting near the bottom of the hill another explosion went off. Grice had found another booby trap, a wired hand grenade, and unwired it and threw it out into the brush. The VC had circled around us and rigged the grenade on the same trail we had cleared going up. By now I was hurting and mad as hell.

As we reached the bottom, shots rang out from the hillside, and we returned fire. I must have fired 10 fast rounds from my M79 grenade launcher in return. Another medevac chopper flew in over the flooded rice paddy. Carroll's body was loaded on and I went in behind him. As we flew towards a field hospital that looked like TV's Mash unit, the chopper's copilot reached back and gave me a cigarette. I gave him a thumbs up. As it turned out it was good that I tied my leg off with that bandana because my main artery had been nicked by the shrapnel and I was doing a slow bleed out.

For Pelton, it was a "million-dollar wound" that ended his tour in Vietnam. Platoon RTO PFC Gerald Carroll was 24 and from LaSalle, CO. A friend of his from infantry training remembered him in a post on the Vietnam Wall of Faces website:

> We talked a lot in AIT. What a bummer the 1st Sgt put you on KP when your wife was there. You, Terry, and I sat on the plane all those long hours. I wish we could have sat together coming home. Welcome home in spirit. You will be with me forever. Rest easy my friend.

Firefights and booby traps weren't the only danger. On one patrol, first platoon's medic and radioman disturbed a nest of tropical bees and were repeatedly stung. Both were medevaced and were out of the field for weeks. Medic Bob Kastner's hands were so badly swollen for a while that he couldn't hold a fork or spoon and had to be hand fed by someone else.

On August 30, 1967, Charlie Company air-assaulted into the Cay Giap mountains on a search and destroy operation and began finding and destroying bunker complexes. On the fourth day, the company entered an area with about seventy-five bunkers and found a wounded NVA officer who had apparently been abandoned by his unit. When questioned by an interpreter, he said he had been sunning himself on top of a bunker four days ago when an airstrike hit. He suffered a severe injury to his foot which became infected and couldn't walk. Captain Lyttle was a strong and stocky man, and he carried the wounded officer a long way down a mountain trail until the company reached a clearing big enough for a medevac chopper to land.

Firefight in the 506 Valley

The 1/5th started October 1967 conducting search and destroy sweeps and rice harvest security operations east of the Suoi Ca Mountains in eastern Binh Dinh Province. By then, all of the valleys in and around the mountains had been declared free fire zones to deny the crops grown there to the Viet Cong and NVA units based there and in the An Loa Valley. The NVA and VC were forced to try to harvest it from abandoned fields in the valleys or to go farther into the lowlands to get rice from local farmers and the 1st Cavalry was moving to find and interdict them in what was labelled Operation Rice Grain.

Most of Charlie Company was securing LZ Ollie with the second platoon at LZ Pony, both conducting search and cordon operations and night ambushes around local villages. Other companies from 1/5th, as well as Special Forces teams and 1/9th Cavalry recon platoons, were running search and destroy sweeps, ambushes, and aerial searches in the area. A battalion of NVA was reported to be in the area seeking rice to take back to their base areas in the mountains.

On October 5, 1967, the company linked up at LZ Uplift and moved from there into the bush. Late the next day, Captain Lyttle was notified by battalion S-3 that an estimated 20 NVA had been spotted near Thach Long, a small hamlet in the 506 valley, and to have the company ready for an air assault early the next morning. The valley was on the northeastern edge of the Suoi Ca Mountains and named for the dirt road that passed through it. Anyone in the valley was considered hostile.

The company rose early on October 7, 1967, quickly chowed down and saddled up. The first wave lifted off at 0720. Only six troop carrying slicks and two gunships were available and it took three or four lifts to move the entire company. On the flight in, John Nowling noted that the villages looked dilapidated and empty and the fields and rice paddies overgrown. Joe "O" Oleszkiewicz, now a sergeant in the fourth platoon, was in the second lift and as it touched down, he jumped out and ran for the perimeter set up by the first men to land. He flopped down next to Sgt Jake Van Meter, then the machine gun squad leader for the second platoon, who looked at him and said "'O', I don't know what I'm doing here—I'm going home in ten days."

Once on the ground, Charlie Company moved out with second platoon in the lead, followed by first platoon. Third platoon and the mortars stayed by the village. Lt Bill Bane, Van Meter's platoon leader and friend (they were both from West Virginia), told him he could stay back by the village since he was so short. Van Meter had been the acting platoon sergeant until a few days before the mission, when second platoon got a career NCO as a replacement. He felt responsible for the men of the platoon, especially since there had been little contact in the past few months and many of the men were green, and he told Bane he was staying with the platoon. One man remembered Van Meter saying sarcastically, "Shit this is fun."

The terrain was fairly open to start, but then the trails narrowed and led into rocky cliffs with large boulders and caves. The point element spotted sandal prints along the trail and about 100 yards farther on saw and fired at a lone NVA. At about 1445, second platoon was climbing up along a steep and rocky trail—possibly a dry streambed—in single file when the NVA sprang their ambush, firing from prepared foxholes and bunkers in the rocks.

Capt. Lyttle, Top Fowler, and Lt Bane took cover and began directing return fire while Van Meter directed his machine gun teams into position. Seeing some wounded men, he exposed himself to bring them to safety and was wounded himself. He was directing machine gun fire against the NVA when he was hit again, this time fatally.

SP4 Neal Wolf, carrying the second M-60 in Van Meter's squad, moved forward as soon as the firing started. Coming to a gap between boulders, he made it across, but his assistant gunner was hit in the leg. Five more men tried to cross the gap but four were hit by the intense NVA fire with only the platoon medic, SP4 Bruce Naile, getting across safely. Joe 'O' also moved up when the ambush was sprung and saw Van Meter lying dead by the trail with a head wound.

For his valor that day, Van Meter was posthumously awarded the Silver Star:

When his unit came under intense hostile fire, Sergeant Van Meter, disregarding his own safety, exposed himself to the heavy enemy fire as he directed his men into covered positions. He again exposed himself to the hostile fire to draw the fire away from his men. Observing several wounded comrades lying in an exposed area, Sergeant Van Meter moved through the open area and pulled the wounded soldiers to safety. While moving the men to a safe position, Sergeant Van

> Meter was wounded, but continued until he had completed his task. At this time, while delivering a high volume of covering fire for the wounded men, Sergeant Van Meter was mortally wounded.

Due to the heavy fire, Van Meter's platoon mates were not able to pull him to safety. Three other men were also killed early on and eleven more wounded, many of them seriously. The firefight lasted for over two hours and because of the terrain, the closeness of the NVA, and the exposure of the some of the wounded, it was difficult for company to call in supporting fire. At one point, an OH-13 scout chopper trying to coordinate artillery fire was hit in the fuel line and disabled. The pilot was able to land safely at the base of the hill, but his observer was wounded.

First platoon was called up to assist the platoons in the ambush. Sgt Dave Combs, a squad leader, was told by Top Fowler to lead the platoon as both the platoon leader and platoon sergeant were out of the field that day. By the time they reached the ambush site, the fire had slackened and the NVA were pulling out. He and Nowling and others in the platoon began carrying the wounded and dead down the hill in makeshift stretchers to an LZ where they could be medevaced.

As night approached, the company had not been able to recover Cartwright's body. Some men could see him up the trail and knew he was dead, but there was still enough incoming fire to make it too dangerous to get to him. Joe 'O' could tell how much it troubled the men of second platoon to have to leave him there, especially knowing artillery and airstrikes would be hitting the area as the company pulled back.

A few days later, John Nowling wrote a letter home describing the battle, saying in part:

According to an NVA defector, there were supposed to be 60 or so NVA soldiers in a draw leading up the mountain. According to the defector, they were all sick and weak and "didn't want to fight Americans"…As it turned out, the 60 NVA had plenty of fight left in them. They were entrenched in foxholes and bunkers dug in on both sides of the draw. The first and second platoons walked into the trap. A good size shooting spree went on for about two hours. We would have broken contact right away and called in artillery but there was quite a bit of trouble getting the wounded out. Several men were wounded trying to get to those who were initially wounded. My platoon was called on and we moved up into the draw toward the shooting. By the time we got into the area of the fight, all wounded and dead, except one body, had been recovered. We helped carry them down the mountain…The defector who led the way on the 7th ran off during the night following the firefight.

At dusk, the company sent out a small patrol to set up a listening post. During the night, they reported hearing numerous NVA moving out of the area. The next morning, Charlie Company went back up the hill to retrieve Cartwright's body and recover weapons and ammo. The NVA had carried off most of their dead, but the company did find two men alive and took them prisoner. A 1st Cavalry Intelligence summary estimated a possible ten NVA KIA from the fight.

Sgt Van Meter was 24 and from Slatety Fork, WV. Three other members of second platoon were killed that day: SP4 Vaun Andrews, 20, of San Fernando, CA; PFC Ronald Cartwright, 24, from Eugene, OR; and PFC James Otis Beasley, 18, of Denver, CO. Cartwright and Beasley had joined the company as new replacements on the same day in late August. Eleven other men were wounded, most from second platoon. Years later, Neal Wolf posted a message to Van Meter on the Vietnam Wall of Faces website:

> Jake. You were an inspiration to the rest of us with your leadership. I will never forget that you would not stay back from our assault up that mountain. You were determined to be with "your" men even though you only had a very short time to go. We will meet again someday so you can tell me more about "West By God Virginia."

Van Meter never got to meet his child, who was born while he was in Vietnam. A friend of Vaun Andrews also left a message on the website:

> I saw your name on the wall on veteran's day after 9-11. We went to boot camp together. Then advanced infantry training and finally Vietnam. In the back of the truck, you asked me to sing a song. It was *You've Lost That Loving Feeling.* I tried to sing it again at the Wall but didn't make it all the way through.

First platoon went back through the area the next day, capturing another prisoner, and killing three NVA who refused to give up. The 1/5th continued to operate around the 506 valley for another five days, with Charlie Company making sporadic contact and at least one air assault into the mountains where Delta Company had tracked the NVA and found a medical complex in the jungle. During this time, Wolf remembers three men wounded by grenade shrapnel on a night listening post, bringing second platoon down to the size of a squad.

The company then went to guard the bridges over the Bong Son River near the division forward HQ at LZ English, fairly easy duty for a while, where they held a memorial service for the four men KIA. In addition to Van Meter, four other men received the Silver Star: Captain Joseph Lyttle, Lt Bill Bane, First Sergeant Robert Fowler (his second Oak Leaf Cluster), and medic SP4 Bruce Naile. A number of men also got the Bronze Star with "V" or the Army Commendation Medal for heroism. Decades later, Joe 'O' wrote about his experiences in combat in Vietnam and said in part:

COMBAT is walking into an enemy ambush.

COMBAT is dragging the wounded to safety while the enemy is shooting at you.

COMBAT is seeing your buddy lying in the dirt…dead.

COMBAT is putting the wounded and the dead on the Medevac.

COMBAT is thanking your God for letting you live another day.

COMBAT is having to do it all again tomorrow.

Last Months in Binh Dinh Province

Despite the ferocity of individual firefights, it seemed that the war was winding down in Bong Son. According to the official history of the 3d PAVN Division written after the war, between September 1967 and January 1968 the Communist units on the northeastern coast of II Corps "suffered [so] many reverses and casualties...that heavy infiltration of North Vietnamese Army troops was still not enough to fill the gaps." For much of that period, only the 1st Cavalry's 2nd Brigade operated in Binh Dinh Province.

The 1st Brigade moved west to support the 4th Infantry Division and 173rd Airborne Brigade around Kontum and Dak To and the 3rd Brigade moved north to Quang Ngai Province to support the newly formed Americal Division as it deployed to Vietnam. Some of the slack was taken up by a newly deployed mechanized infantry battalion which began operating out of LZ Uplift in late September. The 1/50th was an independent battalion with M-113 Armored Personnel Carriers (APCs) and M-42 dusters and it gave the 1st Cav additional firepower in the coastal lowlands of Binh Dinh Province.

Charlie Company spent the rest of October and most of November in Bong Son on routine missions, returning to the An

Khe area in late November for security missions around the division's base camp. Early in this period, Minor Chaney arrived in Vietnam after a year of training and stateside duty and was assigned to the second platoon. Years later, he wrote about his experiences so his grandsons would know what their 'PawPaw' did in the war. He described his reaction when he first met his platoon leader and other officers in Charlie Company:

> They were all 1st lieutenants and had a different demeanor than the 2nd lieutenants I had been used to in the States. They didn't have that mightier-than-thou attitude, and they had much more concern for the welfare of their men. They expected them to do their jobs, but the safety of their men seemed to be their utmost concern.
>
> I was introduced to my platoon leader, 1st Lieutenant Bill Bane. From the beginning I like and respected him and soon realized that the reason this group of lieutenants had been promoted to 1st lieutenant was because of their experience in the field. 1st Lieutenant Dan Terry [the company XO and a former enlisted man] was one of them, along with Charlie Brown, Steve Voelker, and Frank Romiti [also a former enlisted man].
>
> With these guys and with Captain Joseph Lyttle as our CO, I realized I was in a good unit. Then, of course, there was Top, 1st Sergeant Robert Fowler, who had been in the Army more than twenty years and had fought in the Korean Conflict. I learned that he had turned down a promotion to Sergeant Major because that was an office job in the rear, and he wanted to stay in the field with his men. Top loved fighting more than anyone I had ever seen. His experience saved our bacon more than once.

Shortly after Minor arrived, Dan Terry was promoted to captain and took command of Charlie Company and Captain Lyttle went to battalion as the S-3 operations and aviation officer. Lt Bane replaced Dan Terry as Executive Officer and second platoon got a new platoon leader, 2Lt Ron Pape. And at some point in December 1967, the 1/5th got a new battalion commander, LTC Robert Runkle.

Charlie Company's only significant action during this time was on December 2, 1967 when a South Vietnamese outpost northeast of An Khe, manned by a Popular Forces unit and three Special Forces advisors, was attacked early in the morning. The company was notified at 0445 to saddle up and be ready to move by vehicle at first light to relieve the outpost, located near a dirt road named 508 on Army maps. The men were on the move by 0605 and twenty minutes later as their trucks came down a slight hill and slowed for a curve, they were ambushed by some VC with automatic weapons and captured M-79 grenade launchers. But the company expected an ambush and was ready for it and dismounted and returned fire without any casualties. The VC were driven off and the company slowly advanced in a cold rain to secure the outpost and evacuate the PF and Special Forces casualties.

Early on December 22, 1967 the company was unexpectedly pulled back to Black Knights Heights in Camp Radcliff where everyone was issued new clothes and jungle boots. Rumors flew but no one knew what was happening until the next day. Early on the 23rd, the men were trucked to the An Khe airfield, loaded onto C-130's and flown to Cam Ranh Bay for a review by President Lyndon Johnson. Charlie Company was one of two companies of the 1st Cavalry selected to be among the units assembled for the review.

Once at Cam Ranh, the men stood on the tarmac for three hours waiting for LBJ to arrive, after which they stood at attention while he passed by standing in the back of a jeep. They got to sit while he gave a short speech and then flew back to An Khe where Captain Terry scrounged up enough steaks to feed the company and grilled them for the men. No one knew it at the time, but it was the last time the company would return for a standdown to "Black Knights Heights" in the 1st Cavalry's base camp at An Khe.

The respite was short lived, however, and they next day the company went back to Bong Son. On the evening of December 26, 1967, Minor Chaney was sharing a position with another man, Bernie Poblock. Chaney pulled first guard and Poblock was asleep in their two-man hooch as a chopper flying overhead called in artillery on a nearby target. Without warning, a round fell short:

> The first round was white phosphorus, which is used to mark a target. I knew the next round would be a high explosive. I grabbed my radio handset and started yelling "Ceasefire!!!" My radio was set on company frequency, so the pilot could not hear us, but some of the guys pulling guard in the CP had their radios on push, and they got him stopped after one round.
>
> Unfortunately, that round was almost a direct hit on Bernie in our hooch. I yelled for a medic, and Lt. Pape was there instantly. He held Bernie in his hands while the medic shined a light in his face until all the life was gone from his eyes.
>
> The knot in my throat was so big I couldn't say a word. Lt. Pape took it very hard also; so did everyone. The same chopper landed and carried the body back to the rear. That pilot was shaking like a leaf. I don't know how he was able to operate the machine.

Lt Pape and SP4 Chuck Rodriguez were asleep in their hooch when they heard the white phosphorus round hit. Pape recalls:

I sat up real quick and Chuck knocked me down just as quick. Immediately after that, shrapnel ripped thru our hooch which would have killed me! I knew what had happened and immediately went outside to check on things. I saw the wounded soldier, PFC Poblock and ran over to him. He was alive, but literally blown in half. I held him in my arms, comforting as best I could. He died after a few minutes.

Once things quieted down, I called Company Headquarters and told Top Fowler what had happened. There was a big investigation by CID after this. It was found out that for whatever reason the gunnery sergeant at the firebase short loaded the white phosphorus round and then fired a hot shell into our position.

PFC Bernard Poblock was 20 and from Detroit, MI. He had been in Vietnam about seven weeks.

Battle on the Coast

On New Year's Day 1968, the 1st Cavalry received intelligence that some VC or NVA had been spotted in a village on a narrow strip of the coast between the Dam Tra-O Lake and marshes and a wide sandy beach, just south of the Cay Giap Mountains, and a company of the 1/50th Mechanized Infantry was sent to investigate. Early on January 2, 1968, they made contact with three companies of the 2nd VC Regiment of the Yellow Star Division, and another company of 1/50th and three companies of the 1/5th and 2/5th Cav joined the fight. Charlie Company was notified at 1200 hours to break off its search and destroy mission in the mountains and assemble at an LZ for pickup.

Choppers flying overhead with loudspeakers gave the villagers thirty minutes to leave the area and then the arriving companies cordoned off the village. Charlie Company air-assaulted to the west of the village at about 1410 hours and artillery and air strikes began pounding the area. Even so, resistance was fierce. As Charlie moved into position, first platoon set up a blocking position just in time to catch about forty VC trying to escape the village.

Minor Chaney, then in the second platoon, described his view of the day in his memoir:

We were getting some sniper fire from across Dam Tra-O Lake on our right. All of a sudden, Eduardo Hernandez from El Paso, Texas, turned and fired his M-79 grenade launcher at a bush at the water's edge. He blew that NVA soldier ten feet out into the water. We dragged him out on the bank, got his weapon, and searched through his pack to see if there might be anything with information on it.

When we reached the end of the lake, we spun around to the right with the head of the column already advancing into the wood line and the remainder of the column wrapping around and coming up to the wood line, closing off any escape through our lines. The first team into the wood line on our right was in contact and the helicopter gunships were firing a curtain of fire in front of us to keep the enemy in until we were in place. The gunships were firing much too close to us for comfort; in fact, the bullets were hitting an arm's length in front of us.

Lt. Pape broke radio silence and ordered them to back off. We then popped a colored smoke grenade so that they would know where our line of defense was. The pilot responded that he was going to make one more round and back off until he was needed for support. He made that round, and as he was leaving out, his plane took a round in the tail section and went into a spin. He crashed just beyond the tree line where we had come in. Both pilot and co-pilot were killed, but the door gunner jumped and landed in an irrigation canal and was saved.

Ron Pape also remembers the gunship firing on them but doesn't remember it being shot down. Others remember a chopper being shot down later in the afternoon with one man killed. Pape described the day as he experienced it:

The platoon moved on into the Village and started to dig in. Then out of nowhere one of our gunships starts firing on us! I popped a purple smoke immediately, as instructed to do in case we needed to be identified as "Friendly". Unfortunately, the pilot ignored this and fired on us again! Now this was serious because we were taking casualties.

At this point I felt I had no choice but to break radio silence and call the gunship. Much to my dismay, the pilot still would not respond to me. Now I was getting desperate. I called the Battalion Commander and told me my situation and that if the gunship came around again and start firing at us, we would shoot him down!

Almost immediately the gunship pilot broke in. He apologized saying he could not see our smoke?? Yeah right! Anyway, I popped another purple smoke. He still could not see it. So, I popped another smoke out in the rice paddy behind our position. That one he saw. Thank God! Next the pilot explained what he was seeing. There was enemy movement right in front of our position. So, he thought we were part of that movement. Once that was cleared up, he wanted to fire some rockets at the NVA troops to take them out. He proceeded to that and asked if we could check out the results of his firing.

Pape then led some of his men into the village. He directed Neal Wolf, by then the machine gun squad leader, and one of his men to cover their flank while he and the others moved deeper into the village:

I had two key personnel in my platoon, a Staff Sargent named Simcakowski (Ski) and our Forward Observer, Gary Clayton. Both great soldiers for sure. Even though I had only been in country a few months, the three of us had really bonded. They were "short timers" and only had weeks to go before they were going home. I spoke with them both before this mission began and tried to get then to stay behind. They refused!

Ski grabbed a squad and headed out front into the village. Not five minutes later, he comes back shot through both wrists! Now I was really pissed off! I grabbed a couple of men and went look looking for the NVA that had shot Ski! I saw one up ahead and as I threw a grenade, he shot me. I know I killed him because I saw him go flying. Then everything went black! As it turned out, a 2nd NVA soldier hit me with an RPG grenade.

The action was so close that shrapnel from Pape's grenade wounded his radioman, PFC Mike Fey, hitting him in the face and neck, opening up his trachea. Fey had been with the company for two weeks and it was his first action.

Minor Chaney and the rest of the second platoon were still outside the village:

My squad had dropped our packs beside the packs of the first squad, who were farther in the woods. We had to belly-crawl backwards when the gunship was firing so close. Sergeant Albert White said, "I need someone to go out there and get those packs." He didn't order me, but he was looking straight at me, so, like a nut, I volunteered. I told him I would go get them if they would cover me.

They laid down a field of cover fire, and I low-crawled out to the packs. The firing had let up and, all of a sudden, a soldier came out of the woods and I didn't recognize him. My buddy League said, "That's Lt. Pape!" The lieutenant, bloody from head to toe, was just staggering, barely able to get one foot in front of the other. League jumped up calling, "C'mon and help me!" I hurried with him and we got Lt. Pape down and kind of behind some cover. By that time, squad leader Richard Simcakowski had made it back, having been shot through both wrists.

We called for a medevac, but a cargo Huey came in and we got the wounded on it. The door gunner from the crash went in the Huey with them. There were some other wounded, but not as seriously as Lt. Pape and Ski.

The war was over for Pape and Ski, but Mike Fey returned to the company about three months later, rejoining it for Operation Pegasus.

As it started to get dark, Neal Wolf and his gunner cautiously made their way back to the rest of the platoon to hear that Pape, Simcakowski, and another man were wounded, and Gary Clayton was missing. After pulling some wounded men to safety (for which he received a posthumous Bronze Star with "V") Clayton apparently went back into the village to try to retrieve Lt. Pape's rifle when he was hit.

After dark, Wolf and Joe Vivirito, along with Lts Bill Bane and Charlie Brown, crawled into the village through trenches to recover Clayton, with Brown killing one NVA in the trench as they headed in. Wolf tied rifle slings to Clayton's arms and dragged him back a short distance to make sure he wasn't booby-trapped. They then carried him back to his platoon where his body was lifted out the next morning. Clayton was 21 and from Oklahoma City.

The companies surrounding the village pulled back and set up blocking and ambush positions along possible enemy escape routes. Sporadic contact was made through the night with small groups of VC trying to escape the trap. Second platoon set up by an irrigation canal and Chaney thought he would take the opportunity to clean up:

It was my intention to find something to stand on so I could take a bath and not get my feet muddy. I looked around, and right behind our position was an old barn or shack. So, I tore a board off of it and started back towards the water. Suddenly, something hit me in the back, ran past me, and jumped into the canal. It was an NVA soldier that had been hiding in that shack. As he ran by me, he dropped some kind of explosive. My buddy Donnie Sharp from Georgia was hit in the hand by the shrapnel. We threw grenades into the water until we got him.

Late on the first day, as the men sorted out their packs and those of the casualties, they found a VC pack stuffed with Vietnamese piasters. Before he was hit, Lt Pape had killed a VC officer and taken his pack. It's likely the officer was the paymaster for his unit, but the men of Charlie Company were the beneficiaries. The piasters were distributed throughout the company, with second platoon getting the largest share, and as soon as the men got to an LZ where they could relax a little bit, the poker games began.

The next morning, January 3, 1968, Charlie Company was picked up and flown over the village for an air-assault on a sandy beach, where it linked up with Bravo Company, 1/50th Mech. Charlie swept the village, advancing behind the APCs of the mechanized company, destroying the village, and overwhelming the last VC there. Chaney remembered their effect: "Their .50 caliber machine guns and 40-millimeter grenade launchers riddled trees, huts, and everything in their path. We infantry guys just kinda walked behind them and watched the devastation in awe."

As they reached the far side of the village, the two companies turned and swept through it again, encountering a stream of women and children who had remained in the village throughout the battle and final assault, now leaving and carrying their few remaining belongings. John Nowling was down to his last weeks in Vietnam and as he passed an old woman, he pressed his share of the captured Vietnamese piasters into her hand. He moved on as she pressed her hands together and kept bowing to him in gratitude.

US losses at what became known as the battle of An Tinh were six KIA and twenty-eight WIA, against a body count of ninety-seven VC, with twenty-eight weapons captured. Ron Pape spent about a year and a half in Army hospitals and always remembered one incident early on:

> When I came to in a Hospital in Vietnam (no idea after how many days) a nurse came over to my bed and said, "There is a Warrant Officer over there that wants to apologize to you." I could only look at her and then to my right (had a Tracheostomy tube stuck down my throat) to try and see who she was referring to? I could not make him out. But she said he was the pilot of the gunship that was mistakenly firing at us. Sadly, I couldn't even signal to him that it was okay.

When the companies of the 2nd VC Regiment were located and trapped in An Tinh village, it is possible they were establishing positions and weapons caches for the upcoming Tet offensive. While no one in the field with Charlie Company could have predicted the scope and audacity of the oncoming Tet offensive, it was clear that the war was taking a different turn. Starting in the spring of 1967 and increasing greatly in November and December, the North Vietnamese launched major attacks along the DMZ and Cambodian border.

The battles around Dak To in late November were the biggest battles of the war since LZs X-Ray and Albany in the Ia Drang Valley two years earlier. The Marines in I Corps were hard-pressed with many of their units tied down in bases like Con Thien and Khe Sanh, hit daily with heavy artillery and rockets, something rarely encountered before then. In response to the developing threat, General Westmoreland ordered the 1st Cavalry to move north.

Around that time, infantry companies in the 1st Cavalry at least began to get more reliable rifles. First, some of the existing M-16s were retrofitted with new buffers that slowed down the rate of fire. Then units began getting the new M-16A1's with chromed chambers, self-contained cleaning kits, and other improvements. While still a temperamental weapon, the new rifles were much more reliable than the ones the men carried during the company's first two plus years in Vietnam.

Charlie Company had one more mission in Bong Son, a sweep through the Kim Son Valley in the Soui Ca Mountains, familiar territory for the past twenty-two months. On a night ambush patrol on January 9, 1968, SP4 Genie McDonald was killed and three others were wounded. According to the battalion log, one end of the ambush "engaged the other while changing reliefs." Vaughn Wright was the platoon medic that day and recalls that a man with a Starlight night vision scope saw movement and fired, thinking a VC was sneaking up on the other end of the ambush. In reality, one of the men had moved out of position to relieve himself. The man who fired was medevaced with the wounded, hysterical and in shock, and was later transferred to another company where he was reportedly killed in action about three months later.

McDonald had less than a month to go on his tour and was suffering from a serious case of boils on his back. Wright had recommended that he be sent to the rear for treatment but was overruled by his platoon leader. McDonald was 20 and from

Gosport, IN and had an infant son born when he was in Vietnam. He was the last man from Charlie Company to die in the Central Highlands.

Part 3: Operations in I Corps, 1968

North to the DMZ

On the morning of January 16, 1968, Charlie Company was operating out of LZ Pony in the Kim Son Valley when it was ordered to assemble to be picked up for movement to a new location. Alpha, Bravo, and Delta Companies of the 1/5th, operating out of LZ Uplift and other nearby bases, got the same order. By mid-afternoon, the battalion was lifted to Phu Cat Air Base, just north of Qui Nhon, where it went under the operational control of the 1st Brigade.

That evening, the battalion flew by C-130s to Phu Bai, a Marine Corps base just south of Hue, starting the 1st Cavalry's redeployment from the Central Highlands to the northernmost part of South Vietnam and making Charlie Company one of the Cav's first companies to set foot in the division's new Area of Operations (AO).

The next morning, part of the 1/5th and the forward headquarters of the 1st Brigade moved by helicopter to a former Marine firebase renamed LZ Jane, ten kilometers southwest of Quang Tri City. Division headquarters set up outside of Hue and Operation Job Stuart was launched on January 21, 1968. Over the next week, the rest of the 1st Brigade made the journey from Binh Dinh Province to its new AO by air and by ship, followed by the 3rd Brigade. The 2nd Brigade, minus the 1/5th, stayed in Bong Son to wrap up Operation Pershing, moving north to rejoin the division in late February. To compensate, the 1st Cavalry was given control of the 2nd Brigade of the 101st Airborne Division, newly arrived in Vietnam.

At the time of the move, US strength in Vietnam was close to its peak, and General Westmoreland and MACV believed they were on the path to winning the war. MACV controlled nearly half a million American soldiers, Marines, airmen, sailors, and coast guardsmen, along with nearly 60,000 combat troops from South Korea, Australia, New Zealand, the Philippines, and Thailand, backed by Air Force bases in Thailand and Guam and the aircraft carriers of the Navy's Seventh Fleet on station in the South China Sea.

South Vietnamese forces added another 350,000 military personnel, plus an additional 280,000 in Regional and Popular Forces militia units. Against this, the North Vietnamese and Viet Cong had some 280,000 full and part-time fighters, backed by an extensive network of local guerillas and village-based support units.

The 1st Cavalry's new AO was made up of Quang Tri and Thua Thien Provinces, running from the DMZ southeast for approximately 90 miles. It was the narrowest part of South Vietnam, averaging less than 50 miles from the coast to the Laotian border, and the two provinces were particularly vulnerable due to their proximity to NVA bases in Laos and north of the DMZ. Most of the approximately 800,000 people in the two provinces lived in a narrow coastal plain about ten miles wide. The area had been dubbed "La Rue Sans Joie" (The Street Without Joy) by the French in the first Indochinese war because of the high number of casualties they suffered there and the strong loyalty of the inhabitants to the Viet Minh.

To the west, there were rolling hills intersected by river valleys, which then rose to steep and densely forested mountains, rising in some places to over 2,400 meters along the poorly defined border with Laos. The Marine Corps base at Khe Sanh was in the far northwest corner of Quang Tri Province and the A Shau Valley, a major NVA stronghold, was in western Thua Thien, running parallel to the Laotian border.

The primary US combat unit in the two provinces prior to the 1st Cavalry's arrival was the 3rd Marine Division, an outfit of 24,000 headquartered at Dong Ha with five infantry regiments, one artillery regiment, and supporting units. Most of the Marines were tied down in a series of company-size strong points and battalion-size combat bases in northern Quang Tri Province running from the coast to Khe Sanh.

In early 1968, the NVA maintained a higher concentration of units in northern South Vietnam than anywhere else in the country, including some of the best regiments and divisions in their army. Enemy forces in Quang Tri Province included thirteen infantry regiments belonging to five different North Vietnamese divisions, plus an assortment of Viet Cong main force battalions and local force companies. With much less need than the allies to defend fixed positions, the NVA could achieve local superiority by massing troops at the time and place of their choosing.

Highway 1, a two-lane paved road, ran north and south through the two provinces about ten kilometers in from the coast and connected the three most important urban areas in the AO. Farthest north was Dong Ha, a small town on the Mieu Giang and Cua Viet Rivers twelve kilometers south of the DMZ and within range of NVA artillery firing from North Vietnam. Highway 9, a dirt road, ran west from Dong Ha to Khe Sanh and the Laotian border.

Fifteen kilometers further south was Quang Tri City, the provincial capital with about 12,000 people. Another sixty-five kilometers to the south was Hue, South Vietnam's third largest city with about 140,000 people, the provincial capital of Thua Thien Province and the former imperial capital of Vietnam before the French colonized the country in the late 1800's.

By the afternoon of January 17, 1968, Charlie Company was back in the field securing positions in hilly country southwest of Hue. There the company ran patrols, night ambushes, provided security for road sweeps by combat engineers, and searched for weapons caches. Minor Chaney recalled one search after the company received an intelligence report that weapons were hidden in a cemetery:

> I got on a detail to open a fairly fresh grave. We dug down until we hit a box, and we had to tear a board off it to see if there were any weapons. As soon as the board came off, the stench almost knocked us down, Captain Terry said, "Cover that back up and let's get out of here." We covered it way faster than we uncovered it.

A few days later, the company loaded onto trucks and drove up Highway 1 past Phu Bai and Hue and rejoined the rest of the battalion near LZ Jane.

On January 21, 1968, the war along the DMZ took a new turn when the NVA attacked the Marine Corps Khe Sanh combat base in force. Khe Sanh had been established in early 1967 when General Westmoreland ordered the 3rd Marine Division to set up a combat base at the western end of the DMZ. The Marines objected, believing that it would tie down their forces in a position with little strategic value and detract from the more important mission of pacification in the coastal lowlands. Westmoreland prevailed, and by mid-January, there was a reinforced Marine Regiment occupying the base and some smaller outposts on key hills overlooking it. NVA ambushes had shut down road access to the base along Highway 9 and Khe Sanh could only be supplied by air, with C-123s and 130s flying in supplies whenever there was a break in the winter monsoons.

MACV had been monitoring the large buildup of NVA units around Khe Sanh but still seemed unprepared for the size of the attack on January 21 when the base and its surrounding outposts were hit by hundreds of rounds of mortar fire, 122mm rockets, and 130mm and 152mm artillery firing from caves in Laos. The Marine's main ammunition dump exploded and the airstrip was damaged and effectively shut down, raising fears in both MACV and Washington that the North Vietnamese would try to turn Khe Sanh into a new Dien Bien Phu, the Viet Minh's major victory over the French in the first Indochinese war. Ground attacks were repelled by the Marines but a nearby South Vietnamese district headquarters was overrun.

In response to the attack, 1/5th moved into western Quang Tri Province, with Charlie Company operating in mountains overlooking a river valley east of Khe Sanh, conducting air-assaults, search and destroy sweeps, and night ambushes. Chaney described one of their missions:

> The choppers picked us up and flew up to a mountain top. We were told that the NVA were dug in there. The elephant grass was so tall that the choppers couldn't land for fear of getting the grass wrapped around the tail prop. We had to jump about eight feet and walk the grass down so that the rest could at least get down to three of four feet before jumping.
>
> Once on the ground, we advanced towards the top with no re-

sistance. When we finally got up there, we found some tunnels. We threw in CS (tear gas) grenades but got no one out. Finally, we threw in a frag and one of the small guys went in and brought out a young teenage girl of the Montagnard tribe. She had a head wound and was having trouble breathing. Doc Rogers did a tracheotomy on her right there in the field using an ink pen to hold her airway open. We got her on a chopper headed to a hospital. I didn't throw the frag, but I remember distinctly how sick I felt about this deal. We were told that there were some NVA holed up there, and possibly they could have been there and were already gone. There was nothing more we could do but move on, but I still felt awful about what happened.

The Battle for Quang Tri City

A few days later, the company air-assaulted onto a hilltop called LZ Pedro about ten kilometers southwest of Quang Tri on an artillery raid. As the men began building bunkers and filling sandbags to fortify their positions, a battery of 155 mm howitzers was lifted in by C-54 Skycrane helicopters. The men were still at it the next morning, January 31, 1968, when word came down to destroy what they had done and prepare to move out. Chaney recalls:

> Top Fowler came around to our position so excited he could hardly be still. He was yelling, "Destroy those sandbags, leave nothing here that the enemy can use! We're going to Quang Tri City, the NVA are running wild in the streets!"

The Tet offensive had begun. This was an ambitious effort to topple South Vietnam by simultaneously attacking hundreds of government bases across the width and breadth of the country. The Communists launched their major assault before dawn on January 31, hitting twenty-seven of South Vietnam's forty-four provincial capitals, five of six autonomous cities, and numerous smaller targets like district towns and ARVN bases. The largest attacks came at Saigon, Hue, and Quang Tri.

The North Vietnamese hoped that the Tet offensive would inspire a popular uprising that would overthrow the Saigon military government, open the way for a coalition government dominated by the Viet Cong, and force the withdrawal of the United States and all allied military forces, paving the way for the reunification of North and South Vietnam. The first day of the Tet offensive was the deadliest day for the US in the war, with 246 Americans killed.

Charlie Company flew straight into the battle. As South Vietnamese paratroopers fought a main force VC battalion inside Quang Tri City, elements of the 1st Cavalry were committed to attack elements of the 812th NVA Regiment outside the city. Military historian Eric Villard described the fight in his 2008 publication *The 1968 Tet Offensive Battles of Quang Tri City and Hue*:

Shortly after the two companies from the 1st Battalion, 12th Cavalry engaged the rear elements of the K4 Battalion, Companies A and C from the 1st Battalion, 5th Cavalry descended by helicopter on the village of Thong Thuong Xo, about four kilometers southeast of Quang Tri City. Enemy troops in the area shot down a scout helicopter as it buzzed overhead, but prowling gunships quickly suppressed the ground fire and made the landing possible.

According to the commander of Company C, Capt. Daniel C. Terry, he and his fellow soldiers knew very little about the tactical situation when they stepped off their aircraft. His unit had been on a mission near the Laotian border when it had received orders to fly back to Quang Tri City immediately and engage an enemy force that was besieging the capital. Despite the minimal time he had been given to prepare for the assault, Terry was confident in his company's fighting ability and hoped that the speed with which Rattan's far-flung brigade joined the battle would come as a rude shock to an enemy that had never seen the 1st Cavalry Division in action.

Company A established a blocking position near Highway 1 while Company C searched the area north of the village. Company C soon made contact with dug-in enemy soldiers, and by 1840 hours, the entire company was engaged with what turned out to be the heavy weapons company from the K6 Battalion. The sudden appearance of an American unit to their rear spread uncertainty among the North Vietnamese, many of whom abandoned their fighting positions, along with several hundred 82-mm mortar rounds.

Once they had been flushed into the open, enemy soldiers fell by the dozens to allied artillery and gunships. The North Vietnamese soldiers apparently had little experience fighting helicopters; most chose to feign death as an aircraft approached instead of opening fire, making them easy targets for the American pilots. The heavy weapons company from the K6 Battalion eventually broke contact but not before suffering crippling losses.

This was the first time the NVA units attacking Quang Tri had encountered the 1st Cavalry and the results were described by Shelby Stanton in his book *Anatomy of a Division: The 1st Cav in Vietnam*:

The North Vietnamese and Viet Cong were confident and superbly equipped when the battle opened, but their battle experience against the Marines had offered them only limited opportunity to witness airmobile tactics. Marine helicopters were comparatively rare and used as transports rather than as an integrated armada of aerial war machines. The NVA/VC were completely unprepared to cope with the dazzling pace and devastating firepower of air cavalry tactics. Not realizing their vulnerability if caught in the open, the North Vietnamese often "played dead" and seldom returned fire as helicopters approached. This primitive response cost them dearly as division helicopters swarmed over the fields and cut loose with rockets, cannons, machine guns, and grenade launchers into the prone enemy ranks.

As night approached, the enemy began withdrawing from Quang Tri City and the surrounding area in small groups. Some NVA shed their uniforms or wore civilian clothes over them to try to pose as refugees fleeing the destruction in the city. Lt Steve Voelker, one of Charlie Company's platoon leaders, was stunned when he saw two nuns and a priest gunned down by his platoon sergeant as they ran out of a Catholic Church, apparently intent on fleeing the battle raging around them. Voelker's shock and outrage quickly disappeared when they examined the bodies and found three men wearing NVA uniforms under their religious garb. His platoon sergeant, SSgt Elray Ellender, received a Silver Star for his actions that day.

Following the battle, Charlie and the other companies of 1/5th spent the first week of February sweeping the countryside around Quang Tri, counting bodies, picking up weapons, detaining suspicious men and women, and fighting quick and sporadic firefights with small groups of NVA and VC trying to escape. Here are battalion log entries just for Charlie Company for February 1, 1968, the day after the battle:

O845hrs Weapons captured yesterday total 6 AK47, 2 RPG MG, rocket launcher, 1 SKS, 12 rockets, 1 anti-tank, 300 rds small arms

0943hrs Spotted 10 civilians leaving the area. Request scout A/C.

1035hrs Medevac requested for 3 nuns wounded since last night. Blood or doctor not required. C Co standing by w/ smoke.

1110hrs A PF found out from a civilian chief that 1500 NVA passed through AO moving S early this morning about 0700. No further info available.

1135hrs Request medevac for civilian with frag wounds in hips and legs. Ambulatory patient female.

1515hrs Found 34 NVA bodies and a sandbag of documents. Documents picked up by battalion CO. Will be sent through intel channels.

A few days later, Charlie Company was placed under the operational control of the 1/501st Airborne of the 101st Airborne Division for five or six days, but their daily routine remained the same. Fifty miles to the south, the Marines were mired in their second week of house to house fighting in Hue. The 1st Cav's 3rd Brigade and a battalion from the 101st Airborne shifted south to try to block reinforcements and resupply flowing from the A Shau Valley in western Thua Thien Province to the NVA and VC in Hue. About thirty-five miles to the west of Charlie Company, Khe Sanh and its outposts were in their third week besieged and under daily artillery fire. On February 7, 1968 the NVA overran the nearby Lang Vei Special Forces Camp, using tanks for the first time in the war.

Rain, Cold and Short Rations

Except for the occasional rumor, usually inaccurate and overblown, the men of Charlie Company knew little about what was happening in these nearby battles, and even less about the scope of the Tet offensive in the rest of South Vietnam and the political and military reaction to it back home. There were few places more isolated than an infantry company in the field, at least in the pre-internet days.

What they did know was that it rained every day in February. Minor Chaney remembers: "The sun did not shine, even one time. We ran our patrols in the rain; we ate our meals in the rain; we set up our hooches and slept in the rain on the wet ground." And it was cold: a damp dense fog would roll in most nights and the temperatures would drop into the 50's and the men had only their thin jungle fatigues and some newly issued armored vests.

Resupply was often a problem as choppers were grounded due to the weather and supply shortages were created by the rapid buildup of forces in northern I Corps, made worse by the fighting at Hue and frequent ambushes of supply convoys by the NVA along Highway 1. Food and ammunition were sometimes rationed and trip flares, claymore mines, and illumination rounds were all in short supply. Chaney recalls that "our clothes were about to rot off of us, and there was no such thing as hot meals — we barely got enough C-rations to do us." At one point in early February, Top Fowler purchased black-eyed peas from local villagers to augment the men's rations. They were a treat at first, but by the fifth day few men would eat them.

The company spent most of the month operating in the hills of Quang Tri Province, back where they had been before the Tet attacks. One of the more dangerous jobs was searching caves and NVA bunker complexes. On February 16, 1968 first platoon was moving down a hill when its men heard Vietnamese voices and then found a camouflaged cave entrance. As they approached it, machine gunner George Macias threw a grenade into the cave but a NVA soldier threw it out before it exploded, badly wounding him. When medic Domenico Morgera went to Macias' aid, another NVA soldier popped out of a concealed entrance and sprayed the men with his AK-47. Doc Morgera was killed instantly. He was 21 and from Providence, RI.

Charlie Company ended the month under the operational control of 1/8th Cav. Farther south, the Marines retook Hue on February 25, 1968 although small pockets of NVA fought for another week. To the west, Khe Sanh was still surrounded by thousands of NVA regulars. But for Charlie Company at least, March would be an easier month.

Utah Beach and the Street Without Joy

By late February, the supply situation in northern I Corps was so critical that the Army started to build a new installation on the coast so that supplies could be landed by ship. On March 1, 1968 the 1/5th returned to the control of the 2nd Brigade and it's first mission was to air assault into and secure an area near the coast east of Quang Tri City. Over the next few weeks, Army engineers and Navy Seabees would turn the area into a major resupply base called Utah Beach, later renamed Wunder Beach.

Charlie Company helped secure the perimeter and the men got the chance to swim in the ocean and local streams, get hot food on a regular basis, listen to Armed Forces Radio, and stay dry in well-built bunkers. At one point early in the month, Major General John Tolson, the commander of the 1st Cavalry, issued an order forbidding nude swimming in the area and saying, "Minimum wear will be shorts when swimming."

Each day the company was at Utah Beach, a few men were allowed to take an amphibious boat out to one of the Navy ships offshore to have lunch and go to their PX. Chaney remembered when it was his turn:

Those sailors were so good to us. While in the chow line, they would tell us to go to the front of the line. They were truly appreciative of what we were doing. On that ship they didn't eat C-rations—they had the biggest spread I had ever seen. They had green salads, ice cream and cobbler for dessert, and all kind of vegetables and meats on their buffet. I didn't think I was dreaming but it sure seemed like it.

Utah Beach was in the area called "The Street Without Joy" and, outside the perimeter, the war continued with Charlie Company running regular patrols and ambushes through the villages, sand dunes, and foothills. This was an opportunity for Top Fowler to break in new men, especially anyone assigned to work with the company CP. Marv Anklam was assigned to Charlie Company as senior medic by battalion headquarters company, even though he had not been a medic for one of its platoons.

Some of the medics who had been with Charlie Company had complained about having to walk point or go on small patrols with Fowler and were reassigned and he got the job. Anklam was told when he got assigned to Charlie Company to go along with Top, that he was tough and knew what he was doing. After Top 'initiated' Anklam by bringing him along on point on a patrol outside Utah Beach, things were fine and after that Anklam split his time between Charlie Company and the battalion aid station.

Rob Stanley was a member of the battalion commo team but spent time with Charlie Company during his tour from March 1968 to March 1969. On his first night in the field, he volunteered to go on an overnight ambush patrol lead by Top Fowler:

Charlie Company plans on sending out a platoon to set up a night ambush. This guy Granger, a Cajun from Louisiana, tells me he's going out with them and do I want to go too? I said, "Yeah I'll go if they let me."

The sergeant that's running the ambush is Top Fowler, a chunky, bald headed forty-year-old good old boy from Alabama. I could tell when I got over there that the Charlie Company young grunts felt invincible going out with him.

I don't think Top felt as confident about me as he looked me up and down, "You ever been on an ambush before?" "Ah no, not really," I said. "Here," he said as he threw some camouflage markers to me, "have someone put that on your face and make sure you keep in contact with the guy in front of you."

After I had put it on, he took a quick look and said, "OK. Alright it's dark enough, lock and load and put it on safety, let's move out."

I can still see us moving out, single file, stepping over the perimeter trip wires and into the darkness. Top led the way as usual, setting a pretty good pace as we hiked for a couple of hours until we set up the ambush. I laid there staring into the darkness with my adrenalin going faster than it's ever gone in my life.

We stayed there for about an hour and a half. Nothing. Top put the word out we're moving, and off we go to another ambush site. We stayed for another couple hours and nothing again. Off we go again as we moved for a final time to find a place to sleep.

About two hours of sleep in the sand and off we go, up and down hills, through swamps and rice paddies until we reached a small forest area. Top holds his hand up in a stopping motion and gives hand signals pointing toward a large clump of vegetation about a hundred feet to the left of us. Suddenly someone yells, "There they go!" And all hell breaks loose as everybody opens up towards the clump. I think I see shadows moving and blow off about 20 rounds in that direction.

Everything goes quiet and there's a lot of motioning to go towards where we saw the movement. My eyes are wide open as I scan the area for anything that looks suspicious. I grew up watching a lot of war movies and in this situation, you check for tracks and follow the footprints. So, I put my head down and look for prints. When I pick my head up I'm all by myself! My first reaction is 'Oh shit'.

Don't panic I tell myself as I think about all the bad things that can happen to me in the next couple of minutes, shot or taken prisoner by the VC, shot by a trigger-happy American, stay lost in the jungle for the next month! Go back the way you came, that sounds like a plan, which way was that, everything looks the same.

Follow your footprints back, yeah that's a winner. I see a clearing and I'm out. Just as I step into the clearing a Cobra gunship rakes the area I just stepped out of with rocket and mini-gun fire! Wow, talk about dodging the bullet as I get some distance between me and the forest area and get back to the company.

In the excitement of the action, nobody's missed me. I'm happy to be alive, happy to be back, and damn happy that the grunts didn't realize that the commo FNG was missing in action. How embarrassing.

When I get in, I realize why nobody's missed me—Charlie has linked up with Delta Company and one of their Kit Carson Scouts had been wounded and they had a VC prisoner that another Kit Carson Scout was not treating too well. I was now feeling safe as helicopter gunships are flying all over the place.

It's late in the afternoon and I think we're going to hump back in when our radio man gets a call from Alpha Company. They were just in contact with an estimated company sized NVA element and are chasing them towards us and that we need to set up a blocking force. Wow, here we go again I thought as Top spread everybody out in a straight line at about twenty-yard intervals.

I was next to this Black guy who carried an M-60 machinegun, and I was wired again as I looked ahead for any kind of movement that I thought was sure to come. I looked over at the veteran machine gunner as he set himself up against a tree and aimed his gun forward.

About thirty minutes of waiting and I look over at him and he tipped his boonie hat forward and took a nap. I'm thinking how anyone in this situation can be as relaxed as my eyes bugged out scanning in front of me.

About five minutes later a buck sergeant comes by, "Pack up we're going in." We're about five miles out of Utah Beach and it seems like we're sprinting back. The sun's going down as we step back over the trip wires and back into Utah, and me and Granger start heading back over to the commo area.

Top walked over to me and with a paternal look on his face said, "Ya did good kid."

Top could be tough if he thought someone wasn't up to his standards. Patrick Manijo joined Charlie Company's second platoon in late 1967 after spending a month in Alpha Company. Being from Hawaii, his buddies soon began calling him 'Big Kahuna.' In March 1968, he got a minor shrapnel wound to his hand and went to the rear for treatment. When he tried to rejoin the company, he ended up in a convoy that was held up for days by road closures.

After backtracking and finally getting to Charlie Company, he was met by Top Fowler who accused him of deserting the company and threatened to punish him for it. Despite this, Manijo, like most men in the company then, greatly admired Fowler for his leadership and courage, even if they thought he was a little crazy. Manijo was interviewed in 2017 by author and historian John McGuire and described the First Sergeant:

Top was never in the rear. He was always in the field. When the company was on patrol, Fowler was usually 100 yards out in front of the column. He told me, "As long as I'm in this company, we're never going to get ambushed." He'd wear a sweater and usually a ball cap. Fowler never wore a helmet. Gung Ho was not the right word to describe Fowler. Fierce warrior comes close to describing him. Charlie Company had the reputation as the first to get into a firefight. That was in large part because Fowler would volunteer the Company. If you did something wrong, Top would show you tough love. It was his way of teaching you. The men of Charlie Company had a great deal of respect for Top. He was tough. But taught you how to survive in Vietnam.

During March 1968, Charlie Company fought a few firefights with NVA stragglers and lost about half a dozen men to booby traps. On one patrol when the company was operating with a platoon of trigger-happy ARVN Rangers, one man walking point with Top Fowler was severely wounded by a grenade rigged with a trip wire. Shortly after that, 1Lt Steve Voelker tripped a much larger booby trap—a 155mm shell packed with C-4 explosives. But when his foot hit the trip wire, it pulled the firing mechanism out of the explosives and it sputtered and sparked on the ground in front of him and his RTO, PFC Bob Broderson.

In mid-month, an NVA solider who was sick with malaria gave himself up to the company and said there were about thirty wounded NVA in the area, with twenty guards. Based on this intelligence, Charlie Company found and picked up eleven more NVA, some of them wounded. Decades later, Charlie Brown—then one of the company's platoon leaders—was given one of the prisoners ID book from another company veteran who had kept it as a souvenir. Brown sent the ID book back to Vietnam through an intermediary who managed to locate its original owner and return it. Eventually the word got back to Brown that the NVA veteran was grateful he'd been captured that day because he knew then he had a chance to survive the war.

Operation Pegasus

By the middle of March, the 1st Cavalry was finalizing plans to go on the offensive and lift the siege of the Marine combat base at Khe Sanh. With Hue retaken and supplies moving again, all three of the division's brigades would operate together for the first time in months. On March 20, 1968, Army engineers and Navy Seabees began building LZ Stud, a large firebase about halfway between Dong Ha and Khe Sanh that would be the jumping off point for Operation Pegasus.

MG John Tolson, Commanding General of the 1st Cavalry, would have overall command and his plan was for the 1st Marine Regiment to reopen Highway 9 and attack west towards Khe Sanh on the ground while the Cav would air assault into the surrounding hills. On the first day, the 3rd Brigade would seize the hills on either side of Highway 9. The second day, the 2nd Brigade would land its three battalions southeast of Khe Sanh and attack northwest. The next day, the 1st Brigade would air assault just south of Khe Sanh and attack north, followed by an ARVN airborne task force which would air-assault to the southwest and retake the Lang Vei Special Forces Camp.

On April 3, 1968, the 1/5th was relieved at Utah Beach by a battalion of the 101st Airborne and lifted to LZ Stud. A few hours later, all four companies air assaulted onto LZ Wharton, a rough and rocky hill overlooking Khe Sanh, about ten kilometers to the northwest. Wharton was within range of North Vietnamese artillery firing from caves in the Co Roc Mountains just across the Laotian border. The NVA began shelling the LZ that night and continued through the morning. Aside from occasional friendly fire, no one in the company had been on the receiving end of accurate artillery fire before.

When Patrick Manijo heard artillery coming in, he crawled to a fox hole and ended up on top of three men already there. When the next round came in, a hot piece of shrapnel cut the back of his shirt collar and up into his helmet without hurting him. He remembers how the next morning, poncho liners were shredded and hanging from trees, water cans were blown up, and the LZ was generally beat to hell. Minor Chaney remembers one barrage early in the morning lasting about two hours. He wrote:

> Finally, when daylight came, it was so foggy that you could only see a few feet ahead. The choppers couldn't get in to evacuate our dead and wounded or bring supplies. We couldn't do anything but hold our positions.

Charlie Company was lucky. It had men wounded, but Alpha, Bravo, and Delta all had KIAs. Bravo was especially hard hit with three KIA and thirteen or fourteen WIA, including the company commander. LTC Robert Runkle, the battalion commander, appointed Capt. Joe Lyttle, his S-3 officer and Charlie Company's former CO, to take over Bravo Company, and they boarded Runkle's command chopper at LZ Stud to fly out to LZ Wharton. They flew low due to the cloud cover and were shot down by the NVA while on the way.

Contact was lost with Runkle's chopper at 1000 hours but the wreckage wasn't located for another eight hours. The NVA got there first and killed anyone who survived the crash and made off with anything valuable, including code books and maps. Of the seven passengers and crew, Joe Lyttle was the only survivor, with injuries both from the crash and being shot and left for dead. He was partially paralyzed and in a wheelchair for the rest of his life. Another seven men were killed, and twice as many wounded, most from the 2/7th Cav, fighting to secure the crash scene.

The next morning, April 5, 1968, Charlie Company and the rest of the 1/5th moved out of Wharton on foot to assault an old French fort that was held by a battalion of NVA. Manijo described their start in his interview with McGuire:

> Second platoon was in the lead. Before we started moving, an artillery barrage started again. There was no place to hide so we laid on the ground. I heard a whistling and watched as a piece of shrapnel landed right next to me with a thud. The constant artillery was intense. There was one guy who went crazy and just started screaming and tried to run off.

At least four more men of the company were wounded in the barrage. But supporting fire works both ways: Chaney remembers that while on the move, the company caught some NVA in the open and that Top Fowler decimated them by calling in mortar and artillery fire and rockets from gunships.

The assault on the old French Fort turned into a three-day battle, as described by Eric Villard in *Staying the Course: Combat Operations in Vietnam, October 1967 to September 1968*:

> The 1st Cavalry Division met its first real challenge of the campaign

two kilometers south of Landing Zone Thor. As the 1st Battalion, 5th Cavalry closed in on the old French fort that overlooked a narrow switchback on Highway 9, the soldiers discovered that it was already held by North Vietnamese troops from the 8th Battalion, 29th Regiment. The cavalrymen tried to maneuver within grenade-throwing range of the fort but found it impossible to do so without bringing down a torrent of machine-gun and mortar fire. The 1st Battalion, 5th Cavalry, spent the next three days trying to seize the position, but to no avail. Colonel McDonough [2nd Brigade commander] broke the deadlock on the morning of 7 April by airlifting a pair of companies from the 2d Battalion, 5th Cavalry, deep behind the enemy position and then attacking the fort from the opposite direction. The attacking companies faced almost no resistance. Apart from six enemy soldiers who died resisting the morning assault, the bulk of the North Vietnamese defenders had slipped away during the night. The capture of the fort removed the last major strong point between the 1st Cavalry Division and Khe Sanh.

Khe Sanh was relieved on April 8, 1968 with the NVA withdrawing back into Laos and north of the DMZ, leaving large amounts of equipment behind. Shelby Stanton summarized Operation Pegasus in *Anatomy of a Division: The 1st Cav in Vietnam*:

> Tolson's swift and powerful cavalry raid had smashed through the enemy lines and broken the siege of Khe Sanh in the first division scale air assault in history. Every line battalion was helicoptered directly onto the battlefield in the first airmobile division attack to use all three brigades ...
>
> The 1st cavalry Division effectively coordinated an airmobile drive of eight cavalry battalions with a ground advance by seven Marine and four South Vietnamese infantry battalions. The pace of the

division's aerial onslaught was set by waves of helicopters catapulting battalions of Skytroopers over successive enemy barriers...The combination of air assaulting infantry, aerial rocket attack, and scout ship harassment forced the NVA to abandon carefully prepared defenses and to retreat without regard to his planned directions of withdrawal. The hasty enemy departure was evidenced by the staggering amounts of munitions, emplaced weapons, and equipment left in defensive positions.

Operation Pegasus ended on April 15, 1968 but not before Charlie Company got caught up in the last firefight of the operation. Early on April 13, 1968, Charlie and Bravo Companies air-assaulted onto a hilltop south of the Lang Vei Special Forces Camp and almost on the Laotian border. Bob Broderson was now one of the RTOs for Captain Terry and the CP and remembers that the hill was being used as an observation post by the NVA.

The LZ was hot and the first choppers landed on top of a bunker with four or five North Vietnamese soldiers in it, who were quickly dispatched. At one point in the day, the clouds broke and Steve Voelker looked up and could see NVA artillery firing down on them from caves in the Co Roc Mountains in Laos. Before an airstrike or artillery could be called in, the guns had disappeared back into the caves and their positions were camouflaged and impossible to spot.

Early the next morning, Easter Sunday, the hill was attacked by an estimated company of NVA preceded by rockets, mortars, and artillery. Shortly before the attack, Broderson smelled marijuana and thinks it was being smoked by NVA moving into position. They broke through the perimeter and Bravo Company had men killed and both companies had wounded, some by shrapnel from their own supporting artillery. Broderson remembers one NVA yelling "medic" to try to lure a US doc into the open.

The ploy may have worked with Bravo Company, who had eight men killed. As the fight unfolded, some soldiers from Bravo came over and asked for a medic as they had none. Top sent Marv Anklam:

> When I got there, B Co had all the wounded gathered together on the top of the hill, 6-8 best I can remember After checking their wounds, a couple soldiers took me down the hillside to a bunker. I think there were three dead troopers inside, the thought was they fell asleep and were taken out. That night was constantly lit up with flares which lit up the whole hillside. The next morning Top told me, "You did good last night, Doc." Nothing in this world could have made me feel better than to have Top say that.

Even as Operation Pegasus was winding down, the 1st Cavalry was planning its next move. On April 19, 1968, the 1st and 3rd Brigades began Operation Delaware with air-assaults into the A Shau Valley, southeast of Khe Sanh in Thua Thien Province. But while that operation caught the attention of the press in Vietnam, Charlie Company continued to operate in the Khe Sanh area, as the 1/5th and 2/5th went under the operational control of the 3rd Marine Division for Operation Scotland II.

At the same time, the North Vietnamese were planning their next move, a resumption of the Tet offensive. Due to the NVA and VC's heavy losses in February, it would be scaled back with only two main targets: Saigon and Dong Ha. The NVA started their attack on ARVN and Marine units around Dong Ha on

April 29, 1968 and on units around Saigon a week later. May 1968 would be the deadliest month of the war for the US, with 2,169 KIA and many more wounded.

Top Fowler's Last Patrol

At the beginning of May 1968, the 1/5th, now under the command of LTC Clarence Jordan, was operating along the Laotian border west of Khe Sanh and just north of Lang Vei. The battalion CP and a battery of 105mm howitzers were on a small hilltop named LZ Peanuts, guarded by Alpha Company, with Bravo, Charlie, and Delta Companies running patrols and night ambushes in the surrounding hills and valleys. Peanuts received daily artillery and mortar fire from Laos and much of the countryside was open and down to bare dirt, in part due to all the shelling and B-52 strikes in the area during the weeks Khe Sanh was under siege.

On the morning of May 4, 1968, Charlie Company was ordered to sweep south parallel to the border and set up a new position in the evening. It was a long hard hump and the men carried only weapons, ammo, and water. Their rucksacks had been lifted out in the morning and would be flown out to their new position once they reached it. As he sometimes did, Top Fowler grabbed a couple of riflemen and set out in front, walking point about 100 meters ahead of the company. At about 1430 hours, they were caught in the open by an NVA machine gun in a well concealed bunker. Lt Steve Voelker was one of the first to reach them:

I had just returned from R & R in Hawaii and had just taken over the mortar platoon. The company was strung out in line. Coming down a knoll and heading up to a big bald hill in front. I was on top of the knoll and could see the Top, Galindo, and I believe Hurst. They were in the middle of the beaten zone. I had no doubt that they were dead. They went down immediately. I called it in and reported that they were on the east side of the hill and recommended that [Lt Frank] Romiti take his platoon and go up the east side. Their attack stalled. Since my Platoon Sergeant was more skilled at the mortars than me, I walked up the hill and got to the line where first platoon had taken cover. I crawled up and recovered Galindo's body. Our side was not firing, because we could not see a target. There were a lot of bees buzzing by me, if you know what I mean. I eventually got hit in the left inner triceps. Followed immediately by a belly wound in my navel. We did spot the bunker then. I crawled back to receive aid. Romiti said that they took out the bunker with a LAW.

Voelker would spend months in the hospital in the Philippines, Japan, and Ft. Campbell, KY and eventually need seven surgeries.

A few minutes after getting the first report, Charlie Company requested medevac for three KIA and one WIA. One more man would be killed and five more wounded trying to recover the bodies. The NVA fire was intense enough so that RTO Bob Broderson was trying to get more cover by digging with his helmet, as his entrenching tool was with his rucksack. Patrick Manijo heard on the radio that "Top Fowler has been shot" and was one of the men who helped to recover Top Fowler's body. He volunteered to go get Fowler, in part to let him know, "I never deserted the company:"

I ran to a shallow ravine about eight feet deep and could see three men laying dead. I was about to run across the ravine when Lt. Jones stopped me and said the NVA had a clear shot down the ravine. When I got to Top, he was still alive but shot in the chest. We tried to drag him down the hill but couldn't, due to his size. I said to him, "Hang on, I'll get you down" and then he died.

After recovering the dead and wounded, the company pulled back and called in gunships and artillery. The two men killed with Top Fowler were PFCs Edwin Galindo and Ronald Hurst. Galindo was 20 and from Yukon, OK. Hurst was 18, from Swannanoa, NC, and had been in country less than a month. Killed trying to retrieve their bodies was SP4 Roy Barry League, 20, of Tallapoosa, GA.

Robert Fowler was 40 and from Geneva, AL. He had been in the Army for twenty-two years. At the time of his death, he had been in Vietnam just under three years, with only an occasional R & R in Bangkok, Thailand, where he owned a bar. He arrived in Vietnam in October 1965 and became first sergeant of Charlie Company in December 1966. One man recalls that Fowler was carrying $4,000 in his wallet when he was hit and killed.

That night, LZ Peanuts was hit by the NVA. Artillery firing from Laos set off the ammo dump and a sapper company backed by two infantry companies breached the perimeter and destroyed most of the howitzers on the firebase. 1Lt Charlie Brown, who had been a Charlie Company platoon leader for eight months and who replaced Joe Lyttle as battalion S-3 in early April, helped organize the defense and drive out the sappers. Fighting was close range and hand-to-hand with heavy casualties on both sides. Two days later, LZ Peanuts was abandoned.

Battle in the Sand

Charlie Company had already moved on. Since April 29, 1968 two battalions of Marines and two battalions of ARVN had been fighting a running battle with elements of the 320th PAVN Division and the independent 270th PAVN Regiment around Dong Ha, close to the coast. By May 2nd, two more Marine battalions and a battalion of the 196th Light Infantry Brigade from the Army's Americal Division had been fed into the fight, now named the battle of Dai Do for some villages where the NVA had dug in.

As the battle seemed to be winding down, the Marines organized a new mission to try to cut off the retreating NVA. Called Operation Concordia Square, it would put the 1/5th and 2/5th between the DMZ and the NVA. On May 5, 1968 the Marines ordered the 1/5th to move to the Dong Ha area. Charlie Company was lifted to LZ Stud and from there flew to a Marine Corps base south of Dong Ha. Late that afternoon, all four companies of 1/5th set up in a field by the Cua Viet River, about four kilometers northeast of Dong Ha. The next day the battalion began sweeping north towards the town of Gio Linh, about three kilometers south of the DMZ.

Top Fowler's death had deeply affected the men of the company, and many were nervous and on edge. It wasn't just the loss of his leadership and combat skills or the intensity of the past month on the Laotian border—it was the thought that if Top could 'buy the farm' so easily, then the odds just got worse for everybody else. Then as the company moved north, the mood went from nervous to spooked.

Somewhere north of Dong Ha, Charlie Company came upon a Marine encampment with fortified and sandbagged positions, hooches still up, some personal gear strewn around, and no one there. RTO Bob Broderson thought it looked like they just got up and left. George Dickman in the second platoon recalls: "We found wallets, personal gear…things you just don't leave behind. We all knew something strange had happened here." RTO Chuck Rodriguez saw a movie camera and ammo laying there. No one ever found out what happened to the Marines who had left so fast. Captain Terry called the incident in to battalion and sent some of the Marines' personal items in on the next resupply chopper, but there is no reference to it in the 1/5th daily logs.

As the battalion moved north on May 8, 1968 with Charlie Company in the lead, it entered a broad expanse of sand, riddled with bomb and shell craters from earlier battles, and with sparse cover and vegetation. All four companies set up that night in a large perimeter and each sent out ambushes and listening posts. First platoon provided them for Charlie Company: 1Lt Frank Romiti went out with a twelve-man ambush patrol and SP4 Gordon Adams took out a five-man LP. Although the purpose of an LP is to provide early warning of enemy movement, Adam's team didn't have a radio. Of the two first platoon radios, one was with Romiti and the other was back in the perimeter with Sgt Frank Duran, who had become acting Platoon Sergeant after the platoon's career NCO was wounded on May 4.

At one point early in the morning on May 9th, another unit, most likely Marines, fired illumination rounds hundreds of meters away and Romiti's RTO could make out a long line of North Vietnamese stretcher bearers in the distance heading north carrying wounded NVA. They were most likely NVA soldiers wounded in the earlier battles with the Marines near Dai Do.

At 0339 hours, Romiti radioed in that his ambush patrol had counted over 300 NVA moving near their position and requested artillery fire. Bob Broderson was monitoring the radio for the company CP and woke Captain Terry up when he got Romiti's call. The request for fire support was relayed to battalion but was denied by the Marines for unknown reasons. Frank Duran and Minor Chaney were monitoring the first platoon and mortar platoon radios at the time and also heard Romiti's call. Chaney remembered Terry's initial reaction:

> I went on guard about 2 am and my job was to monitor the radio. At about 3 am, Lt. Romiti's ambush called in and said they had movement on their position. A few minutes later, he called again and said that it was a large unit moving from left to right. Captain Terry told him, "Tear 'em up!" Lt. Romiti came back and said, "But sir, there's too many…we'll be annihilated." Captain Terry thought about it for a few seconds and then said, "Okay, hold right where you are and when it gets light, we'll come and get you."

At 0540 hours, Romiti radioed in again and reported that the NVA had returned to the area and were digging in within fifty yards of his ambush position. His RTO remembered the NVA stopping and taking a break only yards in front of their position and then dispersing and starting to dig in, apparently unaware of the ambush patrol and LP. Terry ordered Romiti to move back about 100 yards and set up a defensive position until the rest of the company could relieve them.

According to the battalion log, Adam's LP made it back to the company just after 0610. By then, Terry was getting most of the company ready to move and the returning men joined them heading out, about eighty men in all. Frank Duran remembers that the move was rushed and that platoons were mixed together. The group was strung out with some men not starting out until after Terry had already left the perimeter. The disorganization may have been partly the result of the loss of Top Fowler, one of the platoon leaders, and other experienced men five days earlier. Captain Terry described what happened as he remembered it in a statement he wrote in 2014:

> It was a foggy morning as we set out to link up with Lt. Romiti. When we reached his position, I asked Lt. Romiti where are the positions of all the NVA he referenced to earlier that morning. He reported that they were all along his front and that he could hear them digging as far to the left and right as he could hear. I could see almost to North Vietnam and I could not see anything, He replied that they were out there. What he said was strange to me because there were no trees, very few scrubs and sand dunes to our front. I thought how could so many troops be there and we could not see them.
>
> We started walking forward. My RTO's were besides me. We probably walked about 10 to 15 meters when up jumps two NVA soldiers. We fired on them and killed them. A third one jumps up and I made the decision to try to catch him and see what was going on through our Vietnamese interpreter. We took off running after him. That was a mistake. Suddenly a whole line of fire opened up on us

and all hell broke loose. We were suddenly in the toughest firefight I had witnessed in my eleven months in Vietnam. The NVA appeared out of nowhere. They were everywhere. We were truly out manned and I would estimate at least 600 by the sound of the weaponry and size of the fighting front. The sound of mortars could be heard from their rear and for the first time in combat I witnessed a flame thrower engulfing one of my Platoon Sergeants. It sounded like machine guns were everywhere.

I was hit immediately two times. The first one shattered my left femur into thirty-four pieces, the second one shattered my left tibia and fibula. Falling to the ground, I immediately pulled my belt from my trousers and made a tourniquet to stop the blood spewing from my leg. While doing that, I was wounded by a round to my left arm. I looked and both my RTOs were dead. Then I was wounded in my left hip and right thigh...ducking behind a small sand dune, I called my troops to come forward to the platoon in contact. They were already trying to get to us.

The enemy was about fifty yards in front of us as far as I could see in both directions. I could hear Peter Olivo's M-60 doing a great job. Good thing that it was there. Then a grenade exploded between me and where Olivo's M-60 was firing away, a piece of it hit my buttock. Somehow another RTO made his way to me. I made contact with our command group and requested any fire support they could give us. I do not know what happened after that. I lost consciousness. I awoke on the hospital ship USHS Repose three days later.

Patrick 'Kahuna' Manijo remembered the morning as well:

In the early morning hours of May 9, 1968, Pete Olivo and I were having coffee brewed from our c-ration cans. We had been on high alert all night for the ambush squad sent out the previous night. Before long, we got word to saddle up and move out. The morning was cold, damp, and overcast. When we arrived at the ambush squad, I could see a worn trail, about three-feet wide outlined in the damp sand. It appeared obvious the enemy had passed very close to the ambush squad during the night.

Word arrived for us to get online. We did this and advanced about fifty yards. Suddenly I heard the enemy mortar tubes go off. Instinctively we hit the ground. The mortars were exploding down the line to my left. It was then that all hell broke loose. A significant number of automatic weapons and small arms fire seemed to be directed at only Pete and myself. Pete was positioned to my left on a sand mound. He was concentrating his M-60 on the enemy, an enemy just some one hundred yards to our front. I was approximately ten feet to Pete's right with our platoon leader, 1Lt. Robert Jones, positioned between us.

In seconds I could see tracer rounds kicking up sand all around Pete's position. Doing my best to concentrate my fire on the enemy jumping from sand mound to sand mound, I yelled to Pete to stay down. By this time, the enemy had advanced to what appeared only fifty yards They were close enough for us to see the camouflage leaves stuck to their helmets.

The fighting was intensifying with mortar rounds exploding all about us and I saw an enemy flamethrower spraying the company. Pete called out to me, Kahuna the NVA with the flamethrower! I swung my sniper rifle to the left, but Pete was in the line of fire. I shouted for Stu, who was carrying the M-79 grenade launcher, to shoot that NVA! Stu fired and the NVA exploded in a ball of fire. During all this I remember thinking to myself—holy shit. I called out for Lt. Jones to call in artillery fire. Tragically he caught a round to his forehead. He grunted and fell backward. It seemed the enemy was growing thicker. We couldn't move. It seemed as though thousands upon thousands of deadly rounds were whistling all around us.

I heard an explosion. The NVA had come within range of Pete's position and tossed a grenade killing the assistant gunner and ammo bearer. Pete called out, "Kahuna, I'm hit." I yelled back, "How bad is it?" I yelled for the medic but Pete refused the medic's aide. He yelled back, "I'm okay." Despite being wounded, Pete kept firing his M-60.

It was at this point I saw a log bird fly close above us. I could see in front of me a NVA with some type of heavy machine gun firing on the log bird. The chopper went down. As I tried to get a bead on the NVA gunner I saw that someone had already taken him out. I put two rounds into his weapon hoping I could damage it enough so it couldn't be used again.

Stu 'Shag' Dorethy was the trooper with the M-79. All of this happened in the first half hour or so of the firefight. The 1/5th battalion log recorded this entry at 0710 hours:

All 4 companies are receiving small arms fire from all sides, receiving mortar from N.E. C Co is cut off, B Co is trying to reach C Co, to help pull back. ARA and gunships can't shoot, ceiling too low. Huey was shot down 200m from FOB. The Huey was 2/5 log bird.

The Huey that was shot down was a resupply chopper on a routine mission that flew low over the area, unaware of the intense fight unfolding below it. Minor Chaney had taken cover in a partially flooded bomb crater and it seemed to him that for a minute the NVA stopped firing at them and directed all their fire at the chopper. It turned and tried to fly back to the perimeter but crashed and exploded in a ball of flame, killing the pilot and co-pilot. The door gunner and crew chief were able to jump to safety as it was going down.

The men back in the company perimeter also got hit. Chuck Rodriquez was on one of the company's radios and remembered:

> Listening to the radio, we can tell its mass confusion; the entire company had made heavy contact, which supported the communications of the outpost during the night. We can't make contact with Captain Terry. We don't know what's happened to him and his two radio operators. We're trying to make contact with platoon leaders: 2-6, 3-6, 4-6. While we're doing this, we're using the radio in the back, trying to make contact with battalion, trying to give them information. It's basically mass confusion. Meanwhile, we're still receiving mortar rounds and heavy fire. We're trying to communicate and direct some kind of fire; not being able to communicate with the platoons was an indication that leadership of the respective platoons may have been lost. Then we learned that Charlie Company has been separated. Bravo Company is trying to help but it's having a rough time of it.

The fight continued for about four hours and the men of Charlie Company received no fire support for much of that time. As they had done earlier that morning, the Marines would not authorize artillery for the company and the fog and low ceiling prevented any air support, either from 1st Cavalry's gunships and ARA choppers or Air Force jets (although it's unclear why gunships couldn't get airborne if a Huey could fly on a routine resupply mission around 0700).

When the fighting first started, many men took cover in the bomb and shell craters around them, some partially filled with stagnant water. But the NVA soon began targeting them with accurate mortar fire. Minor Chaney was in one with a buddy when he was wounded twice by shrapnel and realized he had to leave:

I told Yeary to watch me and I was going to try to get over the top of the back of the bomb crater, and this would put us back online with the other guys. I told him, "If I make it, then you come over." As I scrambled over the top, I was shot through the bottom of my foot, but I did make it, and Yeary came on over without getting hit. The fight was still very hot, and I had used up about half of my ammo. All of a sudden, my rifle quit firing.

I tried to pull back the bolt and clear it, but I could not. The blood from my shoulder wound had run down my arm and hand, soaked my shirt, and gotten into my rifle. As I had scrambled around from one position to another, sand had gotten in it also and mixed with the blood and it was jammed tight.

By this point, Yeary was wounded and out of commission, I was wounded and now my weapon was jammed tight and it was a pretty helpless feeling. On our right was a machine gunner from Romiti's group, and he was laying 'em down. And on our left was one of my buddies, Ron Koitzsch, and he was firing away also. I believe that these guys kept the enemy off us. After a while, I heard a splot sound, like a bullet hitting something, and I looked over to see Koitzsch slump down.

The machine gunners in the company played a major part in keeping it from being overrun. Duran still remembers one of the gunners from first platoon, Leonard Silva, who was hit in the cheek while leaning out of his hole firing his M-60. The round had been slowed as it went through one of the bipod legs of his machine gun, but it was hot enough to cauterize his wound and stop any serious bleeding and he shook it off and kept firing. At one point a group of NVA charged his position and Silva jumped out of the hole and stood up and fired from the hip to put more effective fire on the NVA, stopping all of them.

To Duran's right, Jimmy Haskins, the platoon's other machine ginner, was also keeping the enemy at bay. In second platoon, Pete Olivo stayed at his machine gun until he had used up all his ammo and was killed by the NVA. Manijo witnessed Olivo's last minutes:

> I heard Pete yell out that the enemy was trying to flank our right side. I fired on the lead NVA doing my part to stop the flanking attempt. It was at this point when I told Pete that I was out of ammo. Because my sniper rifle used the same ammo as his M-60, I figured it was the best chance I had at continuing to do my part. As he rose to throw me an ammo belt, Pete was hit for the second time. I saw him fall backwards. I yelled out to him, "Pete, are you alright?" Again he called out that he was Okay. Again, he refused receiving any aid from the medic. I was pleading with him to get help.
>
> By this time, the NVA were about twenty feet to our front and I heard Pete yelling. Pete was firing the M-60 nonstop. Over the roar of his machine gun and the deadly chaos all about us I could hear Pete reciting the Lord's Prayer. I took a moment to look his way. He was almost hard to see for the amount of smoke rising from his M-60. Then I could hear him calling out a name over and over again. I recognized it as Edna. I knew the name well. It was the name of his youngest sister. It was as if Pete knew he was making his final stand and would fight until his last breadth.
>
> It was about this time our jets dropped napalm. It exploded in front of us. I could smell the gasoline and burnt flesh and the image of NVA running in the fire ball. We did our best to start pulling back. I yelled to Pete that we were pulling back.
>
> Doug carried Lt. Jones to the back of the sandbank where the choppers evacuated the wounded and dead. I picked up one of our guys who was severely burned and called for help. As I carried him,

I saw that Pete was dead. His lifeless body was outstretched over his M-60. In his right hand was his .45 caliber pistol. A third round from the enemy had killed my friend Pete. Some ten feet in front of his position were dozens and dozens of dead enemy soldiers.

As the mist and fog burned off, the company finally got artillery and air support and the danger of being overrun by the NVA passed. Air Force jets passed low over the company on their bombing runs and men could see napalm canisters tumbling end over end before hitting the ground yards in front of their positions. But with the sun burning brightly, it got extremely hot in the sandy expanse and without water, some of the men began to suffer from heat exhaustion. Company medic Marv Anklam remembers that "it may have been cool early that morning but as the morning went on the heat and thirst were almost unbearable."

Anklam was crawling from man to man providing first aid and to this day carries with him the images of men with severe head wounds and the charred bodies of the soldiers killed by the flamethrowers or the resupply chopper that was shot down. He wrote about his actions that day:

I took a peek over the sand berm, and I probably just thought 'Oh My God!' I'm trying to remember and probably saw ten to twelve wounded and dead soldiers at first who must have been caught in the open when the fight started. It's hard to remember how far away from my location they were but were close enough to seem to be able to tell which ones were dead. Out past them I could see NVA soldiers with camouflage in their helmets. I looked at that scene for a while and at some point, told myself I have to try and do my job.

I got as low to the ground as I could and started crawling toward the wounded. It seemed like all the bullets were aimed at me, but they were going over my head so I just took it slow and worked my way towards them. My web gear held my canteen, .45 and ammo but was making it too difficult to crawl in the sand so I took it off, and it helped a lot. I'd get to a wounded and put on a dressing and in some cases just tried to encourage them and leave them where they were as there was no cover.

Later I got to a soldier that had the side of his head shot away. Blood was still pumping out of his brain matter and as I was thinking how I was going to bandage it, another soldier said, "Save your dressing, doc, he's dead." I didn't bandage the wound. I came to a wounded solider about waist deep in a bomb crater half filled with black water. After treating him I pulled him out of the water a ways and left him in the crater. I took a drink from the water and immediately threw up and then moved on. The last casualty I reached was Capt. Terry. He was shot up real bad and had more holes in him than I had bandages left.

Captain Terry would survive but would spend the next year and a half in the hospital and need more than fifteen surgeries.

Anklam was a big man, over six feet, but Chaney still recalls his gentleness when the medic cut off his boot and shirt and treated his wounds. Shortly after that, the NVA began to pull back and the wounded could be medevaced and Chaney tried to make his way to the rear:

An order came down for all the wounded that could maneuver on their own to head back toward the CP. I thought I could go by putting my weight on my heel, but my foot collapsed at the first step and I fell on my face. A couple of buddies who were only slightly wounded came to me, and they got one on each side of me and picked me up and, like a three-legged race, we took off toward the

CP. I had lost a lot of blood by this time and was about to faint, so I had them put me down and go on. Just as they let me down, I blacked out.

I have no idea how long I was out. As I came to, a small observation helicopter, a Loach, landed right in front of me. The gunner got off, picked me up, and strapped me into his seat. Because there was no more room on board, he stayed in the field until they could fly me to a first aid station in Dong Ha.

Later that day, Chaney ended up lying next to the gunner at the aid station and found out he had stayed on the ground with Charlie Company while his chopper picked up two more wounded men. The last time the chopper went back for him, the gunner was shot through his calf as he stepped onto it. Chaney ended up in a hospital in Hawaii, and from there to the States and an early discharge.

George Dickman had been sent back to the rear with a fever the night before and was at the battalion aid station as the fight unfolded:

Some guy working in the aid station walks up to me and says, "You're from Charlie Company, right?" Before I could answer, he hands me a clipboard with paper and tells me to start taking down the names of the men that were wounded and killed. There was a radio there and I started hearing the names coming over the radio. At first the names were being spelled out phonetically and then a kind of panic set in on the other end; the names of those killed were being said out loud. They were all there. So many. I didn't want to write anymore down but I did. I was just sitting there listening to those names coming over the radio. That was a real bad day.

Charlie Company had at least thirteen men killed that morning and another forty-one wounded, the highest casualty total in its almost six years in Vietnam.[12] PFC Ramiro 'Pete' Olivo was 21 and from Eagle Pass, TX. Both of Captain Terry's RTOs that day were killed in the first minutes of the fight. They were SP4 Robert Alexander, 21, of Washington, DC and SP4 Winford Crabb, 21 of Shafter, CA. Fifty years later, Crabb's fiancée posted a message to him on the Vietnam Wall of Faces website:

Fifty years ago, today, you left me. I didn't know at the moment; I would never see you again. You died in Vietnam on this date. Soon, I would hear from your mother. Your return would not be one filled with joy. Her heart was truly broken, as was mine...

When you arrived home, I was unable to see you, as your physical body had been so compromised. That made it worse, for I didn't believe you were "in that box." We were young then, just 21. We were in love and to be married soon. I still have the pictures and letters...

I couldn't speak at all. I could only wrestle inward thoughts of "What am I supposed to do now? You promised you would be careful and come home!"

Grief knows no boundaries. I long for the life we were supposed to have, but I had to face my reality: "God said no!" As time passed, I moved on as your mother told me I must.

Though half a century has passed, your love, spirit and memory never left the home it had within my heart. Rest in Peace, My Soldier, My Love.

---

12. Some initial reports said there were 14 KIA. If that is correct, one remains unidentified. In addition, it's also possible that some of the wounded died at a later date and are not known or counted as fatalities from the battle.

The other Charlie Company KIAs that morning were: PFC James Bang, 21, Minneapolis, MN; SP4 Robert Capanda, 21, Detroit, MI; SP4 Carlos Cornett, 21, Flatwoods, KY; PFC Freddie Cox, 20, Oakland, CA; SSG Frank Elliott, 23, Streamwood, IL; 1Lt Robert Jones, 21, Delta, PA; SP4 Ronald Koitzsch, 20, Camas, WA; SP4 Mitchell McGuire, 20, Hanoverton, OH; SSG Albert Smith, 34, Clairton, PA; and PFC William Waysack, 20, Orange, CA.

2Lt Don Heth was newly arrived in Vietnam and was in the rear waiting for a chopper to take him to his new assignment in Bravo Company when he was ordered to grab his gear and get down to the landing pad. There he was told he was going to Charlie Company to replace Lt Jones and to get on the next Huey as soon as it was loaded with boxes of ammo:

The whole area was going nuts. As the Huey approached, it was carrying some of the dead and I saw many legs hanging out of the side…it landed and all the individuals were unloaded onto stretchers, no body bags. The pilot got out, grabbed a hose and washed the blood out the floor of his Huey, then the ammo boxes were loaded, and I climbed in to sit on one of the boxes. Within 15 minutes, the Huey corkscrewed into a sandy open area…out to my side I saw the burning wreckage of the Huey that was shot down earlier. We flared in and because the floor was so slippery, myself and the ammo flew out. I hit the dirt not knowing what the situation was…as far as I could tell, the fighting was over, yet I stayed on the sand. I low crawled to a depression in the sand until a trooper asked me who I was!! We stayed in that area that night and I sat next to LT Bane and what remained of 2nd platoon…and that was my first day!

That night, an ambush or LP from the third platoon reported movement in front of their position. This time, the marines authorized a fire mission. A sweep through the area on May 10, 1968 by other companies of 1/5th counted 147 NVA KIA and recovered ten crew served and fifty-seven individual weapons.

Charlie Company spent the next week guarding a bridge on Highway 1 between Dong Ha and Gio Linh and conducting road security sweeps with Marine tanks as new replacements came in to fill the gaps. 1Lt Bill Bane, the company's XO, led the company for the next few weeks until a new commanding officer arrived.

Action continued in the area for a few more days—on May 11, Alpha, Bravo, and Delta Companies of 1/5th made contact with an NVA force of unknown size and lost five men killed and another twenty-one wounded. On May 17, 1968 the 1/5th and 2/5th returned to the control of the 1st Cavalry Division and moved to Utah Beach to start a new operation. The Navy awarded the 1/5th the Navy Unit Commendation Medal for its part in Operations Scotland II and Concordia Square.

May 17, 1968 was also the day the 1st Cavalry ended Operation Delaware in the A Shau Valley, after first extracting companies and battalions of the 1st and 3rd Brigades out of the valley. While the A Shau operation continues to be prominently featured in both official and unofficial histories of the Vietnam War, none of the companies that operated there fought a battle as intense or suffered as many casualties as Charlie Company did on May 9, 1968 in a patch of sand on the Street Without Joy.

Except for Purple Hearts, only a few men in the company got medals for their actions that day. Medic Marv Anklam and Sgt Gene Meredith, Charlie Company's head communications man, both received the Silver Star and about half a dozen men got Bronze Stars. With most of the officers and NCOs in Charlie

Company among the casualties, there was no one left to recommend a man for a medal, as deserving as many of the men were that day.

This was partially rectified more than fifty years later when Ramiro 'Pete' Olivo received a posthumous Distinguished Service Cross (DSC), the Army's second highest medal for bravery, in early 2021 after years of advocacy by Patrick Manijo and other veterans of the battle. The bravery and sacrifice of other men on May 9, 1968 remains unrecognized by the Army and in some cases even unknown to the men who served with them.

In 2018, Manijo traveled back to Quang Tri Province in Vietnam and placed a memorial plaque at the site of the May 9, 1968 battle: "Dedicated to the men of Charlie Company 1st Battalion 5th Cavalry 1st Air Cavalry Division who fought and died on this spot May 9, 1968. May your souls rest in eternal peace. You are not forgotten."

While he was there, his Vietnamese guide told him he had heard from a North Vietnamese veteran that units of the 320th PAVN Division had positioned themselves that night to ambush the 1/5th as it moved out of its perimeter in the morning. It's likely that Captain Dan Terry's movement out to the ambush's position at first light forced the North Vietnamese to launch their attack early. While Charlie Company paid a heavy cost, it may have prevented a worse outcome for the rest of the battalion.

A New Normal

The war would start to slow down in Quang Tri and Thua Thien Provinces, but not before a spectacular parting shot by the NVA. On May 19, 1968 they rocketed Camp Evans, setting off over 10 million pounds of munitions, which ignited an aviation fuel supply dump creating a fireball that rose nearly 15,000 feet. Two of the 1st Cavalry's three helicopter battalions were based at Evans and most of their aircraft were destroyed or heavily damaged and operations were impacted for weeks.

In the four months between Charlie Company's arrival in Phu Bai in mid-January 1968 to the May 9, 1968 battle, the war had taken a new turn. While the Tet and spring offenses of the NVA and Viet Cong failed to achieve any of their military goals, and had cost them tremendous casualties, they had added fuel to the growing debates in the U.S. about the costs, tactics, and goals of the war.

Even before Tet, some of the war's original architects were becoming pessimistic about the chances of a military victory. Secretary of Defense Robert McNamara announced his resignation in November 1967 because he could no longer support what he—as much as anyone else in Washington—set in motion. A few weeks after that, three prominent retired generals expressed their opposition to the bombing campaign against North Vietnam and said South Vietnam was not worth the trouble it was taking to defend it.[13] McNamara stayed on until February 1968 but by that time the political ground was shifting.

1968 was an election year and campaigning had already started. On March 12, 1968 as Charlie Company was enjoying the perks of Utah Beach and risking booby traps and snipers on the Street Without Joy, anti-war candidate Eugene McCarthy almost beat President Johnson in the New Hampshire Primary. A few days later, Robert F. Kennedy announced he was running for president on an anti-war platform.

In response to the growing level of discontent about the war and the loss of public credibility of both the military and his administration, President Johnson convened an informal group of close advisors to be briefed by the Pentagon and review U.S. options. The group, called the "wise men", included retired diplomats and foreign policy experts and three retired generals, Omar Bradley, Maxwell Taylor, and Matthew Ridgeway.[14] The group had met before the previous November and at that time they supported a military solution in Vietnam. This time the group recommended to Johnson that the U.S. "take steps to disengage" from the war.

---

13. General Matthew Ridgeway, commander of airborne forces in World War II, commander of 8 Army for much of the Korean War and former Chief of Staff U.S. Army; Lt. General James Gavin, commander of the 82 Airborne Division in World War II and ambassador to France in the Kennedy Administration; and General David Shoup, former Commandant of the Marine Corps and Medal of Honor recipient.

14. General of the Army Omar Bradley commanded U.S. ground forces in France in World II and was a former Chief of Staff U.S. Army and Chairman of the Joint Chiefs of Staff and General Maxwell Taylor commanded the 101 Airborne Division in World War II and was also a former Chairman of the Joint Chiefs of Staff and ambassador to South Vietnam 1964-65.

On March 31, 1968 as the 1st Cavalry was saddling up for the relief of Khe Sanh, the president went on national television and called a bombing halt over much of North Vietnam, expressed a willingness to negotiate an end to the war, and announced he would not seek re-election in the fall. The first negotiating session between the U.S. and North Vietnam took place on May 10, 1968, one day after Charlie Company's battle north of Dong Ha, although for months the parties bickered over who should participate in the talks and what shape the negotiating tables should be.

Military victory was no longer the stated goal of the U.S. in Vietnam. Men would now fight and die not with the expectation of winning the war, but to give diplomats a better negotiating position.

In the first week of April 1968, as Charlie Company was moving into position to attack the NVA dug in at the Old French Ford outside of Khe Sanh, men heard more unsettling news. Minor Chaney recalled that day:

On the morning that we were to attack the fort, we got word that Martin Luther King had been assassinated. This made everyone feel so bad, especially our black brothers. Here we were fighting for our lives against a hostile enemy that was trying to kill us, and back home, Americans were killing other Americans. It just didn't make sense to us, and that was very demoralizing. Nevertheless, our task at hand had to go on. Artillery and fighter planes had been bombarding the old fort for hours, and now it was time to go.

Back in the States, King's assassination and the resulting riots and unrest in dozens of U.S. cities intensified the debate about whether the war was consuming resources that were needed at home and whether it was worth the rising loss of life on all sides. Thousands of active-duty soldiers from the 82nd Airborne Division and Marines and other stateside units were sent to Washington DC, Baltimore, Chicago, and other cities to restore order, raising fears in the Pentagon and Congress that the military was stretched too thin and that the U.S. would not be able to meet other national and international threats and obligations as long as it remained deeply involved in Vietnam. These and other concerns about the war were echoed and amplified by critical press coverage.

The government had lost confidence in General Westmoreland, and he was replaced in June by his deputy, General Creighton Abrams. One of his priorities was to start the process of 'Vietnamization': building the combat skills and capacity of South Vietnamese units so that they could play a bigger role and eventually take over responsibility for fighting the war. Under Westmoreland, they had often been excluded from any significant role in operations due to concerns they were unreliable and infiltrated by NVA and VC agents and sympathizers.

During the same period, social changes in the U.S. were beginning to impact units in Vietnam, especially concerning race relations and drug use. These issues tended to be much more pronounced in rear areas, where men had easy access to drugs and alcohol, but even combat units were affected.

SSG Lester Tarkington had been the platoon sergeant in Charlie Company's first platoon, where his men called him 'Sgt T', from the fall of 1966 until he was wounded on March 21, 1967. He came back for a second tour in mid-1968 and was assigned as a platoon sergeant in a company of the 101st Airborne

Division.[15] Once there, he was surprised to find that most of the men in his new platoon, including the platoon leader, openly smoked marijuana. He was able to put a stop to it, at least when they were in the field.

At the same time, the North Vietnamese were reeling from their losses at Tet, Khe Sanh, Dong Ha, and elsewhere in South Vietnam:

> Two major offensives had pushed the Viet Cong and North Vietnamese to the limits of their endurance. An official history produced by the Communist government of Vietnam later acknowledged that "our soldiers and civilians had suffered heavy losses of personnel, weapons, and ammunition" in the first six months of 1968. The defection of several high-ranking Communist officers likewise indicated a growing sense of despair among enemy field commanders. As the summer began, the Communists withdrew many of their combat units to rear areas for an extended period of rest.

Eric Villard in *Staying the Course: Combat Operations in Vietnam, October 1967 to September 1968.* Most of the new NVA replacements were not as well-trained or motivated as the men they replaced and some communist soldiers also began to turn to drugs as a release from combat or boredom.

---

15. The 1st Brigade of the 101st Airborne Division had been in Vietnam since August 1965. By the time the 2nd and 3rd Brigades arrived in mid-December 1967 they were airborne in name only and their ranks were filled largely with draftees. In response, the Army designated the 101st to be its second airmobile division. In early summer 1968, it was renamed the 101st Air Cavalry Division and the 1st Cavalry was renamed the 1st Air Cavalry Division. After complaints by Army traditionalists and airborne veterans, the Army reversed itself six weeks later and went back to the 101st Airborne Division (Airmobile) and the 1st Cavalry Division (Airmobile).

For the men in Charlie Company, the political and social changes may have been concerning but they were largely distant and abstract compared to the daily reality of patrols and ambushes, booby traps and snipers, and who would get stuck with ham and lima beans when C-rations were distributed.

Charlie Company and the rest of the battalion spent the rest of May and all of June operating out of Utah Beach and LZ Jane, conducting search and destroy missions in the hill country west of the coastal plains.

Captain Frank Orlevitch, Charlie Company's new commander, was no stranger to the company. He had been a platoon leader in the company from July 1966 until he was wounded in the firefight on March 21, 1967. Like Dan Terry before him, he had been an enlisted man before going to Officer's Candidate School. When he came back for a second tour, he was waiting in a replacement center for orders to the Americal Division when he was offered the chance to return to the 1st Cav. He took it and ended up back in Charlie Company. It was still understrength and disorganized when he got there and he wasn't impressed with the leadership at the battalion and brigade level. It seemed to him that some of the company's missions were makeshift and lacking in any clear direction or purpose. After Tet, it's likely that operations on the tactical level were impacted by the growing uncertainty and drift at both the national political and the MACV military levels.

Orlevitch was Charlie's CO for less than a month. A few weeks into his tour, someone tripped a booby trap jumping off a Huey and he was hit by shrapnel. Orlevitch came back to the 1/5th after some time in the hospital but the shrapnel had aggravated his older wound and he became the battalion's S-2 (intelligence) officer. He stayed in that slot until the division moved south in November when he got the chance to go back into the field, this time as an advisor to a South Vietnamese Regional Forces unit in the MeKong Delta.

Charlie Company's XO again became the acting CO. Records and memories are unclear, but it appears that Bill Bane had completed his tour and left, and the XO was now a Lt Elliott. The company got its new CO, Captain Karl Cropsey, sometime in July 1968 or later. He had been an adviser to an ARVN unit on his first tour and spoke some Vietnamese and remained as CO until late January 1969.

The ongoing mission for the 1st Cavalry for the next five months was summarized by Eric Villard in *Staying the Course*:

The northernmost Army division in [I] Corps, General Tolson's 1st Cavalry Division, spent the summer continuing Operation Jeb Stuart. Begun in January 1968, Jeb Stuart was a search-and-clear operation conducted in the coastal lowlands and piedmont areas of southern Quang Tri and northern Thua Thien Provinces. Tolson's 1st Brigade, commanded by Col. John Stannard, worked the lowlands around Quang Tri City with the South Vietnamese 1st Infantry Regiment to protect the town and the Revolutionary Development areas clustered to the north ...

Meanwhile, Col. Robert M. MacKinnon's 2d Brigade patrolled the region south and east of Quang Tri City, while the 3d Brigade, led by Col. Charles H. Curtis, covered the lowlands to the north of Hue from its base at Camp Evans ... Tolson employed the 3d Squadron, 5th Cavalry, an armored cavalry unit from the 9th Infantry Division on loan to him since February, to guard the logistical facility at Wunder Beach and the lines of communications that radiated from it ...

The three North Vietnamese units that typically operated in the Jeb Stuart zone—the 6th, the 9th, and the 812th Regiments—assisted the recovery effort by staying in their mountain camps for most of the summer. The Viet Cong battalions that operated in the lowlands also kept a low profile.

With the NVA and main force VC holed up in their base areas, the biggest threats were booby traps and occasional small arms fire from squad size or smaller groups of NVA. For Charlie and the other companies of the 1/5th, the scale of operations shifted from battalion and company sized assaults and sweeps to platoon and squad sized missions, with smaller groups fanning out from LZ's and setting up day and night ambushes, often in close coordination with scout choppers and recon teams from the 1/9th Cav.

Units found NVA bunker complexes on a regular basis, some recently occupied and others showing signs of artillery and rocket strikes from past operations. On June 6 and June 8, 1968, Charlie Company found and destroyed two large bunker complexes in the foothills, each capable of holding dozens of NVA and VC. One complex had an underground bunker with forty-eight bunks in it. The bunkers were connected by trenches and tunnels and some had overhead cover of logs and dirt over five feet thick.

In June 1968, the company lost more men to heat exhaustion than to wounds. But luck ran out for one man on June 9, 1968. PFC William Headrick, a new replacement after the May 9 battle, was seriously wounded by a booby trap and died eleven days later on a Navy hospital ship. He was 24 and from Smithville, MO. Five more men were wounded by booby traps in two separate incidents on June 21 and 24, 1968. Headrick died a few days after Robert F. Kennedy was assassinated in Los Angeles, one day after winning the California Democratic

Primary with a campaign that was highly critical of the conduct of the war. On the campaign trail, he had called the Vietnam war "the gravest kind of error."

When NVA and VC units did leave their base areas, U.S. forces were able to rapidly respond and pile on in strength. On June 27, 1968 an armored cavalry troop of the 3/5th Cav operating with a dismounted recon troop of the 1/9th Cav encountered small arms and B-40 fire from the small coastal village of Binh An, about thirteen kilometers northeast of Quang Tri City. Two other armored cavalry troops joined the fight to surround the enemy and cut off their escape routes and a Navy Swift Boat arrived offshore to intercept any NVA trying to flee by boat.

The trapped unit was soon identified as the K14 Battalion of the 812th NVA Regiment, about 300 men strong, and the 3/5th commander requested infantry support to fill in the gaps between the armored vehicles. Charlie Company and Charlie Company of the 2/5th Cav were flown in to reinforce the units already there and placed under the operation control of the 3/5th.

Charlie Company joined Troop B of the 3/5th on the north side of the enclave early in the afternoon as fire support was brought down on the trapped NVA, including aerial rocket artillery, 105mm howitzers, and tactical air strikes. Charlie and Troop B attacked in the afternoon to shrink the NVA perimeter; it was already so small that when Charlie and Troop B attacked, Charlie Company 2/5th and the armored cavalry troop on the south had to take cover to avoid being hit. When Charlie and Troop B pulled back, they attacked.

Late in the afternoon, a Navy cruiser and two destroyers arrived and began shelling the NVA with their 5" guns, firing throughout the night. This is believed to be the largest group of NVA fired on by ships of the U.S. Seventh Fleet during the war.

In the morning, the paint had been burned off the barrels of the guns of the cruiser USS Boston.

Charlie Company and the other units attacked again in the morning and met only scattered resistance. The K14 Battalion was destroyed; over 200 bodies were found, most killed by the Navy's accurate fire, and over forty prisoners were taken. Among the NVA dead were the battalion commander and all his company commanders. Three U.S. soldiers were killed in the fight, none from Charlie Company.

Except for the recon troop from the 1/9th, this was exclusively a Fifth Cavalry "Black Knights" fight involving elements from all three of the Army's battalions with lineage tracing back to the original Fifth Cavalry Regiment in the 1850's. It was the first time all Fifth Cavalry units operated together since World War II.

In late June 1968, LTC Jordan was replaced as commander of the 1/5th by LTC Gregory Troutman after less than three months leading the battalion. In mid-July 1968, Major General John Tolson completed his year as the third commanding general of the 1st Cavalry and returned to the US. Brigadier General Richard Irby, the Division's Assistant Division Commander, led the Division until mid-August when Major General George Forsyth arrived to take command.

Unlike his three predecessors, Forsyth was not a trained aviator and had not been involved in developing air mobility techniques and units before the war. He had been serving as one of General Westmoreland's deputies in MACV Headquarters and Westmoreland had promised him command of an infantry division. Forsyth had to go back to the States and complete a rush aviation course to get his flight wings before he could take command of the 1st Cav.

In early July 1968, General Abrams ordered the Marines to shut down the Khe Sanh Combat Base. Most NVA units that had fought there had withdrawn to Laos and Abrams favored freeing up the Marine units that had been tied down on large static bases for more mobile operations. Still, the abandonment of Khe Sanh so soon after it had been portrayed by the military as something to be defended at all costs just added to the growing public confusion and doubt about the goals and rationales for the war.

Late in July 1968, the 1st Brigade of the 5th Infantry Division (Mechanized) arrived in Vietnam, adding one armored and two mechanized infantry battalions to the U.S. forces in northern I Corps. This was the last major combat unit deployed to Vietnam. Within the next year, units would start returning to the States.

Grinding it Out

No men died in Charlie Company in July 1968, but the daily grind went on. The company started the month securing LZ Jane, fairly easy duty. Then on July 7, 1968 Bravo Company spent much of the day slowly moving through a large bunker complex, fighting small firefights as they moved. Around 1700 hours, Charlie Company air assaulted to support them, taking fire from three directions as it went into the LZ. While moving to cordon off a village, 2Lt Don Heth was hit by grenade shrapnel in his lung and heart and medevaced out of the field. He had led the second platoon for almost two months, almost twice as long as his two predecessors combined.

New men were getting acclimated. Richard Levenson came to the company as a replacement in June and could see the gap between the older men and the new:

C 1/5 was somewhat split into generations: the May 9 survivors, the May 9 replacements, and the August replacements. We all got along well. We were organized into platoons with fire teams of four or five people each. It is difficult to remember the different contact incidents. Basically, we kept tramping around the Ho Chi Minh Trail until we were ambushed in September.

229

Most of the guys who had been through Khe Sanh and Dong Ha didn't put any energy into getting to know the new replacements. It was just assumed some of them wouldn't be around too long. Pat Manijo started walking point all the time. He was angry and just wanted to "provide as much payback to the enemy as possible."

One day, his platoon was sweeping through some villages when Pat offered a small, ragged boy some cocoa and crackers from his C-rations. The platoon was fired on by an AK-47 and the men knew to hit the dirt, but the boy was shot through the neck. Pat lost it then and stood up and yelled, "Gooks shoot me, shoot me." He ran across a rice paddy to the small village where the shot came from "like a wild animal" intending to burn the village. Before he could do anything, the little boy's grandmother came out saying, "GI, GI, no VC, no VC." Manijo stopped and walked away.

On July 20 and 21, 1968 Charlie Company located and destroyed a complex of more than twenty fortified bunkers, along with a cache of rice, salt, medicine, B40 grenades, and some rockets wrapped in plastic. Among the items recovered was an M-79 with "C 1/12" carved into its stock. When the company wasn't finding bunkers or supply caches, it seemed to spend a lot of time digging up gravesites to try to determine if they were NVA and how they died.

August 1968 would be third deadliest month of the war for Charlie Company, largely due to its worst friendly fire incident. It was still operating in the hills around LZ Jane on August 2, 1968 when it engaged a squad or more of NVA in mid-afternoon and killed one of them. A few hours later, as it was digging in for the evening, it was hit by small arms fire from two directions and one man was killed while putting out a claymore mine. PFC Ronald Bakewell of East Millsboro, PA was 20 years old and had been one of the replacements for the men lost on May 9. The jungle canopy was too dense for a medevac chopper to land so it dropped a rope down through the trees. Bakewell's squad mates tied it around his chest and he was lifted through the jungle and flown away, dangling beneath the Huey.

Two days later, the first and second platoons were on a sweep while third platoon and the mortars remained at an LZ. For much of the day, the two platoons dug up graves as recorded in the battalion log:

1140 C 16 & 26. Found 1 bunker (destroyed). 2 fresh graves w/ a fence around the graves. Fence made of vines; One grave marker, name: Vinh. Graves are being dug up.

1236 C 16 & 26. In the 2 graves found earlier, found a body in each. Both bodies approx. 1 month old. One death was caused by chest wounds fm small arms. The other body was too decomposed to tell cause of death.

1309 C Co: 16 & 26. Found a grave w/1 NVA officer's body. Approx 2 weeks old. Cause of death unk. Neg wpns or equip. Grave was very neat.

1333 C Co: 16 & 26. Found 1 grave w/1 NVA EM body, body badly decomposed, back of head blown off is cause of death.

Late in the afternoon of August 4, 1968, the point man spotted fifteen suspected NVA in front of him and opened fire with his M-79. They dispersed and the cloud cover was too low to call in recon choppers or gunships. That evening, as the two platoons dug in, they spotted two NVA about three hundred meters in front of their line and called in artillery. One round fell short and hit a tree within the perimeter, bursting in the air just above the men. The first report to battalion came at 2020:

> C Co: 16, 26 ele has 5 EM wounded by friendly arty. Need Doc and plasma. Also need jungle pene. Medevac requested.

The medevac chopper could only take one man at a time and by its second or third trip, it began taking fire. At 2320, the battalion was notified:

> C Co had: 1 KIA, 1 w/ sucking chest wound and multiple wounds, 1 w/ left leg severed, 2 w/ head wounds, 1 wounded in back of neck, 1 w/ hand wound, 1 can't hear, 1 w/ face wound, 1 w/ arm wound, 1 wounded in back and wrist.

The second platoon, now led by 2Lt Joseph Bravin, was hit hardest, and lost many experienced troopers. Richard Levenson remembered their medic, Doc Dick Boutilier, performing triage in the dark as the medevac chopper was driven off by NVA fire. Some of the men could not be lifted out until the next morning. Four men were killed by that short round. PFC Johnny Earl Frisk, 20 years old, of Purdy, MO, and Sgt Miguel Negron-Rodriguez, 26, of Cayey, PR died that night. PFC Eugene Baker, 21, of Chicago, IL died the next day in a field hospital and SP4 Robert Bumiller died five days later on a hospital ship. He was 20 and from LaDue, MO. Years later, his sister left a message for him on the Vietnam Wall of Faces:

> You have never been forgotten. You will always be a part of me. So

many memories of our short time together before Our Lord took you back home. Know that you are with Mom, Dad, Louy, Ethel and all our relatives. Hope you are watching over us.

Love always...your Sis

Also on August 4, 1968, Sgt James Fowler, 28, of White City, KN died in an Army hospital of encephalitis, most likely caused by a mosquito bite while in the field.[16]

On August 9, 1968, Charlie Company found and destroyed a NVA hospital complex and took one prisoner. RTO Chuck Rodriguez saw fresh dressings and equipment there and it looked like the NVA had left just ahead of the company. Five days later, the company found and destroyed a complex of about fifty fighting bunkers, most with overhead cover. Later in the month, it fought a series of short but sharp firefights with small units of NVA, killing some but losing five or six men to wounds.

In mid-August 1968, the North Vietnamese launched another offensive, ordered by Hanoi over the objections of some of their generals and field commanders. A number of targets were hit from Da Nang down to the Mekong Delta, but there were no attacks in Quang Tri or Thua Thien Provinces, only a slight uptick in violence. The NVA's decision to bypass the two provinces was likely due to the buildup of allied forces there and the rapid response capabilities of the 1st Cavalry and the newly airmobile 101st Airborne. Combat was heavy for about a week in Tay Ninh Province northwest of Saigon, but otherwise the NVA's August offensive went nowhere and further weakened their forces.

---

16. No relation to Top Robert Fowler (66-68) or SFC James "Pop" Fowler (1970).

On the evening of August 26, 1968, Charlie Company was setting up its night perimeter around a small one ship LZ on a ridge when a resupply chopper brought in containers with a hot meal for the men. PFC Rick Higgins of the third platoon, one of the May replacements, was digging his foxhole while PFC Richard Daugherty, his best friend in the company, went for chow. As men lined up, the NVA walked in thirty to thirty-five 60mm mortar rounds. Six men were hit, two of them fatally. Daugherty, 19, of Waterloo, IL, died that night. Higgins got to see him one last time before he was medevaced but knew he wasn't going to make it. SP4 Allen Griffin, 28, from Houston, MS died the next day in a field hospital. Allen had completed two years in the Army and got discharged in 1965. After a few months, he enlisted again, did a tour in Germany, and then ended up in Vietnam.

During the night, the men were mortared again. A little later they were surprised when a small plane flew over dropping flares and lighting up the sky. At first light they were told to roll up their gear and were then lifted out one ship at a time and flown to a new LZ in a valley six to eight kilometers away. Once there they found out that the plane was flying a night reconnaissance mission and had detected a large group of NVA just up the ridge from their position, possibly massing to assault them. From their new LZ, they watched a B-52 Arc Light strike devastate the ridge they had just left.

Two days later, after sweeping through a small bunker complex, the company ran into about sixteen NVA and was hit by small arms, mortars, and grenades. Three men were hit and one died before he could be medevaced. PFC James Glover was 21 and from Hannibal, MO.

Almost 9,000 miles away, the Democratic Presidential Convention opened in Chicago on August 26, 1968. Over 10,000 protesters came to the convention with a number of issues, but for most of them, ending the war was primary. Around the same time PFC Glover was hit and killed, major riots were developing around the convention site, with demonstrators, bystanders, convention delegates, and reporters tear-gassed and fights lasting into the night between demonstrators and Chicago Police. While a majority of Americans no longer supported the war as it was being conducted, this didn't translate into support for anti-war demonstrators.[17] Some historians believe that the public reaction to the events outside the Democratic Convention helped elect Richard Nixon later that fall.

Charlie rejoined the battalion on September 12, 1968 for Operation Comanche Falls, a search and destroy operation in the Hai Lang Forest, some heavily wooded hills southwest of Quang Tri called Base Area 101 by the NVA. On the morning of September 17, 1968, the company air assaulted onto a hill-top clearing called LZ Green and began spreading out, finding bunker complexes with overhead cover and spotting a small group of NVA in the distance.

At about 0830 the next morning, second platoon was pushing through a bunker complex when some well concealed NVA opened up on them. 2Lt Joseph Bravin rushed to the front to lay down suppressive fire and was hit almost immediately. PFC Kreg Viestenz rushed to his aid and was giving him first aid when he was hit as well. Richard Levenson recalled that morning:

---

17. In August, a Gallup poll indicated that for the first time a majority of Americans (53 percent) believed that America's participation in the war had been a mistake. Others continued to support the war, but disagreed with how the administration and military were conducting it.

I was carrying a grenade launcher when we were ambushed. I was toward the back of the column and heard a few shots. Then I heard the solid "chunk" of an American M-60 machine gun. An American machine gun could be distinguished because it sounded as if it was made from castings rather than stampings. When I heard that I thought we were controlling the situation, but I was wrong because the M-60 had been taken earlier from an American company.

I went forward to help make a perimeter. I loaded a shotgun shell into my grenade launcher due to the close range of the ambush but did not have to use it. Artillery fire helped suppress the ambush. Then two Air Force jets arrived and told us by radio to pop green smoke grenades to show our position. The other side, not being fools, monitored our radio frequency and green smoke popped all around us. We then popped a different color smoke and told the planes what color we used so they could identify us. Then, as they bombed, strafed, and napalmed, we made our way back up the hill.

A resupply chopper landed briefly when we got to the top of the hill. I'm not certain why it picked that particular moment to arrive. Our new platoon sergeant (August replacement?) got on it and left us there. So, we muddled along until the rest of the company arrived.

The Lt. was shot in the head and died almost immediately. Kreg Viestenz was shot across the middle and died about 1/2 hour later. There must have been shock involved because he did not appear to be suffering. Kreg hung on in the fetal position until he had to be stretched out to be attached to a stretcher basket lowered into the jungle from a Medevac helicopter.

Lt Bravin was 21 and from New York City and had been commissioned from ROTC after graduating from Penn State. He replaced Lt Don Heth who had been wounded in early

July and lasted in the field just slightly longer than Heth did. Kreg Viestenz was 19 and from Eugene, OR. He had been in country about six weeks when he rushed to his platoon leader's aid.

At about the same time, another platoon from Charlie Company got hit on a hilltop about 800 meters away. Two men died there as well. PFC James McCoy was 20 and from Travelers Rest, SC. PFC Robert Gray, from Corbin, KY, was 19. In 2014, this message was left for Gray on the Vietnam Wall of Faces website: "I love you as much now as i did when i was 3 and watched you walk out the door for the last time'!.........LOVE YOU DADDY."

The next day, the company swept back through the bunker complex where Bravin and Viestenz had been killed. Per the 1/5th battalion log, it estimated at least ten NVA had been killed based on "arms, legs, clothing and other pieces of body; result of Arty & ARA." A few days later, a patrol encountered and shot two NVA. As soon as they were hit, they yelled "Chieu Hoi" and were then treated and taken prisoner. By then, many NVA soldiers carried Chieu Hoi leaflets as a form of insurance.[18]

Charlie Company spent the first twelve days of October under the operational control of the 2/5th Cav, operating in the same general area. Contact was minor and sporadic for the rest of the month, with no fatalities and only a few minor wounds and "non-hostile" injuries recorded. On October 21, 1968 the second platoon found and destroyed an arms cache containing Chicom claymore mines, 60mm and 82mm mortar rounds, B-40 rocket

---

18. "Chieu Hoi" literally meant "open arms." Chieu Hoi leaflets were widely dropped by Army Psychological Warfare Units to encourage NVA and VC to defect or surrender with promises of safe conduct and incentives.

grenades, and ammo for AK-47's and .51 caliber heavy machine guns. Also found and turned in to battalion were a U.S. M-60 machine gun and some NVA operational maps.

On October 25, 1968 General Abrams ordered the 1st Cavalry Division to move south for a new mission: guarding the approaches to Saigon, South Vietnam's Capital, about 600 miles to the south. Three days later, battalions began being pulled from the field and flying south. The second Brigade moved last and Charlie Company would lose one more man killed in Quang Tri Province before leaving its area of operation. On November 1, 1968, PFC Gregory Heggen of Denver, CO was killed in action when the second platoon swept through a bunker complex. He was 19 and had been in country three weeks. The next day the company loaded onto Chinooks and flew to Camp Evans and from there boarded C-130's for the flight south.

Part 4: Cavalry Screen on the Cambodian Border

New War, New Mission

When the 1st Cavalry moved north in January 1968, it was in response to the rapid buildup of enemy forces there and the threat of large scale NVA offenses. By fall, the situation south of the DMZ had stabilized and the division was doing little more than routine searches for food and weapons caches, not the best use of the Army's most mobile division. The NVA and VC generally avoided contact, and other Army units were now established in the area.

Now the bigger threat lay 600 miles to the south as MACV intelligence detected a major buildup of enemy forces along the Cambodian border north of Saigon, which had been a major target of the 1968 Tet and Spring offenses. In late summer 1968, the North Vietnamese moved their elite 1st PAVN Division south from the Central Highlands closer to Saigon to join three divisions already there: the 7th PAVN Division and the 5th and 9th VC Divisions (which were filled largely with NVA replacements after their losses earlier in the year). Its deployment raised fears that another major attack against Saigon was imminent.

The Army already had significant forces in the III Corps Tactical Zone area, which included eleven provinces and forty percent of South Vietnam's population. By September 1968, they were the 1st and 25th Infantry Divisions, part of the 9th Infantry Division, the 3rd Brigade of the 82nd Airborne Division, the 199th Light Infantry Brigade, and the 11th Armored Cavalry Regiment, as well as brigade size Australian and Thai units. The South Vietnamese Army had four divisions in III Corps and two more south of Saigon in the Mekong Delta, plus some airborne and ranger battalions.

The 1st and 25th Infantry Divisions had previously operated closer to the border, but during the NVA's 1968 Tet and Spring offenses they had been pulled back to establish a protective ring around Saigon. In late 1968, they were paired with ARVN units and assisted pacification operations in more heavily populated provinces around the capital. General Abrams ordered the 1st Cavalry to move south to fill the gap and take up operations along the border.

Abrams gave the order on October 26, 1968 and Operation Liberty Canyon started the next day. Shelby Stanton described it in *Anatomy of a Division: The 1st Cav in Vietnam*:

> The task of moving the 1st Cavalry Division represented the largest allied intra-theater combat deployment of the Second Indochina War. The division withdrew its scattered battalions from the jungled mountains at one end of the country and moved them more than 570 miles air, land, and sea for commitment into flat territory against an unfamiliar enemy at the other end. Operation Liberty Canyon commenced 27 October 1968 as Brigadier General Irby began sending the cavalry battalions south at the rate of one per day.

Charlie Company and the 1/5th were in the field in III Corps by mid-November. While the terrain and some of the enemy units may have been unfamiliar, the 1st PAVN Division was no stranger to the 1st Cavalry. Elements of both divisions fought repeatedly in Pleiku and Kontum Provinces in 1965 and 1966, starting at LZ X-Ray and LZ Albany in the Ia Drang Valley. Charlie Company fought through one of their bunker complexes in the Chu Pong Massif in August 1966 and was ambushed by one of their regiments in the Ia Drang in November 1966.

As the 1st Cavalry was moving south, Richard Nixon was elected president. During his campaign, he called for an end to the draft, repeatedly said that the U.S. should not be fighting other people's wars and pledged to seek an "honorable end to the war in Vietnam." At the time of his inauguration in January 1969, there were about 545,000 U.S. servicemen and women in Vietnam, with thousands more offshore in the Seventh Fleet and at bases in Thailand, Guam, Okinawa, and the Philippines. By then, U.S. units had been fighting the VC and NVA for over three and a half years. Over 30,000 Americans had died, about half of them in 1968, plus hundreds of thousands of Vietnamese on both sides and caught in the middle.

The New Area of Operations

Operation Liberty Canyon wrapped up in mid-November and the 1st Cavalry launched Operation Sheridan Saber. Most of the NVA and VC base areas close to Saigon had been plowed over, defoliated, depopulated, and otherwise neutralized in operations in 1967 and 1968, but they still had a strong presence along the Cambodian border in War Zones C and D and maintained sanctuaries and large supply depots in Cambodia. The NVA had built a series of major trails through the jungle from the border aiming in towards Saigon, well camouflaged and impossible to spot from the air.

The Division's new mission would stretch across three border provinces containing War Zones C and D and most of the NVA's known infiltration routes. Tay Ninh, Binh Long, and Phuoc Long Provinces arced from northwest to northeast of Saigon along about 100 miles of border with Cambodia. Most of it was sparsely populated, consisting of rolling and heavily jungled plains with few major hills or mountains, broken up by small streams, swamps, and low hills and ridges, and intersected by the Saigon River and two tributaries, the Song Be and Vam Co Dong Rivers.

On the western end of the arc, parts of Tay Ninh Province

closer to Saigon were heavily populated with flat rice fields leading into the Plain of Reeds and the northern edge of the Mekong Delta. A few kilometers north of Tay Ninh City, the largest
mountain in III Corps—Nui Ba Den or "Black Virgin Mountain"—rose by itself almost 1,000 meters off the jungle floor. On
the other end of the arc, in eastern Phuoc Long Province, the
foothills of the Annamese Mountains began.

In Binh Long Province, about halfway between Nui Ba Den
and the Annamese foothills, the most prominent feature was the
Razorback, a ten-kilometer-long ridge rising about 300 meters
out of the jungle and overlooking the largest Michelin rubber
plantation in South Vietnam. Passing through this area was the
Serges Jungle Highway, a network of well-camouflaged trails
that was one of the largest NVA infiltration and supply routes in
the 1st Cavalry's new Area of Operations.

Whenever the NVA and VC planned an offensive, they would
send supply units ahead and stockpile supplies and munitions
close to their target. Their infantry units could move rapidly from
their bases on the border, pick up supplies, and go on the attack
with little advance warning. They called this the "One Slow, Four
Quick Steps" and it was a central element of NVA and VC tactical doctrine.

The "Slow" step was planning and preparation, which could
last for weeks or months. In the 1st Cavalry's new Area of Operations, this involved maintaining their supply trails and moving supplies and weapons to forward depots before an offensive.
The four "Quick" steps were quick advance, quick assault, quick
clearing of the battlefield, and quick withdrawal. The Cav's new
mission was to interdict the trails and ambush their supply units,
to find and destroy their forward bases and supply caches, to keep
the NVA and VC off balance, and disrupt them before they could

finish their first slow step. In addition to the move of the 1st PAVN into III Corps, Army intelligence reported in late 1968 that the NVA had increased the flow of supplies to their advance depots.

With about 4,800 square miles to cover and its nine battalions dispersed, the Division would serve as a cavalry screen on the approaches to Saigon, using its air mobility and experience in ground-air operations to locate and disrupt the NVA before it could launch an offensive. Unlike the relief of Khe Sanh seven months earlier, where all the division's battalions and brigades acted in unison, this was now a war of platoons and companies, operating out of a string of firebases, permanent and temporary, much like frontier forts in the west in the cavalry's early days.

Charlie Company and the rest of the 1st Cavalry would operate in this way for almost two and a half years, longer that any of its previous missions. But now it would be to buy time for a political endgame and every man carrying a weapon in the field knew it.

The 1st Cavalry set up its headquarters at Phuoc Vinh, a former 1st Infantry Division firebase in Binh Duong Province, just south of Binh Long Province and about sixty kilometers north of Saigon. The 2nd Brigade moved into another 1st Division base at Quan Loi in central Binh Long Province, forty kilometers farther north, about halfway between Phuoc Vinh and the Cambodian border. After first spending a few weeks operating in Tay Ninh Province, Charlie Company spent much of December and January operating out of LZ Eleanor, set up next to the Chi Lin Special Forces Camp on the border of Binh Long and Phuoc Long Provinces. In late December, Charlie Company and the 1/5th got a new battalion commander, LTC Robert Peterson.

For the first time, small American units were operating in

War Zones C and D on an ongoing basis. This had been NVA home turf for years and they had built numerous well camouflaged bunker complexes and supply depots as described by Shelby Stanton in *Anatomy of a Division*:

> Search operations in War Zone C's tropical rain forests pitted the cavalry against well-fortified, superbly camouflaged bunkers built for mutually interlocking fire and always designed in unique arrangements. Fields-of-fire, invisible to the advancing cavalrymen, were cut in the thick overgrowth only a few feet off the ground. Caught in such killing zones, entire platoons could be wiped out in a matter of seconds. The lethal bunker complexes could be mastered only by using carefully coordinated, overwhelming fire support and airpower. Even in the absence of such fieldworks, maneuvering cavalry was targeted by increased use of close-range enemy B-40 rocket launchers. The companies reduced this danger by changing locations daily, aggressively sweeping the flanks of moving units, stalking out night ambush sites, and establishing listening posts around perimeters at night.

Firefights Out of LZ Eleanor

While on a sweep through dense jungle on December 29, 1968, the company ran into some of those concealed bunkers about five kilometers northeast of LZ Eleanor. 2Lt Eugene Rathmann was leading the third platoon. He had been in country a little more than a month and this was his first firefight. In that time, he had gone from being a new OCS lieutenant trying to assert his authority to someone willing to learn from the veterans in his platoon and was well-liked and respected.

As it approached the bunkers, Rathmann's platoon drew fire. He put his men online and as they worked their way closer, the volume of fire increased. He and SP4 Tom Hoover crawled forward, giving each other supporting fire, and knocked out three bunkers with grenades. An NVA machine gun in a fourth bunker kept much of the platoon pinned down and Rathmann threw a grenade at it. As he rose to fire his M-16, he was hit and killed by someone firing from a bunker they hadn't seen. His RTO, SP4 Rick Higgins, saw that he had been hit by one round between his eyes, most likely by a sniper. Rathmann was 22 and from San Diego, CA.

The firefight continued until the platoon had to break contact and pull back to a defensive position as night approached. The

NVA gunner was killed and his machine gun and a few other weapons were captured. The bunker that had fired on Lt. Rathmann was knocked out and in it the men found the bodies of four NVA women soldiers, most likely from an NVA supply unit guarding an infiltration trail. The next morning, after Rathmann's body was hoisted up through the canopy, the platoon renewed their attack on the bunker complex. Don Phillips, a PFC also in his first firefight, described that day's action:

> We did not know if the NVA had abandoned the fight or had pulled back to fight from other positions. We had to clear the bunkers as we entered the area and my squad was tasked with that operation. The bunkers were well camouflaged and difficult to see until very close to them. When we spotted a bunker, the rest of the squad trained their weapons on the bunker while one trooper ran up to the bunker and threw a grenade in the opening. When my turn came to frag a bunker, I remember running to the bunker, grenade in hand with the pin pulled, feeling very exposed and vulnerable. I clearly remember thinking, "If there is a gook in that bunker, I am dead." One by one we cleared 6-8 bunkers with no contact from the enemy; they had abandoned the fight.

After the bunkers were searched, a demolition team of combat engineers flew in and destroyed the complex in one massive explosion.

About ten days later, three more men were lost in another sweep about ten kilometers farther north. On January 9, 1969, Charlie Company was on a joint operation with an ARVN unit looking for an infiltration trail battalion S-2 believed to be in the vicinity. RTO Rick Higgins was now carrying the radio for Fencepost 6 and remembered it as one of the strangest days of his tour. The men were cutting through dense triple canopy jungle with a scout dog when they encountered a huge python. The dog freaked out and was useless for the rest of the mission and the ARVN's wanted to capture the snake and bring it along for their next meal. Not long after that, the company found a well-used trail and started to follow it.

The trail split and Charlie Company headed up what looked like the main trail when the point man spotted twenty to thirty men on the trail standing together and talking. Charlie Company stopped without being spotted and the point man told the CO and Higgins that the men were tall, Caucasian, and were wearing clean tiger stripe uniforms like those worn by Special Forces units. He could hear them talking but couldn't make out what they were saying or what language they were speaking.

Captain Cropsey called battalion and was told there were no friendly units in the area, so he instructed the point man to call out to see if they were friendlies. When he yelled, "Hey G.I.'s" the men fired on him, wounding him in the leg. The rest of the point element returned fire and the men in the tiger stripe uniforms broke and ran into the bush.

The company didn't find any bodies or weapons but did find some blood trails and followed them for a short distance. Continuing their sweep, the men went another two or three kilometers and were climbing up a hill to a ridgeline when first and second platoons were hit from concealed positions and began taking casualties. SP4 Juan Bausa-Perez, a platoon medic, began crawling out and treating and bringing wounded men to safety. Higgins remembered him as very popular in the company, always joking and full of life. On his third or fourth time out in front of the lines, he was hit in the head. When the company was ordered to pull back, the men couldn't retrieve his body and had to leave him where he fell.

Rick Higgins and the third platoon were down the hill trying to cut an LZ to medevac the growing number of wounded.
They were able to cut a small clearing just big enough for a Huey
to drop straight down, with its rotors hitting tree branches on
either side. The first medevac chopper took as many wounded
as it could carry and pulled straight up and out at full power. A
second medevac chopper then dropped in and also took its max-
imum load. When the pilot found out there were still two WIAs
to be evacuated and no more choppers likely to get there before
darkness fell, he told the men to load them on as well. Somehow,
he was able to lift out of the hole in the jungle and get the men
to safety.

The next morning, Charlie Company set up a blocking position while Alpha Company swept the ridgeline from a different
direction. They recovered the medic's body but reported that from
the amount of blood in his helmet, it looked like he may have still
been alive and bled to death after the company had to pull back.
Juan Bausa-Perez was 21 years old and from Rio Piedras, PR.

The other two KIAs were PFCs Ralph Terry, also 21 and
from Cannel City, KY, and Wilbur Jerry Siegrist, 19, from John-
stown, PA. According to information on the Coffelt Database of
Vietnam Casualties, all three men started their tour in Vietnam
on the same day, December 7, 1968. At least a dozen more men
were wounded. In 2007, Siegrist's sister posted this message to
him on the Vietnam Wall of Faces website:

> I was almost 5 when you were taken away from our family. I don't
> remember much about you, but you are always in my thoughts every
> day. It is so sad to think that we never got to see you grow old. I think
> about what you would look like today and where you would be living.
> You had a little girl born a month and a half after you died. You would

be a grandpa now. I cannot wait to meet you in heaven Jerry. I will give you all the love, hugs, and kisses that you missed here on earth. Your sister, Becky.

In late January or early February 1969, Captain James Cain took over as CO of Charlie Company. The new Fencepost 6 had been the battalion's S-2 (intelligence) officer for six months and was anxious to lead a company in the field. Rick Higgins stayed on as one of his RTOs. As Cain was settling into his new position, the company moved back into Tay Ninh Province for a large multi-unit operation. Charlie Company made only sporadic contact during the operation, but one of their ambush patrols blocked what might have been a major assault on the company. Gerald Ruesler, about halfway through his tour, was in the third platoon:

We found a lot of big well used trails that looked like small roadways. At one place they had the trail covered with bamboo mats so they could travel on it in the rainy season. We also found what we thought was a well that went down around 30 feet, all dug by hand. I remember running into small groups of 3 or 4 NVA but no big firefight.

My squad was on ambush one night, set up on a big trail. We heard someone go past us down the trail toward the company's night position. About half hour later we heard the pop of mortar rounds as they walked them down the trail, past our ambush site and then on to where the company was at. After about another half hour we could hear them come down the trail in line going for the company and we thought they were going to try and overrun it that night. They got close enough to us so that we could hear them whisper.

When we set off our claymore and opened fire, you could tell they were all around us. After we sprung the ambush, we could still see a large force moving toward us. We were a couple hundred yards out from the Company and took off running down the trail as hard as we could. When we were close to the company perimeter, we yelled out we were coming in. We knew we would hit the trip flares when we were close.

Just before we got to the flares, one of our guys ran over someone on the side of the trail. After we were back inside our perimeter, we realized that it was the NVA observer who was calling in the mortar rounds. The next day we went back out there and found blood trails and some weapons, but that was all.

A few days later, the squad was itself ambushed by the NVA and lost two men to serious wounds. Point man Mike Tomic was hit by a burst from an NVA machine gun and ended up losing his left leg at the hip and part of the use of his left arm. He was told at the hospital that he had been hit seventeen times. Around February 19, 1969, Charlie Company moved to LZ Dolly in northeast Binh Duong Province, located on the highest point of the Razorback and overlooking the Saigon River to the west and large Michelin plantations to the east and south, all known NVA infiltration and supply routes.

The company got a few days break on the perimeter, but intelligence reports indicated that elements of the 1st and 7th PAVN Divisions had left their base areas and were moving south along Saigon River infiltration routes for the long anticipated 1969 Tet offensive. The 1/5th moved about twenty kilometers northeast to Binh Long Province to operate along Highway 13 between the towns of Loc Ninh and An Loc.

On February 23, 1969, the NVA attacked seventy South Vietnamese cities and U.S. and allied military positions, mostly with mortars and rockets. The NVA's Fourth General Offensive sputtered out after four or five days. A few attacks nationwide caused concern, but in all of them the NVA were defeated within a day by U.S. and improved ARVN forces. Six of the 1st Cavalry's bases were hit; the attacks were all repulsed. Hardest hit was LZ Grant, defended by a company of the 2/12th, where the attack was repelled by 155mm howitzers firing Beehive rounds. In the weeks before the offensive, the 1st Cavalry's raids and patrol had disrupted the NVA supply line in III Corps and limited or delayed many planned attacks. The offensive had little impact on U.S. plans or operations, and it seemed like the NVA too were playing for time.

Battle in the Rubber Plantation

During the offensive, NVA units were spotted in the Michelin Rubber Plantation and the battalion, along with units of the 25th Infantry Division, was sent in to find and engage them. Earlier in the war, the Army avoided operating in any of the Michelin properties: the French company charged the Army more for a damaged rubber tree than the Army had to pay as compensation for a Vietnamese civilian killed by accident elsewhere in the country. The NVA offenses in 1968 had shown that they freely used the plantations to move men and supplies and restrictions against operating there were lifted.

On the last day of February 1969, luck ran out for one man. SP4 Glen Venet, 24, from Kenosha, WI, was killed by a shell from a mortar while on a night observation post. A day or two later, Charlie Company joined an operation in the vast Michelin Plantation and found itself in a three-day battle against well entrenched units of the 101st Regiment of the 1st PAVN Division, including a heavy weapons detachment. John Zajdlik, then a sergeant and squad leader in the company, was interviewed in 2011 by Don Moore, a reporter doing a series on veterans and their stories for the Charlotte Sun in Port Charlotte, Florida. Zajdlik remembered the start of the fight:

We were in the process of setting up our defensive perimeter and here comes this guy in black pajamas bicycling down the road. About 30 guys opened up on him.

Right after that we sent out patrols and they immediately came under heavy enemy small arms fire. The fire fight at the rubber plantations was very personal. I could see the guy that was shooting at me and he could see me shooting at him. It was a one-on-one thing.

We called in artillery. The first round came in right about where it was supposed to land. The second round came in a little shorter. The third round of 105 Howitzer hit the top of the tree we were all laying around. We would have all been killed if the tree hadn't absorbed the round.

Because we were only a rifle company, they sent a mechanized unit out of the 25th Infantry Division to support us. Our job was to push the North Vietnam Army troops through the rubber plantation into the 25th Infantry's blocking force with its tanks and armored personnel carriers.

Charlie Company was on its own the first day and the fire from the dug in NVA was so heavy it made little progress. The next morning the company was reinforced by a mechanized infantry company from the 2/22nd Infantry, mounted on armored personnel carriers with .50 caliber heavy machine guns and it resumed the attack. The men were interspersed among the APCs with some between them and some in front and Captain Cain warned them not to get too close to the armored vehicles as they were prime targets for rocket powered grenades. One APC was knocked out and its gunner killed as Cain and Rick Higgins moved alongside it.

The NVA stood their ground and the two companies again made little progress, with many men hit and wounded. Late in the day, Captain Cain was wounded when shrapnel from an RPG rocket ricocheted off the side of an APC and hit him in the nose and lodged in his neck. Cain didn't feel it at first, but Higgins was sprayed by blood from his wound. After a minute, the pain kicked in and the CO was loaded onto a medical APC for evacuation. As he left, he ordered Higgins to help pull the men back to their previous night's position, where a lieutenant, the last remaining officer in the company, took over.

Don Phillips in the third platoon also recalled the battle:

We were engaging a large NVA force and had joined forces with elements of the 25th Infantry Division which had armored personnel carriers (APC). We were intermingled with the 25th Infantry troopers and online assaulting NVA positions entrenched in bunkers. The APCs were online about 75 feet behind our front-line positions where their gunners could fire to the front and over us. I suspect the APC's operated behind the front line to better avoid being hit by armor piercing rocket propelled grenade (RPG) rounds…

When our assault bogged down due to heavy enemy fire, the Air Force was called in to bomb the enemy positions. We were so close to the enemy positions that we had to retreat back to the rear when the bombing runs came in to avoid being hit by shrapnel and debris…

The best cover we had when the bombing runs came was behind the APC's. The Forward Observer would let us know when the bombing runs were coming and we would fall back to the rear and wait until we heard the planes coming in and then get behind the APC's.

Despite this, a few men were wounded by shrapnel and bomb fragments from the air strikes. Between the airstrikes and the gunfire, many rubber trees were shredded and latex sap dripped on the men taking cover below them, hardening into bits of raw rubber and fouling their equipment. Phillips had one close call that day:

> Prior to one of the bombing runs, we had retreated back and I was standing about 2 feet from the front of an APC looking forward for any possible enemy movement until the planes approached. Two or 3 other troopers were nearby. Somewhat surprised, I saw and heard an explosion about 50 feet in front of me. An RPG had hit a broken tree branch about 4 inches in diameter that was nearly horizontal and several feet off the ground. I have always considered myself lucky that the RPG hit the tree branch and not its probable intended target, the APC that I was standing near. I never positioned myself near the front of an APC for the remainder of our time operating with them.

On the third day, the two companies again attacked the bunkers, but the NVA had melted away during the night, leaving behind about 100 dead, and dropping a few mortar rounds on the advancing troops as a parting shot. Higgins took a small piece of shrapnel which lodged between his heart and his lung and was medevaced. Back in the rear, he was told it couldn't be operated on and he was back in the field in less than a week, as was Captain Cain. No one from Charlie Company was killed in the three-day action, but the company was seriously depleted.

LZ Dolly

From early March through July 1969, Charlie Company operated out of LZ Dolly, running patrols and sweeps off of the Razorback into the surrounding lowlands and rubber plantations. On March 12, 1969, the NVA attacked and tried to overrun the company's night defensive position, but were driven off without the company having any men killed. On the 15th, Charlie Company was setting up its night defensive position in deep jungle when an observation chopper sighted boxes of munitions stacked by a bunker about 150 meters away. It was too dangerous to send a patrol out that late and Captain Cain reported the company would check out the sighting in the morning.

That night about ten NVA stumbled into the company's position. They were walking wounded headed to a field hospital in the nearby bunker complex. Charlie Company had unknowingly dug in on the edge of a complex combining an NVA hospital and munitions cache. Most of the NVA were killed by claymore mines and gunfire, but one panicked and ran into the perimeter where he was tackled by PFC Tom Kruger. Another NVA was apparently captured by Platoon Sergeant Raymond Clark when he sat down next to Clark in the darkness and said something in Vietnamese.

The next day, the company found and destroyed scores of boxes of mortar and rocket rounds, all stacked above ground and with Chinese markings. The hospital complex had at least forty bunkers, one of which contained fresh cut flowers and a calendar with the current date scratched off.

Ten days later, early on the morning of March 26, 1969, the company was back at LZ Dolly when it was hit by rockets and mortars, followed by an attack by NVA sappers who breached the wire and hit positions inside the perimeter with hand grenades and satchel charges. Sgt. John Zajdlik remembered the attack in his 2011 interview with reporter Don Moore and recalled feeling that the LZ was in danger of being overrun:

> We had a landing zone on the top of the hill called "Dolly." It overlooked a trail the Communists used to supply their forces. Our base was supposed to be a secure area, but one night we came under heavy mortar and small arms fire from two different directions. I think it was the 9th NVA Division that was attacking us.
>
> The only way to stop enemy mortar fire was to start firing our mortars at the enemy. We began firing at them as fast as we could. Our artillery went to direct fire on the enemy. This means they dropped their barrels down and shot straight ahead with rounds that burst at a certain distance after coming out of the barrel.
>
> We had helicopter gunships coming in to help us out. Phantom jet air strikes were called in to hit the enemy with rockets and bombs. 'Puff the Magic Dragon' was even there with its Gatling guns helping us out.

Twelve GIs were killed on LZ Dolly that morning, five of them from Charlie Company. One of them was SP4 Patrick Benze, 22 and from O'Neill, NE, nicknamed 'Cowboy' by his squad. Ken Alfman, another member of his squad, later wrote a letter to Benze's family telling them how he and the others died:

On the morning of March 25, our company was airlifted back to the landing zone, the same one we were at before we had to go back to the field. About 4 in the afternoon our platoon leader came to our squad and said he needed two guys to go on an ambush that night. Well, this made everyone in our squad mad because that meant two of us had to go out from the LZ and set up an ambush by ourselves, which was really risky, and then come back to the LZ in the morning.

We had a thing in our squad that whenever we had to choose who had to do something, we would draw straws to see who had to do it. So, we drew straws to see who had to go on ambush that night. Pat was one of the first to draw and he got a long one, which meant he didn't have to go. I drew next and got a short one, which meant I was one of the two who had to go.

There were seven guys in our squad, so that left five guys to stay on the LZ that night, plus the rest of the company. I thought I was getting a bum deal by having to go on ambush while everyone else got to stay back, but we did draw straws, so what could I say, I lost.

So that evening, myself and the other guy went about halfway down the mountain and set up our ambush. Everything was fine until about 2 a.m. Then all hell broke loose at the LZ. The fighting went on until dawn. All we could do was listen over the radio and hear what was going on all night.

When morning came and everything was over, we got clearance to come back to the landing zone. When we got there, we couldn't hardly believe our eyes. It looked like a tornado had gone through the place. I was on my way back to the bunker our squad was in when the company commander stopped me and said that Pat and the rest of our squad had all been killed. They were all inside the bunker when it was hit by a rocket, killing everyone inside of it.

I just couldn't believe it, all those guys killed so senselessly. That afternoon we had services for all the guys that were killed.

The four other members of the squad killed in the attack were PFC Edward Green Jr., 18, Hardeeville, SC; PFC Edward Lamoreux, 19, from Plainfield, CT; PFC Donald Forest, 24, of Rochester, NY; and SP4 Carlton Monroe, 19, and from Portsmouth, VA. All had joined the company after its move south the previous November.

Another man who was at LZ Dolly believes there was one survivor in the bunker, PFC Robert Snyder, who was protected from the full force of the blast by another man's body but was temporarily blinded by the explosion. Snyder returned to the company after a few days in a field hospital only to be killed in the company's next firefight.

PFC Tom Kruger was a squad leader in the second platoon and was almost captured by the NVA that night:

I was sitting on top of the bunker talking to Frank Marshall when an enemy sapper fired a B-40 rocket into bunker. Two soldiers were killed, Don Forrest and Ed Lamoreaux. The sappers split going in different directions wreaking havoc in their wake. JD Crossland and I carried Ed Lamoreaux to the aid station where he died before anyone could help him. I was carrying him at the time and talking to him when he died. I returned to my bunker to help anyone else when two sappers returned.

I couldn't find my M-14 or any other weapon and I quickly laid down and played dead. Then the enemy poked one of the wounded and he moaned and that's when all hell broke loose for me. I knew I would be next and I reacted by jumping up and attacking him and his fellow gook. I took both of them out and as I was finishing, two more showed up. One beat me on the head with a chicom grenade and knocked me senseless. When I came to, they were dragging me outside the wire. Captain Cain and Crossland came up to our bunker. I was awake and raised my hand to let them know I was alive and where I was. Luckily, I was still lying on the ground as Captain Cain opened up and fired a clip over me, forcing the sappers to leave me and retreat.

Kruger received a Silver Star for his actions that night. His M-14 was never found and was presumed taken by enemy.

Pinned Down at a Bunker Complex

About two weeks later, Charlie Company was checking out an NVA bunker complex and stepped in it again. Alpha Company had assaulted the complex the previous day and now Charlie was ordered to go in. With them on April 7, 1969 was the battalion chaplain, Captain Claude Newby, who later wrote about the fight in his book *It Took Heroes: A Cavalry Chaplain's Memoirs of Vietnam*. Newby described the opening minutes of the battle:

> A little before noon we swept through a new, fancy bunker complex and held up in a north-south running ditch just beyond it. There we waited out an Air Force bombing attack that we hoped would soften up our objective.
>
> New NVA fighting positions were spaced about every ten feet down the center of the ditch. The condition of the newly dug soil suggested the NVA diggers had abandoned these positions barely ahead of our arrival. The fighting positions confirmed what we already knew. The NVA were ready for us, and they knew exactly where we were. I confess to hoping that our foes were waiting where we expected them to be, right where the bombs were raining down. The NVA were even nearer to us, as it turned out.
>
> PFC Robert Snyder and his machine-gun team had moved for-

ward of the ditch when we stopped to wait out the bombing strikes, as had PFC James Derda with his 90mm recoilless rifle ... A moment later I fell in with the CP element as it passed. I was about six men back from PFC William Allen Jr. who had the point. The time was 1433 hours.

We moved forward with Second Platoon and the Company CP element in a column on a well-used path with the First and Third Platoons in columns on our left and right flanks. The platoon on the left faced tough but safer going through thick jungle with no trail to follow. The other platoon entered an open field after moving five meters from the ditch where we had waited out the air strikes.

An NVA machine gunner opened fire at 1435 hours from a well-concealed position about a hundred feet ahead, where the trail turned sharply to the left and where the open field on our right ended ... With his first burst, the machine gunner killed Allen instantly and drove everyone ahead of me to the ground ... Captain Cain and two radiomen dived behind a large termite mound to the right of the trail. Simultaneously, [artillery FO] 1LT Bill Haines, his RTO, and the company medic dove to cover behind a mound on the left side of the trail.

Up ahead, Gator [Benny Gerrell] hit the ground behind the meager protection of a tree, unhurt. All the other troopers between the NVA machine gun and Cain's CP were wounded ...

Several AK-47s joined the enemy machine gun almost immediately, firing on our front and left flank. Simultaneously, our platoon on the right flank moved into the tree line from the open field, unhurt— presumably the NVA hadn't covered the field because they couldn't imagine Americans approaching in the open.

"Get the 90 [recoilless rifle] and machine gun up here!" yelled Captain Cain.

A moment later Snyder came into view with Hoover right behind him. In response to Cain's call for the machine gun, Snyder hurried forward at a crouch, keeping to the right of the trail for the little protection that Cain's termite hill offered. Dropping to one knee as he drew even with me, Snyder looked directly into my eyes, a look that haunts me still. "Goodbye, Brother," his eyes seemed to say.

Then he leaped forward and threw himself onto the path slightly ahead of where Cain crouched behind the termite hill. Instantly, the machine gunner shifted his fire from me to Snyder...From ten feet away Captain Cain watched helplessly as Snyder's head jerked backward from the impact of a bullet between and just above the eyes. Snyder died instantly.

Derda had arrived perhaps a moment behind Snyder, keeping left of the trail. Dashing to the left, Derda dropped to one knee and fired a flechette round, which he had already loaded, against the NVA forces that were assaulting our left front. The Third Platoon yet struggled through thick undergrowth, trying to get into position to protect our flank.

From behind Cain's termite hill, Hoover yelled, "Gator! Snyder's hit! Here!" With that he threw his heavier-hitting M-14 rifle to Gator and dived for Snyder's machine gun. Hoover died before he could pull the trigger.

"Hold this for me, Chaplain," Derda said, tossing me the strap he used to carry the heavy 90mm recoilless rifle. Then he too was gone around the termite hill into the line of fire. Perhaps the blast of the recoilless rifle had temporarily dampened enemy enthusiasm, for Derda made it to slight cover. But upon seeing that Snyder and Hoover were hit, Derda abandoned the recoilless rifle and dove behind Snyder's machine gun. He took a round in the head before he could fire and joined Snyder and Hoover in instant death.

The firefight lasted close to four hours before Charlie Company got the chance to pull back. Per Newby's account, at one point Captain Jim Cain charged forward and knocked out a NVA machine gun position with grenades. The company moved back about 200 meters under cover of artillery and air strikes. The men killed were PFC William Allen, 19, of Cantonment, FL; PFC James Derda, 23, from Albuquerque, NM; Sgt. Thomas Hoover, 22, Dayton, OH; and PFC Robert Snyder, 23, from Springville, UT.

According to Newby, Captain Cain considered Snyder "the best combat soldier I ever saw." Derda and Hoover may have been left behind as the company pulled back as they were initially listed as MIA and not declared dead until three days later. Derda, Hoover, and Snyder were all awarded the Silver Star. At least nine men were wounded, including Ken Alfman, whose squad had been wiped out at LZ Dolly a few weeks earlier.

Charlie Company remained on full alert that night and was ordered to renew the attack the next morning. Just after dawn, one of the platoon sergeants sought out Chaplain Newby:

> Sergeant Clark looked very somber. "Chaplain, when I looked at my men this morning, some of them had no features where their faces should have been. It was like no soul existed behind each blank face." Clark interpreted the illusion, if illusion it was, as an omen that those particular soldiers would soon die…
>
> In fact, several of Clark's men would give their lives in days to come, but he wouldn't be around to confirm whether those who died were the same faceless ones in his "vision." Clark had about six hours to go in the field at the moment he shared his premonitions with me.

The company advanced on the bunker complex behind air strikes, as described in Newby's account:

The circling Air Force forward air controller (FAC) warned us that the first bombing run was coming in. Casually we took cover in holes or behind trees just before the jet screamed across our front from the south, and almost instantly the jungle floor slammed like a sledge-hammer into our chests or whatever body part we rested on. Concussion and the sound of the exploding bombs came so close together that I couldn't tell which arrived first. Waves of concussion swept over us with such power that even the largest trees seemed to lean away. The blasts were so loud that I doubted our tender eardrums could survive. Waves of shrapnel and debris flashed straight outward from the blasts, over and around us, sounding like thousands of giant, angry wasps. Secondary shrapnel and debris rained straight down from the sky moments after each concussion wave swept past us.

Despite the airstrikes, some NVA remained in their bunkers and Sergeant Clark and four more men were wounded securing the area. Clark also received a Silver Star for his bravery and leadership in the two-day fight. Both Don Phillips and Rick Higgins were among the men wounded, neither very seriously. Over the next few days, both Alpha and Bravo Companies were heavily engaged in the same area.

Transitions

In early May 1969, the 1st Cavalry got a new commander, Major General Elvy Roberts, previously the Division's Assistant Division Commander. He had been a colonel with the 11th Air Assault when it was first developing airmobile tactics at Ft. Benning in 1963 and had commanded the division's 1st brigade when it deployed to Vietnam in 1965. With the war in its final phase, but without an end date in sight, one of Roberts' major concerns was troop morale. J.D. Coleman, then the senior information officer for the 1st Cavalry, described Roberts' approach in *Incursion*, a book he wrote after the war about operations in III Corps and Cambodia in 1969-70:

> When Roberts came back to the division, he further liberalized an already liberal award and decorations program so that he could better reward his soldiers. To criticism that the awards were being cheapened, his rejoinder was that a handful of medals was a small price to pay for a division that retained its fighting spirit. He said he considered every soldier in Vietnam to be a volunteer. "But," protested a staff officer, "most of them are draftees." "That's true," said Roberts, "but you have to remember, many of them had a choice. They could have

run to Canada or Sweden, or they could have wriggled out of the draft by being clever or getting some kind of deferment."

Roberts also knew that in any good infantry division, a brutal and terribly unfair filtering process existed that ensured that only the most highly motivated men finally ended up in line companies. The drones, troublemakers, and cowards were "punished" by being sloughed off into rear-echelon jobs because line-company leaders, from squad leaders to company commanders, could not take chances with undependable and unmotivated soldiers. The good soldiers tended to be sons of working- and middle-class families where values were taught and retained. That is why author Arthur Hadley once wrote that in line units in Vietnam, "it is the best of the middle class that gets blown away."

A few weeks after Roberts took command, the NVA launched mortar and rocket attacks, and some ground assaults, on the 1st Cavalry's headquarters at Phuoc Vinh and every battalion firebase in the Division's AO except LZ Dolly.

By now, Charlie Company and the rest of the 1st Cavalry had adopted new tactics for their interdiction mission on the border. Companies would work out from a firebase and spend three weeks at a time in the field, moving to a new position or ambush site almost every night, sometime by Huey but mostly on foot, and then spend a week on the perimeter of the firebase. The closer to the border a firebase was, the more likely it was to be regularly hit with rocket and mortar fire. The border area was basically a free-fire zone and the company rarely if ever had contact with civilians or villagers.

Sometimes in Bong Son and I Corps, companies followed trails in a long file, about the only way to move in the mountains and high ridges. In III Corps that was an invitation to disaster.

Companies learned to move in platoon and squad columns and to stay off trails—to go parallel to or crisscross them and search for the supply caches and bunkers on either side. Small ambush patrols went out almost every night—Charlie Company had added a third M-60 to each platoon so that each squad had its own machine gun and the gunner would usually be the person designated to trigger the ambush.

A new tactic was the remote ambush, rows of claymore mines hooked up to battery powdered detonators set up along a well-used trail. Platoons and squads would set them up and move about a hundred meters away and wait to see if someone (or an occasional animal) triggered them. Sometimes they would leave them up for a few days. If nothing triggered it, the ambush would be dismantled and set up in another location. After a while, some NVA units began driving chickens or livestock down trails in front of them.

Not only did Charlie Company move differently than it had in the past, it also learned to dig in deeper and faster. Chaplain Claude Newby had done a previous tour with the 1st Cav in Bong Son in 1967. While operating with Charlie Company outside of LZ Dolly, he noted:

> These troops dug in differently now than had those in 1966 and 1967. First, Cain selected the site of the FOB, a different and more difficult process in the trackless jungle than it usually had been in the more populated areas around Bong Son—areas where land features, rice paddies and villages offered points of reference.
>
> With the FOB site chosen, the platoon leaders promptly sent out cloverleaf patrols to sweep a hundred meters or so in front of their respective sectors of the perimeter. Each cloverleaf patrol went forward a specified distance. Then each patrol turned in the same direction,

right or left, and looped back to the perimeter; by this means the patrols usually, but not always, avoided running into one another.

With patrols under way and OPs going into position, it was time to dig foxholes. Every trooper switched back and forth between guarding the perimeter and digging. Each NCO and officer who was not otherwise occupied with vital duties took his turns at pick and shovel. Enough holes had to be quickly dug to permit every man a place under cover from which to stand and fight, if necessary.

After the foxholes were dug in relative silence, the men filled sandbags—each trooper carried a few empty bags in his rucksack for this daily protective routine. At each foxhole, once the sandbags were filled with dirt from the excavations, the men stacked a few bags at each corner of the foxhole and put the remainder aside for later use. Then with holes dug and sandbags filled, noise discipline was relaxed enough to permit the troopers to chop down small trees for overhead cover. Next, short wooden crossbeams were laid across the stacked bags at each end of the hole and four to six long poles were laid across these. Finally, the remaining sandbags were laid across the logs. Thus, in an hour or so almost every day, we dug five-foot-deep fighting positions and constructed overhead cover for protection from mortar, artillery, and rocket bursts, including overhead bursts in the trees.

After dark, ambushes were set and listening posts (LPs) replaced observation posts (OPs). The dissimilarities between how we now dug in 1969 and how we had dug in 1966–1967 reflected the differences in the war itself.

Despite the new ways of operating in the field, the attrition rate due to casualties remained high and most companies remained under strength. Newby recalled that they were generally smaller than they had been in Bong Son two years earlier. He also noted another difference:

In 1966–1967 a wounded trooper could usually expect to be in a chopper en route to expert medical care in sixteen minutes, on average. In 1969 in War Zone C, the wounded waited as much as ten hours for evacuation by a medevac chopper or slick ship. This change I attributed to the loss of so many great medevac crews; exhaustion of the ones remaining; the difference between fighting VC and NVA regulars; and the effect of war protests on everyone, especially on the pilots, who generally were better educated than infantrymen.

Marty Ponist came to the company in late March 1969 as a "shake and bake" sergeant, fresh out of the Army's newly developed NCO program. This had been set up in 1968 to deal with a critical shortage of infantry sergeants caused by both the rapid buildup of forces then and the high attrition rate among NCOs in the field. Although Ponist came in as a well-trained squad leader, he was still green, and he relied on some experienced men in his squad to break him in. In one of his first firefights, he watched Captain Cain move to the front and engage the NVA with his .45 pistol and still remembers Cain as a brave and aggressive CO.

Time caught up with Captain Cain. He had been wounded twice in his months as CO and suffered from severe and debilitating headaches and was replaced in late May or early June by Captain William Keogh. Keogh was on his second tour with the 1st Cavalry and to some men appeared very impatient with the more cautious style of movement required along the border. He took the company down trails, sometimes too fast to put out any useful flank security, and to one experienced point man, he seemed very cavalier about safety. The company lost a few men in this period, but it is unclear just when Cain left and Keogh took over.

On May 25, 1969, Alpha and Charlie Companies located and destroyed a large cache of food, weapons, and munitions. As they approached it, third platoon came under heavy automatic weapons fire from the NVA. One of the first men hit was their platoon sergeant. Don Phillips, then about halfway through his tour, wrote about the fight:

We were engaged in an intense firefight with NVA in fortified positions. We were online and slowly advancing. Multiple NVA small arms and automatic weapons were firing and a lot of bullets were coming our way. Our squad leader was to my left and got my attention. When I got to the squad leader, he said Sgt. Phillips [no relation to Don Phillips] had been hit and I was to help get him back to the Command Post where they were clearing an opening to bring in a medevac chopper. The CP was about 200 feet to our rear and out of sight.

When I got to Sgt. Phillips, the medic was still with him but left soon after I got there. Sgt. Phillips had a bandage on his forehead and seemed a little dazed but could walk and talk. Two or three times he said, "How bad is it?" and asked me to look at the wound. One of us removed the bandage enough for me to see the wound which looked ugly but it did not appear to have penetrated the skull. I told him he had a bad cut but the bullet had not entered his skull and he would be fine.

As we were leaving to go back to the CP, I picked up his helmet to take with us. There, stuck in the forehead of the steel helmet was a bullet. The point of the bullet had penetrated all the way through the steel but was lodged. I showed it to the sergeant which reassured him his wound was not serious. I then guided him back to the CP and he was later evacuated. Sgt. Phillips never returned to our Company and I never heard any follow up on his condition. In any case, the steel helmet undoubtedly saved his life.

Also hit in the firefight was PFC Donald Deevers, in his first month in country. He was well liked in his squad and was nicknamed "Snuffy Smith" after a cartoon character. Phillips saw Deevers as he was medevaced and thought he seemed conscious and had a survivable wound. Their squad was surprised to hear that he died later that day. Deevers was 18 and from Hinton, OK.

On June 1, 1969, third platoon got hit again, this time when following communication wire strung along a trail. They traced it down a hill and found an antenna hidden in a tree and some small hooches and caves or bunkers. Sgt. Ray Knoll, a squad leader who preferred to carry an M-14, was walking point that day, one of his first patrols since getting back from R and R.

The platoon found some trees cut close to the ground and was crawling through the underbrush. Knoll went into a gully and found some warm food that had just been left. As he turned to pull back, he spotted some NVA and both sides opened fire. Knoll was hit in the first exchange of fire and the NVA fled into the jungle. He was 21 and from Muskegon, MI. His platoon had to carry his body back quite a distance and clear an area to get him lifted out. They then humped three or four kilometers back to LZ Dolly and from there watched a B-52 strike devastate the area where Knoll was killed.

Two weeks later, on June 13, 1969, Captain Keogh had the company setting up for the night. Each platoon sent out a cloverleaf patrol in front of its section of the perimeter and one stopped in the path of another. It could hear the other patrol approaching and the patrol leader radioed the CP and asked that all friendly troops freeze in place. The patrol received confirmation that all friendlies were stopped but continued to hear movement coming closer. The point man opened fire, killing two men, one of them a close friend of his. PFC Theodore Heriot was 19 and from Herndon, VA. SP4 James Burton, 21, came from Gordonville, TX.[19]

Months later, the friendly fire incident may have taken another life. Trooper Charles Hoeft fired the fatal shots, or at least believed he did. That December Jim Christensen had completed his tour with Charlie Company and was in the rear processing out when he met Hoeft, who was also heading home to get discharged. Being from different platoons, they had not known each other but they exchanged addresses and said they would stay in touch. Less than a month later, Christensen got a letter from Hoeft's sister saying he had died in a car-train collision. The family had found Christensen's address in Hoeft's wallet.

In July 1969, the battalion got a new commander, LTC Ronald Rasmussen. Around the same time, Captain Kehoe was relieved after less than two months as company commander and replaced by Captain William Vowell. Bill Vowell was also on his second tour. In early 1968, he was a First Lieutenant in the Special Forces, leading a platoon of Cambodian mercenaries in and out of Laos on secret Studies and Observation Group (SOG) missions. From this he learned the virtues of patience, stealth, and thinking like the enemy. His platoon was at Khe Sanh when the 1st Cavalry launched Operation Pegasus and he looked up and saw the "damn sky black with helicopters." When he got the chance to go to the Cavalry on his second tour, he took it.

It turned into a good mix. Vowell was a big man, more than six feet tall, and he led from the front, wielding an M-14. Some men grumbled about having to hack through jungle instead of taking a trail, and digging in deeper at night, but most under-

---

19. The records in the Coffelt Database of Vietnam Casualties list Burton as being in HHC, not Charlie Company, but his MOS was 11B20 and he was with the company that day.

stood his reasons and respected his leadership. Vowell retired as a colonel after twenty-six years and still claims that Charlie Company was made up of "the finest troops I was ever privileged to command and be with." Vowell also felt that LTC Rasmussen was the best commander he ever served with.

Buying Time

As this was happening, events outside of the 1st Cavalry's Area of Operations were having an escalating impact on the course and eventual outcome of the war. In March, President Nixon ordered a series of B-52 raids into Cambodia, officially a neutral country. While the military had been asking for such raids for months, Nixon chose to keep them secret from the public and press, as well as from Congress. When information about the raids was leaked to the press, Nixon ordered the FBI to illegally wiretap a number of members of his own National Security Council, along with four journalists, starting a series of illegal actions that would lead down the road to Watergate and his resignation in 1974.[20]

In May 1969, the 101st Airborne Division (Airmobile) had over 400 casualties in seven days trying to take Dong Ap Bia Mountain in the A Shau Valley, only to abandon the hill and the valley a few days after they finally took it. The soldiers dubbed it Hamburger Hill for the men killed and wounded there and some

---

20. President Clinton declassified most military records on the air war in Indochina in late 2000, in part to assist efforts to locate men missing in action. It was then revealed that secret bombing raids into Cambodia had started as early as 1966 during the Johnson administration. Prior to 1970 they were mostly tactical airstrikes in support of more than 2,000 secret ground incursions conducted by the CIA and Special Forces.

disgruntled veterans of the fight offered a bounty for the fragging of their battalion and brigade commanders.

Public and political reaction to the news and images of the battle was highly negative and grew even more so in June 1969 when LIFE Magazine published a special issue entitled "The Faces of the American Dead in Vietnam: One Week's Toll." Inside, it printed the photos and names of 242 young men killed in a seven-day period "in connection with the conflict in Vietnam." The result was increased pressure on General Abrams and MACV to avoid large unit operations and to keep casualties down.

Then on June 8, 1969, Nixon held a press conference with South Vietnamese President Thieu where he used the term 'Vietnamization' for the first time. He announced that the US would begin to unilaterally withdraw troops from Vietnam. In August 1969, two brigades of the 9th Infantry Division, which operated to the south of the 1st Cavalry, returned to the States. Around that time, Henry Kissinger began holding secret meetings in Paris with the North Vietnamese negotiators, first through an intermediary and then face-to-face, often cutting the South Vietnamese out of the loop.

By now infantry units in the field were mostly filled with draftees, some of whom came into the Army with doubts about the war, and it was inevitable that men began asking themselves, "Why should I be the last to die in a war we're not trying to win."

In the field, the war went on. At the end of June 1969, Charlie Company was operating near LZ Lori, about eight kilometers northeast of the Razorback and LZ Dolly in Binh Long Province, when the 1st Cavalry's commander, MG Roberts, flew into the LZ for a briefing. On his way in, he spotted some NVA from his command chopper and Charlie Company was sent to check it out. Marty Ponist's platoon found the NVA and got into a fire fight which lasted for two or three hours.

PFC Ron Edwards and some other men flanked the enemy position and laid down suppressive fire. Edwards exposed himself and through a combination of words and gestures convinced seven NVA to throw down their weapons and surrender to the platoon. Bennie Atkins, called 'Sugarbear' in his squad, was about two months into his tour and remembered guarding the prisoners that day:

> I was still green and kind of jumpy, and until that day, June 30, 1969, I had never seen an NVA that was alive, face-to-face, up close. I was standing there holding my M-16 on him. He realized I was a little scared, and he looked at me with those dark eyes and said something directly to me in Vietnamese. I suppose, as jumpy as I was, if he had shouted at me, I would have shot him to death!

A month later, First Lieutenant Kevin Corcoran joined the Company. He described his first days in country:

> Got to Vietnam on July 23, 1969. At Cam Ranh Bay reception station, I ran into an OCS classmate who was on his way Stateside following his tour as an Infantry platoon leader. He looked and acted haggard and very nervous. Told me his field experiences were horrifying. He named two other classmates of ours who had been KIA. I was stunned. Could not believe he looked so bad and that two guys I knew well from OCS were now KIA. Not a good start to my Vietnam tour.
>
> Was flown from Cam Ranh to Bien Hoa which was then the 1st Cavalry's rear. Got checked in, underwent a few days of orientation training and then was flown by chopper to Quan Loi, the location of our Brigade and 1/5 CAV Bn rear areas. Soon I was on a bird being

taken to a fire base where the Bn forward HQ was located along with one company for base security.

As soon as I arrived, I was taken to the Bn Tactical Operations Center (TOC) to meet LTC Ron Rasmussen who told me that he wanted me, a newly minted Ranger, to be the BN Recon Platoon leader but only after I had spent 30 days as a platoon leader with C 1/5 under the watchful eye of its company commander, Capt Bill Vowell. The next day I arrived at C 1/5's field location via resupply chopper. There I met Capt Vowell who gave me a few minutes of instructions before the LZ came under heavy enemy small arms fire…my first firefight. The shooting lasted about 15 minutes but to my knowledge no one was hit.

I never fired my weapon in that fight as I was totally bewildered the entire time. I learned later that another guy new to C 1/5 by a few days before me also experienced his first combat on that LZ…Steve Branham. For the next 30 days I served in C 1/5 as a platoon leader, spending most of our time humping the boonies and engaging in frequent but light enemy contact. My recollections of that 30-day period are vague, centered mostly on watching and learning from Captain Vowell who was an exceptionally competent and caring commander from whom I learned an enormous amount during my time under his command.

"Frequent but light enemy contact" characterized Charlie Company's experience for much of the next four months. No men were killed between mid-June and early November, the longest stretch without a KIA since November 1965, but men were wounded and injured on an ongoing basis. It rained hard for much of June and July, slowing down NVA activity, and LZ Dolly was torn down in late July. The 1/5th moved about thirty kilometers north and began operating out of LZs Shirley and Eagle 1, both west of the brigade headquarters at Quan Loi and the provincial capital of An Loc.

In early September 1969, Ho Chi Minh died at age 79 of heart failure. Any hopes that his death would lead to a change in North Vietnam's policies and approach to the war were soon dashed. For men in the field, his death had no impact.

For most of this time, the company continued to operate in deep jungle in Binh Long Province, with frequent contact with squad sized or smaller groups of NVA. If they came to a village, it had been destroyed in earlier operations and its inhabitants dead or removed to refugee camps far in the rear. One day, the platoon was searching a bunker complex that had been hit by a B-52 strike. The earth was chewed up and barren, with the vegetation destroyed and body parts strewn around. Ponist heard a soft click and realized he had hit the trip wire of a booby trap. A 90mm rocket was rigged to the trip wire but failed to go off, his closest call in Vietnam.

Charlie Company lost another man in late October or early November 1969. Tom Kruger was in his bunker at a firebase one night when a man ran in and said that Sgt Richard Moorehead was sick and needed help. Kruger ran to Moorehead's bunker only to find him already dead. He had contracted malaria, thrown up in his sleep, and asphyxiated in his own vomit. Moorehead was 19 and from Detroit and had been in-country for almost eleven months. His military death certificate wrongly states that he died in Saigon and lists "unable to determine" for his cause of death.

LZ Jerri

Larry Touchstone joined Charlie Company not long after Lt Corcoran and wrote about some of his experiences walking point during a search and destroy sweep in early November 1969 when the company was deep in the jungle and far from any of its firebases:

That day we were checking out an enemy trail that had been heavily used. We would never walk down the trail; instead, you would zigzag back and forth, crossing it, and look up and down it while you were crossing. After a couple of hours of this, we crossed it again and something didn't look right. I was on point and saw that the trail didn't seem to have as much traffic at this location. I notified the CO of what I saw and he made the decision to set up an ambush right there. We set our ambush and got in position, camouflaged ourselves and got out of sight. After about ten minutes of waiting, there was a lot of small arms fire directly over our heads, with leaves and limbs falling. If we had been standing up, many of us would have been hit or maybe even killed.

We got up and assaulted in the direction of the firing. Just about 40 yards in the jungle we crossed another trail. The trail split and the enemy heard us coming and had set up their ambush for us on the wrong trail, but we had stopped before we got to that branch in the trail.

Since I was point man, if we had kept going, I may not have caught this and we would have walked right into their ambush, and many of us could have been killed. It was nothing but pure luck that it turned out this way.

The next day, the 2nd platoon rotated to the rear of the column. As we moved later that day, I saw a man about 75 yards out in the jungle on the right side of us. We had a Kit Carson scout. They were enemy soldiers that had given up, and they came over to our side to work for us and we had mistakenly killed one of them in the past.

This one I saw was alone and I wanted to make sure he was not one of ours before I fired. I sent word up to Captain Vowell and asked if we had any friendlies on our right side. The word came back no. I had him in my sights and squeezed off a round, he went down and five other men fired at him after I did. We went to check to see if he was alive, but he was gone, not dead, just gone.

Touchstone was a skilled hunter from rural Georgia and an excellent shot. He never knew what happened to the NVA. That afternoon, the company was ordered to hold in place while Captain Vowell flew into brigade headquarters to be briefed on a new mission. While he was gone, a few NVA probed the company's position. Touchstone recalled:

We moved on a few hundred yards more and set up a night position. It was still daylight and as we sat there eating our C-rations, we heard one of our M-60 machine guns open fire on the other side of the position. We were nervous but then it was quiet again.

The M-60 gunner in the third platoon had been on guard with

his assistant gunner. There were some NVA regulars about 50 yards out trying to sneak up on us. Sherman saw them but kept his cool and acted like he didn't see them. He and his assistant moved around to get into the right position to fire, while they were talking to each other as if nothing was wrong. He got a grip on the M-60 and rolled over suddenly and opened fire.

The NVA were likely killed with the first ten rounds, but he fired most of a 200 round belt to be sure they were not going anywhere. They went to check them for any intelligence information. They were young NVA, probably draftees. There were no others and we slept peacefully that night.

'Sherman' was the men's nickname for Steve Branham, a big man who guys said was built like a Sherman tank. His platoon sergeant was Marty Ponist, now close to halfway through his tour and a staff sergeant and sometimes acting platoon leader.

Vowell returned to the company the next day and it resumed its sweep. A few days later, the men were ordered to saddle up for extraction, issued extra ammo, and told they were heading to LZ Jerri, in northeastern Phuoc Long Province, about forty kilometers northwest of their current location.

LZ Jerri was almost on the Cambodian border and three miles southwest of the South Vietnamese district headquarters town of Bo Duc and the Du Bop Special Forces Camp, a major jumping off point for clandestine reconnaissance missions into Cambodia to monitor the Ho Chi Minh Trail. Just across the border were two NVA base areas and the beginning of the Serges Jungle Highway, one of the NVA's largest networks of infiltration and supply trails leading into the interior of South Vietnam. Now intelligence indicated that 141st and 165th NVA Regiments of the 7th PAVN Division had launched a new offensive in Phuoc

Long Province. The Special Forces Camp and Bo Duc were under siege and in danger of being overrun.

LZ Jerri had been set up as a firebase for operations over the summer but was abandoned in August. As a former firebase, it was well known to the NVA and an easy target for mortars and rockets. The 1/5th went under the operational control of the third brigade and early on November 7, 1969, Charlie Company assaulted into the LZ to reopen the firebase. The men expected the assault to be hot, and it was.

The entire company went in one lift, twenty-five Hueys each with six or seven fully loaded troopers. The LZ was heavily 'prepped' by artillery, airstrikes, and ARA gunships and 1Lt Dan Barlow, leading the third platoon, remembers it as the heaviest prep fire he saw in his tour in Vietnam. But the NVA were waiting and had heavy machine guns set up inside the tree line. As an empty Huey flew over the area ahead of the assault, it was hit and burst into flames. The crew chief and door gunner jumped out to avoid the fire but both were killed by the fall. The pilot and co-pilot rode the chopper down and survived the crash but were badly burned.

Third platoon led the way into the LZ and took small arms fire going in. At one point, men from the company were fighting NVA on the other side of a large tree down and laying on the edge of the LZ. Once on the ground, Captain Vowell led the company in an assault into the tree line to knock out the NVA machine guns. Later, the company found a large command detonated mine buried in the LZ, but the wire to it had been cut by the artillery and rocket fire prepping the LZ before the company landed.

The LZ was secure at noon and the men began to fill sandbags to rebuild bunkers and to stretch razor wire around the perimeter. Two batteries of artillery were lifted in and the men were told to expect an attack. That night the LZ was hit with mortar and rocket fire and the men could see enemy movement outside the wire as flares lit up the area. Suppressive fire was directed at the NVA and they broke off their ground attack before it even started, but Charlie Company's mortar platoon was hit by rockets as it fired illumination rounds.

SP4 Ronald Rodrigues was hit but his wound appeared minor. He told his platoon sergeant and a medic to take care of "Peppy", another man in the mortar platoon who had been hit in the stomach and whose intestines were spilling out. "Peppy", Rodrigues, and two other men were medevaced that night. "Peppy" survived but Rodrigues died the next day in a field hospital of a chest wound that had been missed because it was so small.

Rodrigues was 22 and from Fallon, NV, and was nicknamed "Sad Sack" by his platoon. Although a mortarman, he liked to volunteer to go out on small patrols and ambushes until his platoon sergeant ordered him to stop and remain in the relative safety of the mortar platoon. Also wounded that night was PFC Robert Schares, 21, from Jesup, IA. He died ten days later in a field hospital outside of Saigon. Years later, members of his high school class established a scholarship in his name for deserving graduates.

LZ Jerri was hit by mortar and rocket fire, as well as by ground probes, on a nightly basis and got sniper fire during the day. Some artillery rounds were unsecured and the wood pallets they were on caught fire, causing some of them to 'cook off', adding to the danger on the LZ. On the third day, a squad on patrol found a large amount of NVA ammo and explosives stockpiled in the tree line and had to move it all into a cleared area to be blown up.

On November 10, 1969, a recon platoon from Echo Company

was ambushed outside of the LZ and Touchstone's platoon was the relief force and had to clear a bunker complex, losing a few more men from the company to wounds. Early the next morning, LZ Jerri was hit by the heaviest mortar and rocket barrage yet, along with more small arms fire. The attack began around 0215 and lasted close to an hour and was coordinated with attacks on a number of firebases and installations throughout South Vietnam, possibly intended to coincide with a large antiwar demonstration about to take place in the States.

Larry Touchstone's platoon was on a section of the line that was hit hard. A four-man sniper team from division had come out to the LZ earlier on the 10th and were to join Charlie Company on a mission the next day. Two of them were killed when their bunker took a direct hit from a 120mm rocket. Everyone in Touchstone's position was hit. His wound was minor but the other three men had more serious injuries and he yelled for a medic. One of the company's medics, SP4 Clark Douglas, was moving to help a wounded man caught out in the open when he was hit and killed by a mortar round. Two other men from different units were killed that night and about twelve were wounded.

Clark Douglas was 21 and from Corning, NY and was scheduled to go on R and R to Hawaii later in the month to meet his wife and see his infant daughter for the first time. He received the Distinguished Service Cross for his bravery that night. His citation read in part:

Specialist Four Douglas distinguished himself while serving as a medical aidman at Fire Support Base Jerri in Phuoc Long Province, During the early morning hours of 11 November 1969, a massive enemy shelling broke the silence, raining destruction on the compound and inflicting severe casualties among the men manning the perimeter bunkers. Without hesitation, Specialist Douglas moved immediately from the safety of his bunker towards cries for assistance. Although thrown to the ground by the burst of an impacting round only meters from his position, he crawled persistently forward in the fusillade. As soon as he reached the first wounded man, he began rendering assistance in a calm, professional manner. Just then, an enemy mortar round struck the ground nearby, inflicting mortal wounds to Specialist Douglas.

Other units moved into the Bo Duc area, including an ARVN regiment, an ARVN Ranger battalion, a Special Forces Mike Force battalion of Cambodian mercenaries, and elements of the 11th Armored Cavalry Regiment, operating under the operational control of the 1st Cavalry. The Mike Force battalion charged into the jungle outside LZ Jerri early in the morning of November 11, 1969 and attacked the NVA before they could launch their ground attack against the firebase. With these units in place and the NVA retreating back across the border, Charlie Company flew to Quan Loi for a break, six days pulling perimeter duty at Brigade headquarters.

At around the same time, the largest antiwar demonstrations in the history of the United States took place. On November 15, 1969, an estimated 500,000 people gathered in Washington, DC to protest the war. Another 250,000 demonstrated in San Francisco, and thousands more demonstrated in other cities across the country. Included were many middle-aged and middle-class citizens demonstrating for the first time, as well as some recently discharged veterans and active-duty service members. In Vietnam, more and more soldiers were wearing peace medallions or drawing or painting peace symbols on their helmets or vehicles.

A few days before the demonstration, newspapers had broken

the story that a company of the Americal Division had killed hundreds of civilians in the village of My Lai in Quang Ngai Province in the spring of 1968. As the demonstration took place, the 3rd Marine Division was in the process of withdrawing from Vietnam and returning to Okinawa. On 1 December, 1969, the Selective Service System held its first draft lottery in an effort, far too little and too late, to make the draft more equitable across race and class lines. A few weeks later, the 3rd Brigade of the 82nd Airborne Division began pulling out of Vietnam to return to Fort Bragg.

Meeting Engagement in the Jungle

The third platoon and November had a history together going back to the Ia Drang Valley, and this month would again bring intense combat to its men. Resuming operations in the field, a third platoon ambush killed five NVA with no friendly casualties on November 24, 1969. Then two days later, it was Thanksgiving and the company got a hot turkey dinner in the field while both sides observed a twenty-four hour ceasefire.

The 141st Regiment of the 7th PAVN had now moved south from the LZ Jerri area and was following the Song Be River deeper into South Vietnam and the 1st Cavalry was shifting battalions around to try to locate and engage them. After Thanksgiving, Charlie Company went under the operational control of the 1/8th Cav and was tracking a NVA unit of unknown size parallel to the river in western Binh Long Province.

The morning after Thanksgiving, November 28, 1969, the company had saddled up and was moving out. First and second platoons were already underway when the NVA mortared the company's night defensive position, catching third platoon in the open and wounding five or six men, including the platoon medic. After the WIAs were medevaced, the company continued tracking the NVA unit, guided by radio intercepts picked up by a specially equipped Huey, although the unit's exact location and size remained unknown.

The following day, Charlie Company was moving parallel to the NVA unit in a column of platoons, first platoon on point, followed by the CP, second platoon and third platoon "walking drag." Just after noon, Captain Vowell directed the first platoon to veer to the left and it almost immediately made contact. When the third platoon heard the fire from the first platoon, everyone hit the ground and faced in the direction of the fire. Machine gunner Steve "Sherman" Branham and his assistant gunner Troy Schwartz, a Texan nicknamed "cowboy" by his squad, laid down on a trail the platoon was crossing and set up their gun.

Almost immediately some NVA came running down the trail and third platoon opened fire, starting a short but intense firefight. Dan Barlow thinks that the NVA were trying to avoid contact and that by moving to bypass first platoon they ran head on into third platoon. The NVA responded with small arms fire, grenades, B-40 rockets, and 60mm mortar fire at close range.

Schwartz was hit by a B-40 and had his leg blown off below the knee. The platoon had no medic and Branham moved to cover him with his body, still firing his M-60, until another man could reach him. Squad leader Joe Armstrong got to Schwartz and improvised a tourniquet on his leg and Branham got up on his knees and continued to fire directly into the oncoming enemy, even after being wounded by shrapnel in his face. With his fire and that of the understrength platoon, the NVA broke off their assault and retreated.

The size of the element that hit third platoon was unknown, but the larger NVA unit was at least battalion sized and included a heavy weapons detachment with .51 caliber heavy machine guns. As Charlie Company was engaged, they set up and shot down four 1st Cavalry helicopters, the Huey tracking them, two LOH light observation choppers, and a Cobra gunship, killing six aircrewmen. As a result, the division stopped all flights into the area, including medevac ships.

With four men wounded, one of them critically, a small group of men made a field litter out of bamboo and a poncho liner for Schwartz while Platoon Sergeant Marty Ponist kept the rest of the platoon ready for another assault from the NVA. Fortunately, a LOH pilot heard the company's radio calls and flew to the scene in defiance of the division's order grounding all aircraft. It located the third platoon and led it to an opening in the jungle big enough for a chopper to land. As he was carried in his makeshift litter, Schwartz was conscious and aware that his leg had been blown off and was even singing "The Yellow Rose of Texas."

A Huey on a resupply run also flew into the area in defiance of the division's order and picked Schwartz up. By this time close to two hours had passed—with no medic on board the supply chopper, it appeared to Barlow that Schwartz would likely die on the aircraft before he got to an aid station. As it was, he survived although he needed forty-nine units of blood. After multiple surgeries, "Cowboy" got out of the Army and went back to Texas where he eventually ended up heading the Prosthetics Department at a Dallas area VA Hospital.

Shortly after that, the battalion commander of the 1/8th Cav flew into the clearing to consult with Captain Vowell. While he was on the ground, Barlow convinced the crew of his command chopper to fly Branham and the other two wounded men to an aide station, leaving the Lieutenant Colonel temporarily stranded in the clearing. For his actions that day, Branham received the company's second Distinguished Service Cross in less than a month.

A few days after the firefight, Charlie Company again flew into LZ Jerri, this time to dismantle it. The men worked for three days, cutting open sandbags, and filling in the bunkers they had dug only a month before, and doing everything else necessary to make the firebase unusable to the NVA.

In early December 1969, Charlie Company was on a search and destroy sweep deep into the jungle and far from any of its firebases when it dug in for the night. Larry Touchstone recalls:

> We set up for the night and started our guard duty as usual. When it came my time for guard, about 2300 hours, I had just gotten up and I heard mini guns firing from a Cobra directly overhead. There were no tracers and you could not tell where it was coming from or where the bullets were hitting. You could actually feel and hear the bullets come through the jungle canopy and hit the ground near us.
>
> I thought they must know what they were doing until I heard Captain Vowell yelling loudly on the radio. We knew something was seriously wrong then because you would not make noise that would give your position away. The CO finally got this stopped and later we learned what happened. There had been mistakes made and we were in an area where there wasn't supposed to be any friendly troops.

The choppers were running a "sniffer" mission. They were equipped were sensors developed during the war that could detect small amounts of ammonia from sweat and urine and when they 'sniffed' Charlie Company's position below the jungle canopy, they assumed it was an NVA unit and opened fire. Luckily no one was hit.

Friendly fire wasn't the only danger in the jungle. Early on December 13, 1969, the company was in its night defensive position when the men on guard heard a loud thumping noise. Then one of their trip flares ignited and men grabbed their weapons and braced for a night attack. Instead, a large wild boar, panicked by the flare, charged into the perimeter, and ran over second platoon sergeant "Snake" Lewis as he tried to get out of his bedroll. The boar ran in a circle and then hit Lewis again, knocking him over, before it found its way out of the perimeter and disappeared back into the night.

Later in the month, the company flew back to the rear and got a well-deserved standdown over Christmas at Bien Hoa, one of the Army's largest and most secure bases. The men had to turn in all their weapons, ammo, and grenades, but got to spend a few days in a compound where they could drink all they wanted, at least until Charlie Company and Headquarters Company got into a brawl. After its break, Charlie moved to another firebase, LZ Fort Granite, overlooking the Song Be River about seventeen kilometers south of LZ Jerri, which would be its base of operations for the next two months.

Year Five and No End in Sight

By 1970, the Army in Vietnam was on a downward spiral. A post war history written for the Army described the problems it faced in the last phase of the war:

> As American forces were withdrawn by a government eager to escape the war, the lack of a clear military objective contributed to a weakened sense of mission and a slackening of discipline. The short-timer syndrome, the reluctance to take risks in combat toward the end of a soldier's one-year tour, was compounded by the "last-casualty" syndrome. Knowing that all U.S. troops would soon leave Vietnam, no soldier wanted to be the last to die.
>
> Meanwhile, in the United States, harsh criticism of the war, the military, and traditional military values had become widespread. Heightened individualism, growing permissiveness, and a weakening of traditional bonds of authority pervaded American society and affected the Army's rank and file. The Army grappled with problems of drug abuse, racial tensions, weakened discipline, and lapses of leadership. While outright refusals to fight were few, incidents of "fragging"—murderous attacks on officers and noncoms—occurred frequently enough to compel commands to institute a host of new security measures within their cantonments.

All these problems were symptoms of larger social and political forces and underlined a growing disenchantment with the war among soldiers in the field.

—*American Military History, U.S. Army Center of Military History,* **Richard W. Steward, General Editor.**

While the 1st Cavalry Division was not immune to these problems, it was probably less affected by them than any other Army division or brigade, at least among the infantry battalions in the field. Marijuana use may have increased when companies were securing a large firebase, but when men were in the boonies, they mostly remained disciplined and focused, knowing it increased their odds of making it through their twelve-month tour.

Charlie Company started the year running search and destroy missions in its assigned area, still under the operational control of the third brigade, and making light and sporadic contact with small groups of NVA and VC on an ongoing basis. On January 8, 1970, LTC James Anderson replaced LTC Rasmussen as commander of the 1/5th and Captain Vowell flew to the rear for a change of command ceremony. Anderson had been General Abrams' aide before coming to the 1st Cavalry and had gotten the battalion ahead of some more senior officers, placing him under additional scrutiny and pressure to perform both within and out of the division.

During the change of command ceremony, Vowell got word that Charlie Company was in a firefight and he immediately left it to grab a chopper and fly back to the company. Roger Byers, then one of the company's medics, wrote in 2014 that he thought Vowell looked like an "avenging God of War" as he arrived back to the field, riding the skids of a Huey into a small LZ hacked out of the jungle by the company, holding his M-14.

Charlie Company had stumbled on a bunker complex on a ridgeline about six kilometers east of Loc Ninh. Second platoon was hit by small arms, B-40, and mortar fire, pinning them down and killing two men and wounding another. After artillery fire was called in, the NVA broke contact and evaded to the north, after which another man was wounded by a booby trap. The men killed were PFC Michael Vickery, 21, of Gatlinburg, TN, and SP4 John Rice, also 21, of Indianapolis, IN.

A few days after that, the company was lifted to LZ Vivian for a week of perimeter duty. Then on January 20, 1970, Charlie Company went under the operational control of the 11th Armored Cavalry Regiment and spent most of the next eight days working with Troop H, a tank unit, on road clearing and security missions. The roads running from An Loc to Loc Ninh to the border, particularly highway 14a from Loc Ninh to Bo Duc, were often heavily mined and subject to NVA ambush, and the 11th Armored Cavalry was bringing in massive Rome Plows to take down the jungle for 100 meters on either side of the road. The plows also cleared areas along the borders, especially near the most heavily used infiltration routes. After the vegetation was stripped by the plows, the cleared areas were sprayed with Agent Orange.

January 1970 ended with Captain Vowell moving to the battalion and taking over Headquarters Company. Men were generally guarded and anxious whenever they got a new company commander or platoon leader, but this time the new CO was a known and respected quantity. 1Lt Kevin Corcoran took over the company—he had previously been a platoon leader and then led the battalion's recon platoon in Echo Company. Corcoran took over as "Grey Ghost 6" and got his Captain's bars a few weeks later.

February 1970 was generally uneventful, but the drudgery of days in the field continued. The threats from NVA elements may have diminished, but the leeches and insects didn't get the word. The Serges Jungle Highway, the main infiltration route in the area, was pretty much shut down and the emphasis switched to Vietnamization and the continued neutralization of NVA base areas and supply caches. For much of the month, Charlie Company was under the operational control of other units in the division, and it appears that only one company member was wounded during February.

Around this time, Charlie Company was joined by an NCO who specifically asked to be assigned to it. First Sergeant 'Top' Robert Fowler was one of the most memorable men to serve in Charlie Company until his death on the Laotian border in May 1968. Now his younger brother joined the company, claiming he had come to Vietnam to seek revenge for Top's death.

James Bonard Fowler was in his mid-30's when he came to Vietnam in 1969. He was a Navy veteran from the Korean War and had been an Alabama State Trooper and a member of the Alabama National Guard for years prior to coming to Vietnam. He was fired from the State Troopers in 1968 after a dispute with his supervisor and rejoined the Army in early 1969. With his prior service and State Trooper training and experience, he was able to skip basic training but did go to jump school and possibly received some NCO training.

Fowler came to Vietnam as a Staff Sergeant in August 1969 and was originally assigned to an engineer battalion, but after four or five months managed to get transferred to Charlie Company and soon got promoted to Sergeant First Class and became the platoon sergeant for 2nd platoon. At a point in the war when most men didn't see much point in taking risks, he became a controversial figure in the company. Like his brother before him, he apparently extended his tour at least once to stay in the field and spent more than a year with Charlie Company.

While he soon became known and respected for his bravery in combat, a trait he shared with his brother, some of the men in the company felt he was overly aggressive and hot-headed. He was called 'Pop' both because of his age and to distinguish him from his brother 'Top' Fowler and some men nicknamed him 'Pop Frag' after an ambush patrol in March when some grenades he threw hit overhanging brush and fell short, wounding several men. While in Charlie Company he was awarded two Silver Stars and two Bronze Stars for bravery in combat.

Pacification in the Villages

On February 24, 1970, the company assembled at LZ Fort Granite for a new mission. The 1st Cavalry Division initiated a test project: individual platoons would be co-located in villages with South Vietnamese Popular Forces (PF) and Regional Forces (RF) platoons and companies to train and operate with them and give them the skills to fight the NVA and VC as the US drew down its forces. Of all the companies in the division, Charlie Company was picked by third brigade commander Colonel Robert Kingston for this job. At the LZ, the men in the company began a concentrated training program to prepare them for operations in selected hamlets.

The men in the company underwent seven days of intense training in infantry techniques—weapons, patrolling, calling in artillery, and more. While much of this was second nature to the more experienced men, they had to learn how to teach these skills to the PF and RF soldiers, many of whom were too old to be drafted into the regular South Vietnamese Army and who weren't the most gung-ho or motivated troops around. After that, a second phase of the training gave the men some knowledge of Vietnamese language, culture, and traditions.

On March 4, 1970, the company split up. Each of its platoons went to a different village, along with one mortar from the mortar platoon. The Company CP was based in the Loc Ninh District Compound. There, Capt Corcoran coordinated activities with District Officials and the MACV Advisory Team. The platoons were located in villages chosen by the An Loc and Loc Ninh District officials based on the VC activity in the village areas. The Company XO, Lt Dan Barlow, was based in the An Loch District HQ to provide admin and logistical support to the platoons in that area. The platoons moved to their selected villages and began building small triangular compounds with the mortar in the middle.

Much of March 1970 was spent winning the trust of the PF and RF soldiers and local villagers. Patrols started with the Vietnamese units learning new techniques and pushing farther out into the bush than they had previously gone to set up ambushes. Some officers and NCOs were invited to eat with the village headmen. Now that they were in a more populated area, some men found other sources of recreation and rates of venereal disease began to go up. Probably the hardest working men in the platoons were the medics, who had to go out on all patrols and ambushes and who also began treating the local villagers for a variety of ailments.

Joint US/RF ambushes accounted for a few VC and NVA and five members of second platoon were wounded early in March when it bumped into a NVA unit. Only one company member died that month and it was not by enemy fire. On March 18, 1970, PFC Lawrence Miller, 18 years old and from Biloxi, MS, was shot and killed by a Vietnamese Kit Carson scout attached to Charlie Company.[21] The scout claimed it was an accident, but

---

21 Kit Carson scouts were former VC or NVA who had come over the government's side and agreed to work with US units.

apparently he and Miller had argued earlier in the day. The Army called it an "intentional homicide" and the scout was arrested and driven to the rear and delivered to military police by company XO Dan Barlow, but he was later released. Miller had been in-country just over two months.

About two weeks later, two men who had served with Charlie Company were killed at a different location. 1Lt Cleveland Bridgman and Sgt Robert Lane were a forward observer team from B Battery, 1/77th Artillery and had operated with the company for months before returning to their parent unit in February. On April 1, 1970, they were with their battery at Fire Support Base Illingworth on the Cambodian border in Tay Ninh Province when it came under heavy rocket and mortar fire, followed by a ground attack which almost overran the base. Twenty-six Americans died in the attack including Bridgman, 23, from South Dartmouth, MA, and Lane, 19, from Concord, TN.

About a month into the mission, Charlie Company CO Kevin Corcoran was interviewed by "The First Team," an inhouse quarterly magazine of the 1st Cavalry Division, and described the progress of the pacification program:

> We've had encouraging successes in all our objectives—ambushes, sanitation, base defense, coordination of fire, and civic action. It's tough to break some of the habits they've picked up but we've shown them that our methods work. You can't judge the results of a thing like this by body counts or cache finds. You have to use a subjective standard. Our goal is to strengthen the RF and PF fighting skills and help them defend their villages, which will eventually lead to winning the full confidence of the people. That in turn will destroy the VC.

The program must have shown promise for in April 1970, the

VC began targeting the platoon outposts with mortar attacks. They were small and mostly harmless but did wound a few men in the company and the attached RF and PF units. Some small caches were found by patrols but often they drew a blank. Typical was a sweep on the morning of April 14, 1970 as recorded in an after-action report:

> At 0600 hours the 4th Plt. of C 1/5 at Minh Duc received 5 rounds of 60 mm impacting approximately twenty meters outside compound. The suspected enemy location was engaged with M-60, M-79 and 81mm. A sweep of the area netted 1 V.C. boonie hat.

The most serious contact in April 1970 came four days later. On April 18, 1970, a platoon of Charlie Company patrolling with a PF platoon spotted some suspected VC about 300 meters away and called in mortar fire. A short round hit the unit, wounding three platoon members and one PF soldier. PFC Jerome Bowers died of his wounds later in the day. He was 23 and from Ridgway, PA.

In his interview for "The First Team," Corcoran also said that it would take time, "possibly six to eight months," for the pacification program to achieve its objectives. But time was running out. In April 1970, the 1st Infantry Division, the longest serving unit in III Corps, returned to the US, as did a brigade of the 4th Infantry Division from the Central Highlands. On April 20, 1970, President Nixon announced that another 150,000 troops would be withdrawn in the next year and that "we finally have in sight the just peace we are seeking" in Vietnam. Charlie Company's Pacification mission was abruptly terminated at the end of April when events in neighboring Cambodia gave the Nixon Administration and MACV the opportunity to go on the offensive.

Crisis and Opportunity in Cambodia

The Army had long wanted to take the war into Cambodia. A power struggle in that country would give it the chance to do so. In mid-March 1970, Cambodia's leader, Prince Norodom Sihanouk, was overthrown by Lon Nol, both his Prime Minister and senior Army General, giving the US a more amenable government there.

For years Sihanouk had proclaimed Cambodia's neutrality while tolerating a large North Vietnamese presence along his eastern border with South Vietnam. The Ho Chi Minh Trail ran through this area and it contained base areas and supply depots essential to the North Vietnamese Army. Somewhere in the southern part of this corridor were the B-3 Front, the major NVA headquarters for units operating in the southern part of South Vietnam, and the Central Office for South Vietnam (COSVN), the communists' main political headquarters.

These bases were especially important in early 1970 when US operations in III Corps and farther north destroyed arms and ammo caches and severed infiltration trails within South Vietnam. Many of the NVA and VC strongholds from 1966 and 1967—the Iron Triangle, Hobo Woods, the Crow's Foot, and the An Loa Valley—were now denied to them, depopulated, burnt out, plowed under, and sprayed with Agent Orange until they were no longer a source of rice and recruits.

As long as the NVA stayed in their corridor along the border, Sihanouk pretended they weren't there. When the US ramped up B-52 raids into Cambodia, he made no complaints, even when a raid mistakenly flattened a Cambodian town. He probably had no choice given how much stronger the NVA were than Cambodia's puny army. It was also very profitable to him and the Cambodian military and political elite. The Ho Chi Minh Trail may be better known but by 1970 the NVA across the border from the 1st Cavalry were getting more than half of their supplies by sea.

Shiploads of arms, food, and other needed supplies came from Russia or China to the Cambodian port of Sihanoukville and were trucked directly to the border. Unlike the heavily bombed Ho Chi Minh Trail, most of this route was outside the allowed area for US air strikes. The North Vietnamese set up their own trucking company under a front and used it to buy off many of the Cambodian elite. Relatives of Sihanouk owned a piece of the trucking company, as did many key generals. At one point the CIA considered bribing Cambodian generals to shut down the port but realized they couldn't match the amounts the generals were getting from the trucking business.

With the Serges Jungle Highway and other main infiltration trails shut down by the 1st Cavalry and other units, supplies were backing up in the border corridor. Then the Cambodian coup removed one of the main obstacles to expanded cross border operations. Lon Nol demanded that the North Vietnamese leave Cambodia. In some early clashes between the NVA and the Cambodian Army, the Cambodians were routed and the NVA expanded their corridor, taking over some towns for the first time and moving a division closer to the Cambodian capital, Phnom Penh.

In Washington, the question of how to support an unexpected new ally merged with how to set back the NVA and buy time in Vietnam. In Paris, Kissinger was having direct meetings with Le Duc Tho, the main North Vietnamese negotiator, and accomplishing nothing. In Congress, some senators were preparing legislation to bar US air strikes and ground operations in Cambodia. In the White House, President Nixon had watched the movie "Patton" several times and was looking for a chance to show the same kind of strength and resolve he saw in the film. He told Henry Kissinger: "This is what I've been waiting for."

In mid-April 1970, some ARVN units began a series of cross border raids, minus their US advisors. There were firefights and some small caches were found and destroyed but one effect of the raids was to alert the North Vietnamese that other attacks were likely. The NVA had already anticipated the possibility of an offensive into Cambodia; in mid-March 1970 the B-3 Front had issued an order to all units to "break away and avoid shooting back...Our purpose is to conserve forces as much as we can."

On April 24, 1970, General Abrams issued the first orders for a limited incursion into Cambodia, at first limiting planning to only a few high-ranking officers. On April 26, 1970, Nixon gave the go ahead. The plan developed by MACV called for two separate attacks into Cambodia: one conducted by ARVN units into the Parrot's Beak, an NVA stronghold on the eastern border of Tay Ninh Province, and the other led by the 1st Cavalry into the Fishhook, a wedge-shaped piece of Cambodian territory between the northwest edge of Tay Ninh and eastern Binh Long Provinces.

For the attack into the Fishhook, the 1st Cavalry created a

task force led by Assistant Division Commander Brigadier General Robert Shoemaker. TF Shoemaker consisted of the 2nd Brigade of the 1st Cavalry with three battalions—the 2/5th, 1/7th and 2/7th—plus two squadrons of the 11th Armored Cavalry Regiment, a mechanized infantry battalion from the 9th Infantry Division, a tank company from the 25th Infantry Division, and three battalions of ARVN paratroopers.

The incursion was named Operation Toan Thang (Total Victory) 42 and H Hour was set for April 30, 1970. TF Shoemaker's portion was named Operation Rock Crusher/Toan Thang 43. The military recommended to President Nixon that the announcement of the operation be made in the ordinary course of Saigon press briefings to keep it as low key as possible. Nixon vetoed the idea and decided to make a major address to the American people and H Hour for US forces was pushed back a day to accommodate his speech.

On April 30, 1970, the South Vietnamese began the attack with twelve battalions of infantry, armored cavalry, and rangers crossing the border from Tay Ninh Province into Cambodia in the Parrot's beak. The next day, four more ARVN tank-infantry task forces attacked from another direction. That night Nixon gave his speech justifying the incursion and announcing US involvement.

Some of his advisors recommended he present it as a relatively minor operation designed to speed up the withdrawal of American forces from South Vietnam by eliminating NVA/VC bases, but he choose to frame it essential to America's status as a world power, stating: "If, when the chips are down, the world's most powerful nation, the United States of America, acts like a pitiful helpless giant, then the forces of totalitarianism and anarchy will threaten free nations and free institutions throughout the world." He compared the incursion to the "great decisions" made by Presidents Woodrow Wilson in the First World War, Franklin Roosevelt in the Second, Dwight Eisenhower in the Korean War, and John F. Kennedy during the Cuban missile crisis.

Nixon also announced that the operation had the special objective of capturing COSVN, "the headquarters of the entire communist military operation in South Vietnam." His speech came as a surprise in many quarters. The Army and General Shoemaker were surprised to hear that the capture of COSVN was now one of its objectives. Nixon and some senior commanders appeared to think COSVN was a large static base, sometimes referred to as the 'bamboo pentagon', but military intelligence had known for years that it was dispersed and spread out among, and frequently moved between many bases in the border area. Per his orders from MACV, Shoemaker had only planned for an incursion about seven days long.

In Cambodia, Lon Nol had not been consulted with or informed in advance and he learned about it only after the attacks were launched from the head of the US Mission in Phnom Penh, who himself only learned about it from hearing Nixon's speech broadcast by the "Voice of America." Lon Nol was shocked. Rather than supporting the incursion, ordered in part to prop up his regime, he publicly declared that the incursion was a violation of Cambodian territorial integrity.

In the US, the anti-war movement erupted. It had been fairly quiet since the start of troop withdrawals the previous December, but Nixon's speech threw gasoline on a smoldering fire, especially since his speech made the incursion seem like more like a major escalation of the war than the limited military operation intended by MACV. Some of Kissinger's staff members resigned in protest. Demonstrations started across the country and on May 4, 1970, four protestors were shot and killed by National Guardsmen at Kent State University in Ohio. The killings sparked more protests and over 400 colleges and universities were shut down by protesting students and professors. Over 100,000 demonstrators marched on Washington, DC on short notice and circled the White House, with other demonstrations in cities across the country.

Shaken by the scope and outrage of the response, Nixon announced on May 7, 1970, that the incursion would be limited to no more than sixty days and would not penetrate more than thirty kilometers into Cambodia. After Kent State, this did nothing to appease the anti-war movement, but it was a gift to the NVA. When Cambodian leader Lon Nol was informed that the US would leave Cambodia by the end of June, he broke down crying.

Into Cambodia

As Nixon was giving his speech on the evening of April 30, 1970, it was the next morning in Vietnam and Operation Rock Crusher started on schedule with B-52 strikes and an hour-long artillery barrage into Cambodia. Units of the 11th Armored Cavalry Regiment and the mechanized infantry/tank task force of the 9th Infantry and 25th Infantry Divisions charged across the border as companies of ARVN paratroopers air assaulted into Cambodia. Early in the afternoon, two companies of the 2/7th Cav air assaulted into a clearing named LZ X-Ray after the 1965 battle, making it the first Cavalry battalion in Cambodia.

Few of the men in any of the units going into Cambodia knew the background of the incursion, only that it was a new and highly dangerous mission. Maybe some saw it as a relief from the monotony of past months and operations. Later in the day, the 2/5th landed in X-Ray by Chinook and moved out to link up with ARVN airborne units. Only two US soldiers died on the first day, both from the 11th Armored Cav, a sign that the NVA remaining in the Fishhook were caught off guard by the size and speed of the day's events.

Charlie Company's turn came next. On May 2, 1970, the 1/5th returned to the operational control of the 2nd Brigade and joined TF Shoemaker. Early on the morning of May 3, 1970, the battalion assembled at Loc Ninh and the men got a hot meal and resupply. At about 1000 hours the entire battalion air assaulted into Cambodia in the heart of the 7th PAVN Division's base area. Charlie Company was the lead company and assaulted into a small clearing near a trail system spotted by a recon chopper the day before. The rest of battalion assaulted into LZ Terry Lynn. Captain Kevin Corcoran recalled the day:

> In early May'70 I was instructed by the BN CDR to move all of C 1/5 to the airstrip at Loc Ninh and await further instructions there. When we arrived at the airstrip, I was told by LTC Anderson that we were air assaulting into Cambodia...we were issued maps and other needed items and soon thereafter we boarded Choppers and flew at tree top level into a cold LZ in Cambodia where soon after landing we were greeted by two Cambodian villagers and a few small kids. For the next day or two we humped the jungle toward an area observed by air as a possible location of a NVA Division training/resupply site.

While Charlie Company set out to find and follow the trail system, the rest of the battalion set up a firebase at LZ Terry Lynn and renamed it FSB North. J. D. Coleman described Charlie Company's mission in *Incursion*:

> The undergrowth under the triple canopy jungle was the thickest that any of the company's veterans could remember, and progress was measured in feet per hour. The company, exhausted from beating against the jungle all afternoon, set up a night defensive position at a location that was later determined to be within one kilometer of the perimeter of the supply installation. So impenetrable was the jungle undergrowth that it took Corcoran's company the better part of the

morning of May 4, 1970 to reach the perimeter. As Charlie Company approached a clearing at the edge of the base, the point squad received light AK-47 fire from two of the enemy's defensive bunkers. The skirmish cost the NVA four dead, and there were no American casualties. The door to the huge complex was wide open and Charlie Company was about to enter.

When the company stopped late on the afternoon of May 3, 1970 to set up a night defensive position, Corcoran came under tremendous pressure to keep moving. Both LTC Anderson and Task Force commander Brigadier General Shoemaker radioed him to try to get him to keep going but he refused, knowing that entering a bunker complex of unknown size as night fell was tactically insane and would put the soldiers of Charlie Company in grave and unnecessary danger.

The supply complex became known as "The City" and was one of the largest such depots found by US troops in the war. It covered over three-square kilometers and had been in operation for over two years without being detected. Over 180 storage bunkers were discovered, each sixteen feet long, ten feet wide, and eight feet deep, filled with weapons and ammunition. There were also eighteen mess halls, training areas, a small animal farm, and a swimming pool in the area.

Charlie Company remained in the area for close to two weeks, running patrols in the day and ambushes at night and helping to move what was valuable from the bunkers and destroy what was left. Combat engineers came in and built a road through the jungle to South Vietnam to help move the captured material. Captured records indicated that the depot was a main supply base for the 7th PAVN Division as well as a training camp for new NVA recruits sent from North Vietnam. It may also have been a base for some COSVN functions. Among the NVA supplies found at "The City" were:

1,282 individual weapons
202 crew served weapons
Millions of rounds of ammunition
Over 2,000 grenades and 58,000 pounds of plastic explosive
30 tons of rice, 8 tons of corn, and 1,100 pounds of salt

One of the bunkers contained dozens of new Chinese made SKS carbines. Since they are semi-automatic, a soldier could bring one home as a souvenir. Battalion commander LTC Anderson authorized any member of the company who wanted one to take it.

There was sporadic contact while the company was at "The City", mostly at night, and one Charlie Company trooper was killed on May 8, 1970. PFC Michael Tuff was hit when his night position was hit by about ten rounds of 75mm recoilless rifle fire. One other man was wounded. Tuff was 20 and from Anaheim, CA.

While Charlie Company was occupied cleaning out "The City", the Cambodian operation got bigger. Task Force Shoemaker was dissolved and the Division took command, sending in more battalions. While Charlie Company was at "The City", it and the rest of the 1/5th Cav went under the operational control of the 1st Brigade while the 2nd Brigade shifted east to assault NVA Base Area 351 in Cambodia across from the Du Bop Special Forces Camp. There the 2/7th Cav found another large arms depot they dubbed "Rock Island East". Unlike "The City" it appeared to have been recently set up as all of the weapons and munitions found there were stacked on pallets above ground and covered with plastic sheeting.

At the same time, brigades of the 9th and 25th Infantry Divisions attacked into different parts of the Parrot's Beak. Farther north, a brigade of the 4th Infantry Division, backed by a battalion of the 173rd Airborne Brigade and ARVN infantry, armor, and rangers, attacked into Cambodia west of Pleiku. As more US units poured into Cambodia, NVA attacks increased, for the most part diversionary and harassing as their major units pulled back beyond Nixon's thirty-kilometer line.

The 1st Brigade and the 1/5th operated in the Fishhook until May 19, 1970 when it leapfrogged over the 2nd Brigade to assault into the O Rang area, across the border from the eastern most part of Phuoc Binh Province. Charlie Company assaulted into a clearing which would become FSB David, the tactical headquarters for the battalion. It was the most remote firebase set up during the Cambodian incursion, in hilly country populated mainly by indigenous tribespeople. After a few days securing the perimeter, the company headed back into the jungle, operating in that area for the remainder of the Cambodian incursion.

At about the same time, Captain Corcoran was transferred to battalion HQ to take over as a S-3 staff officer and 1Lt Terrance Laughlin, one of the platoon leaders, took command of Charlie Company. Changes took place at the division level as well, with MG Roberts replaced as commander of the 1st Cavalry on May 12, 1970 by MG George Casey. Casey had led the 2nd Brigade, including the 1/5th, for much of the Bong Son campaign in 1966 and 1967.

On May 23, 1970, Charlie Company found a small cache with communications equipment and munitions. Early that evening the company made an air assault looking for an NVA supply route. The LZ was a two-ship clearing in the jungle and the NVA were waiting. A Huey in the third lift was hit by a B-40 rocket grenade in the cockpit and crashed, killing the pilot and wounding four Charlie Company members.

A firefight erupted as men moved to secure the downed chopper in the fading light. Sgt Steve Branham and a medic got the wounded co-pilot into a foxhole and covered him through much of the night, but he died before he could be medevaced in the morning. One man from Charlie Company was killed. SP4 John Hughes was found the next morning in a small clearing just outside the company's lines with a dead NVA lying close by. It appeared to the men who found him that he and the North Vietnamese soldier had shot and killed each other.

Hughes was 21 and from Houston, TX. In the weeks before the Cambodian incursion, Hughes had told members of his platoon in a very matter-of-fact way that he knew he would not make it through his tour. Larry Touchstone posted this remembrance of Hughes on the Vietnam Veterans Virtual Wall website in 2006:

> John arrived in Vietnam January 12, 1970. I had been there since September 1969 and had gotten to the point that I did not want to get close to anyone new because it was too painful to lose a friend. We talked a lot, and it didn't matter how hard I tried not to, we became friends before I knew it.
>
> After I had known him a few weeks he told me that he was certain that he would not leave Vietnam alive. I tried many times to talk him out of that idea but had no luck. After that I just made an effort to put it out of my mind, but it was always there.

Operations around O Rang continued and the monsoons

began, making life that much harder for the men in the field. Jim McKeever came to the company in March and remembers the operation as the worst humping of his tour. The company would follow ridgelines and the trails would become so slick that men were constantly slipping in the mud. If a man slipped going downhill, all he could do was aim for a tree and hope to slide into it.

On June 14, 1970, while Charlie Company was in the bush, two battalions from the 174th NVA Regiment attacked FSB David through early morning fog and drizzle. Some sappers broke through the perimeter but the FSB held, losing twenty-nine WIA but no KIA. A sweep of the perimeter in the morning found twenty-eight dead NVA. The defense was led by Delta Company, now commanded by Captain Bill Vowell. Captain Corcoran was also there and recalled: "It is my strong opinion, having been in the TOC on FSB DAVID during the attack, that Capt Bill Vowell's superb actions as Delta Company CO saved FSB DAVID from being completely overrun that night." It was the largest attack on any US unit or base in the Cambodian incursion.

By mid-June 1970, casualties were having an impact on Charlie Company. The third platoon leader had been medevaced after being shot in the neck and second platoon had not had an officer for days, if not weeks, and was being led by SFC Jim "Pop" Fowler. Company commander Terry Laughlin, now a captain, was still fairly new and the company had no artillery FO, so company XO 1Lt Dan Barlow came out to the field. Ranger trained and with nine months of field experience, he took over both third platoon and FO duties and otherwise helped Laughlin run combat operations.

On June 19, 1970, a Charlie Company patrol found a cache

with 33,000 pounds of rice. As the company moved in to seize and remove it, it was surrounded by the NVA and pinned down in place on a small hill for the next two days. Early in the fire-fight, first platoon leader 1Lt Dennis Tenney, machine gunner Sgt John Myers and another man moved out to assist another platoon under fire and were all wounded by a B-40 rocket grenade. Myers was medevaced but died in an Army hospital over two weeks later of gangrene following the amputation of his leg. He was 21 and from Moneta, VA, and left a wife and infant son.

Tenney was wounded in his shoulder but would not allow himself to be medevaced, telling Barlow he would refuse to go to the rear even if directly ordered to do so. They had known each other since Ranger training and he didn't want to leave Charlie Company shorthanded. He continued to lead the 1st Platoon while wounded. 'Pop' Fowler led the second platoon through the fight and Barlow thought his leadership was outstanding and helped keep his men focused and prepared.

After the initial contact, a stalemate developed. Every time a patrol or platoon tried to move forward, it drew heavy fire from the surrounding jungle. Men in the company had to blow down some very tall trees with C-4 to create a narrow shaft for medevac choppers to land. They had to descend and climb out slow and straight and Jim McKeever remembers several guys saying that if they were slightly wounded, they would rather stay and take their chances in the encircled position than risk being shot down on a medevac chopper.

On the evening of the second day, Barlow called in so much artillery support for the company that the battalion commander, LTC Anderson, radioed him and asked him if he realized how much the shells cost. Barlow said no and Anderson told him it was $25,000, clearly implying it was too much. After the call ended, Barlow called for more artillery and in the morning called for air strikes to drop napalm fifty meters from their lines. Only after that did the NVA break off and withdraw, giving the company the chance to destroy the rice cache and start to head back to Vietnam.

As they prepared to move, the company lost two more men, the first by friendly fire. As a wounded man was being medevaced, the medevac chopper was fired on and its door gunner panicked and opened fire, spraying the area, and hitting and killing Sgt Richard Grieme. Grieme was 23 and from Raleigh, NC. A few months before he died, his platoon was flying to a new location on an Air Force C-7 Caribou, a two-engine transport plane. Grieme had learned to fly before joining the Army and after talking to the flight crew, he was invited into the cockpit and got to fly the plane for part of the trip.

Later, as the company was starting to move out and Grieme's body was being picked up by a LOH observation chopper, there was a small quick firefight and SP4 Mark Brantley was killed. McKeever wrote about his experience that day:

Just after getting out of our entrapment in the rice cache, we started humping to eventually get out of Cambodia before Nixon's June 30th deadline. Off the right flank near the rear, we received small arms fire. It lasted only a minute or two and sounded to be from no more than four or five NVA. I was walking rear security with Jesse Ariza. I had an M79 but no sidearm .45 pistol (couldn't get one) and Ariza had an M16. I was covering the right flank and Ariza was covering the left, both of us overlapping the direct rear.

When the firing started, Ariza and I had no nearby cover or concealment, so we just set up behind our rucksacks. When the firing started, I faced to the right in the direction of the fire and told

Ariza to watch the entire rear and left flank. About ten seconds after the firing stopped, about 15 meters in front of me, three NVA who had been moving parallel to our file from the direction of the firing made a right turn and were running full speed directly at me. One of them had a B-40 rocket. However, their attention was focused on their right, where moments before the firing had come from our troops. Nobody else saw them except me. I had no way to take them all out and was sure I was about to die. At that moment I had a paranormal experience which included an exchange with an unseen presence — yeah, I believe it was the Big Guy. I took this to be part of the dying experience because a calm came over me and the fear of death left.

I had a high explosive round chambered in my M-79 but it wouldn't be of much use. The NVA were too close and the fuse in the round wouldn't engage at that short distance.

I had no time to call for fire because in seconds they would literally be on top of me--the closest one was now less than five meters away--so I fired into his chest, figuring that would draw attention from our men, even if Ariza and I were both dead. Simultaneously, I grabbed the shoulder of Ariza's fatigues and pivoted him around. Unbelievably, the NVA I had shot went down dead, and the two remaining NVA totally freaked out upon seeing me for the first time and reversed course into the jungle without firing a shot. My body was now the fighting position for Ariza and I could feel my ass being whacked in sequence with his firing. I thought that in his panicked state his bullets were grazing it, but it was just the muzzle gas. The two NVA got away and I couldn't believe I had survived the event. I said a huge thank you to the Big Guy and every day since.

Brantley was hit at about the same time. Gardy Morton remembers that he was hit by a B-40 rocket fired by an NVA who popped out of a concealed position and fired at such close range that the blast also killed the NVA who fired it. In the confusion, some men thought Brantley had been killed by running into the blade of the chopper picking up Grieme's body.

Mark Brantley was 21 and from El Monte, CA. The company didn't want to risk bringing in another medevac at that location so his body was wrapped in a poncho and tied to a bamboo pole. Morale was down and by that time, any sane soldier was hesitant to take risks, but when Barlow asked for volunteers, some of the men stepped forward. Ray Bell volunteered to walk point and Willie Harris and Paul Carper volunteered to carry Brantley's body.

They carried and sometimes dragged Brantley's body for most of a day until they reached a spot where it could be lifted out. Al Garcia had been wounded by shrapnel around the same time Brantley was hit and he chose to stay with the company rather than risk being shot down in a medevac chopper. The company headed south and humped for days until it reached the border with Vietnam.

At the end of June 1970, all US units were pulled out of Cambodia, although ARVN units continued to operate there for months. Most of the 1st Cavalry battalions and companies were lifted out, but Charlie Company returned to South Vietnam by foot, crossing a wide and swift river on the border. Dan Barlow and Dennis Tenney flipped a coin to see who would be last to cross and Barlow ended up as the last man of the 1/5th Cav to leave Cambodia.

COSVN was never captured. As the Nixon administration made that a major goal at the onset, some critics declared the entire operation a failure. The Cambodian coup and the incursion also unleashed events and forces in that country which would in a few years have tragic consequences for its people.[22] But in the military terms originally envisioned by MACV and the 1st Cavalry when the operation was first planned, it was a success. Shelby Stanton described the results in *Anatomy of a Division*:

> The overall invasion success was verified by the vast quantities of foodstuffs and weapons captured by the allied forces. The NVA/VC lost enough rice to feed more than twenty-five thousand soldiers for one year, or nearly thirty-eight thousand soldiers on reduced rations for a year. Enough individual weapons were taken to equip fifty-five full strength Viet Cong infantry battalions, and enough machine guns and other crew served weapons were seized to outfit thirty-three full-strength Viet Cong infantry battalions.

The incursion set back NVA activity in III Corps for months, possibly over a year, buying time for "Vietnamization" and more troop withdrawals. In response, the NVA shifted part of its focus farther north to operations in I Corps. In July 1970, parts of two PAVN divisions fought elements of the 101st Airborne Division in a twenty-three-day battle around FSB Ripcord near the A Shau Valley. Casualties were heavy and the firebase was abandoned on July 23, 1970. It was the last large-scale battle between the NVA and US forces in the war.

Some of the ARVN units that went into Cambodia per-

---

22. The Nixon Administration continued B-52 raids into Cambodia for more than three years after the incursion ended, expanding the areas bombed far deeper into Cambodia. The bombings became one of the most effective recruiting tools for the Khmer Rough insurgency. By the time the bombing stopped, the Air Force had dropped more tons of bombs on Cambodia than had been dropped by the allies during all of World War II, likely making Cambodia the most heavily bombed country in history.

formed well, particularly their airborne brigade partnered with the 1st Cavalry. ARVN leadership remained mixed with many of their officers still in command on the basis of political loyalty instead of competency, skill, and aggressiveness. Unfortunately, two of their best generals died in helicopter crashes, one at the start of the incursion and the other in February 1971.

The Army lost one of its best generals as well. On July 6, 1970, a week after the last Cav battalion exited Cambodia, MG George Casey also died in a helicopter crash. He was flying in his command chopper from Phuoc Vinh to Cam Ranh Bay to visit 1st Cav troopers wounded in the incursion when it crashed in a monsoon storm, killing him, his aide, the division Command Sergeant Major, and four others. He was replaced by MG George Putnam, formerly the division's artillery chief, who then led the 1st Cavalry for its remaining ten months in Vietnam.

Winding Down

Once Charlie Company was back in South Vietnam, LTC Anderson met it and asked for 1Lt Barlow. When Barlow presented himself, his fatigues torn and muddy and still stained with the blood of casualties, Anderson ordered him to shower and get a clean uniform before approaching him again. The 1/5th remained under the operational control of the 1st Brigade and an ARVN unit replaced it on the border. After a short break to clean up and re-equip, Charlie Company started operations in southern Phuoc Long Province. By mid-July 1970, it was back to running interdiction missions against the NVA's Serges, Adams Road, and Jolley infiltration trails in War Zone D.

For a while, the company resumed pacification missions with platoons supporting South Vietnamese RF and PF units in their villages, but it seemed more haphazard than the earlier attempt before Cambodia. One platoon was withdrawn when it became clear that the local village chief and PF platoon had little interest in the effort.

LTC Anderson was replaced in August by LTC William Burkhart. Captain Laughlin was replaced in September by Captain Robert Parrish and Charlie Company operated in and around firebases in the 1st Cavalry's Area of Operations for most of the rest of 1970. The 1st Cavalry, like other US units, basically remained in a "defensive posture" as Vietnamization continued.

1Lt Mike Kline had arrived in Vietnam in May 1970 while Charlie Company was in Cambodia and joined it shortly after it returned to South Vietnam, taking over the 3rd platoon. Not long after that, battalion headquarters ordered Kline and his 3rd platoon to operate directly under the control of battalion S-3. Kline recently described how the move came about:

We were part of a Brigade sized operation designed to pin and destroy the NVA "84th Rear Service Group" which supported NVA Combat units in our AO. C Company was assigned a sector of the encirclement that included a flat paddy area where we landed facing a steep rise to a ridge line. The ridge had a series of narrow fingers leading down to the flat. The CO, Captain Laughlin, had 1st and 2nd Platoons form a perimeter around the company HQ and assigned 3rd Platoon the task of climbing the center finger to recon.

The sub-ridge we ascended was so narrow that the ground fell away sharply on our right and left and we could see the ridges paralleling us. A very steep and lightly used trail followed the spine of the ridge. About one kilometer up the ridge, we found a flat area about 75 feet in diameter where the vegetation was clearly broken down, looking like men with packs had stopped to rest. We paused, and Willie Harris, who was walking point, moved forward with the "slack man" to look up the trail beyond the flat area. They returned and we had an earnest discussion about how much farther we were prepared to go.

At that moment, a solitary figure emerged from behind a clump of bamboo and entered the clearing. I raised my rifle and Willie and the slack man spun around. The figure ran from left to right toward the nearest defile and we all fired into him. He fell on his back, dragged down by his rucksack. The lead M60 team moved to our right and fired its 100 round "starter belt" up the ridge. We received no return fire but could hear people shouting above us approximately where the ridge we were on joined the larger ridge.

I sent the point team back across the clearing for security and stripped the body. He was about 40 years of age, well dressed, with a recent haircut. There was an AK47 slung around what remained of his left shoulder and a Tokarev TT 30 pistol on his belt. He had a wad of paper in his left breast pocket and a gold Omega wristwatch buttoned on the pocket flap. I secured those and cut loose the rucksack for later examination. I cut away his pistol belt and threw his AK-47 down the hillside. Willie Harris tore off a Cav patch from the multiple patches stitched to his boonie hat, rolled it up and tucked it into the dead NVA's mouth.

My Platoon Sgt, Stan Berg, had made his way to the front of the file and I advised him that we would reverse direction and descend. He would lead and I would use the point team and M60 team as rear security. My logic was that our recon was blown and that we had an unknown force above us. The ridge was too thin to allow maneuver and the parallel ridges would give the enemy the ability to fire into our flanks if we remained or ascended.

When we returned to the company perimeter, I gave Willie and the slack man the pistol and the wristwatch and kept the belt buckle for myself. The rucksack was found to contain a lot of paper and articles (like foot powder) that still had the Saigon PX price tags on them. The papers from his pocket and the rucksack were delivered to LTC Burkhart, the Battalion Commander.

We learned later that our kill was a South Vietnamese with rank equivalent to an NVA Major, who had been twice to N. Vietnam for training (indoctrination) and who was responsible for conscripting villagers for the 84th "Rear Service Group".

Shortly after this incident, the S3 reviewed our actions and recommended that we function as an independent platoon.

For months, Kline's platoon searched for infiltration trails
based on reports from S-2. When they found one, they would
move parallel to the trail until they found a good spot for an ambush. Contact was rare and it was clear the NVA were laying low
throughout much of the III Corps area.

For men on the ground, there didn't appear to be much difference between being in a "defensive posture" as compared to anything else in the past five years. There were fewer air assaults but
men continued to hump the boonies and patrols and ambushes
were still caried out almost daily. It remained hot, wet, and dangerous work and men still died.

The terrain continued to be as much of an obstacle as the
enemy and there were sometimes disconnects between how a
headquarters viewed the ground from maps and flying over it
in command choppers and how a unit experienced it on a mission. On one occasion, Kline was at battalion HQ planning a
mission for his platoon when LTC Burkhart came over, looked
at a map, and directed him to set up his ambush where a trail
crossed a stream, a blue line on the map. Kline tried to explain
the maps weren't very accurate, were five years out of date, and
that the stream shown on the map could be anywhere on the
valley floor. Also, that with the arrival of the monsoon season,
it could easily flood. Burkhart cut him off and told him to follow orders. Kline and the third platoon moved out and set up
along the stream as ordered. It rained hard that night and by
midnight the platoon was chest deep in water and struggling to
get to higher ground.

On September 18, 1970, the company was on a sweep near

the NVA's Jolley Jungle Trail in Binh Thuy Province, miles from the border, when 2Lt James DuPont was killed. Charley Joyce recalled that day:

My squad was positioned second behind Lt. DuPont and the point squad as we encountered an 18-inch wide hard-packed trail suggesting, of course, that it was heavily used and likely used to transport large amounts of equipment and personnel. I also remember that on a previous day our new CO Parrish sent a warning to avoid walking on any trails.

As my squad approached the trail which was on a slight elevation of 5 to 6 feet, the VC opened up and the bullets flew. We hit the ground and protected our flanks. Soon after, we could hear the M60 team which was positioned on the trail call out for more ammo. I left my squad, crawled up to the trail where I found myself less than a foot from Lt. DuPont who was still alive but bleeding heavily from his neck and his head being cradled by his RTO, Alan Fielding.

I crouched and crawled down the trail while collecting bandoliers of M60 ammo from men on both sides of the trail. By the time I reached the gun, the shooting stopped. Beside Jim DuPont, I witnessed only one other wounded member of that squad. He had some shrapnel wounds from a grenade that he threw and that unfortunately hit a vine and came back at him (his words). Fortunately, he wasn't seriously wounded.

Bob Parrish had only been company commander for one or two weeks at the time and he later described his actions and thoughts that day in an unpublished book:

I turned to Vaughan, but before I could say anything, a burst of AK-47 fire came snapping through the bush. In a fraction of a second, more VC opened up and immediately some of DuPont's people began returning fire. I low crawled up the trail, yelling for the troops still not engaged to move forward. The two leading squads were firing, but the people in the trailing squad were just hugging the trees. Over the sounds of the firing, I heard someone yell, "Medic!" The troops around me were scared shitless and I literally had to kick some of them to get them to move up to help their buddies.

I stopped for a moment and nearly got knocked over by Lieutenant Knudsen. He had been chasing around behind me, trying to get instructions. "Take your people and move around on the left flank. I want you to give DuPont some help, but don't go charging into the VC without orders from me."

I continued to work my way forward until I reached what I thought was our front line. I grabbed a young sergeant and asked him where Lieutenant DuPont was. "He and the point team are somewhere up ahead. At least one of them is hit."

Over the sound of the firing, I yelled for everyone to move forward, but to be careful because we had friendlies out front. There was some reluctance to move, but after more yelling and cussing, the people began to slowly crawl forward…Like almost every other fire fight I had been in, everything was confused. Bullets were flying everywhere and no one seemed to have a good fix on the VC positions. Some people were just blasting away at full auto and others were just lying there, waiting for a target.

I called DuPont on the radio but got no answer. Between calls, Knudsen reported that his platoon had gotten around to the left flank but couldn't spot the VC. I told him to hold for a minute until I got this goat-fuck sorted out. I still had to locate DuPont and his point team and get a handle on what we were up against.

Suddenly someone yelled, "Friendlies coming in!" Moments later a small group of people appeared in front of us, dragging a man. The

VC were still firing, but the thick jungle was stopping many of the rounds and the others were going over our heads.

Crouching over, I ran to meet the returning point team. I grabbed one of the wounded man's arms and helped drag him behind a large tree. It was Lieutenant DuPont and his chest and shoulders were covered in blood. An AK-47 round had hit him in the neck, but fortunately it missed his jugular. He was unconscious, in shock, and gray from the loss of blood, but there was a chance he'd survive. Doc Kniffen began working on him and I yelled for my battalion radio operator to call for a priority Dust Off (medical evacuation chopper). Two of the other men had been lightly wounded but were in no immediate danger.

Parrish estimated that Charlie Company encountered about a platoon of VC in bunkers. He deployed the rest of the company and called in artillery support and Cobra gunships, but the VC broke contact. Lt DuPont was 23 and from Westerville, OH.

ARVN units assumed more responsibility for offensive combat operations and US units continued to slowly withdraw from South Vietnam with the rest of the 4th and 9th Infantry Divisions and the 199th Light Infantry Brigade all leaving by the end of 1970. As units pulled out, not everyone went with them. Men with months to go on their tour were generally reassigned to other units, a practice that sometimes negatively impacted morale and unit cohesiveness.

Charlie Company's last fatality of the war came at the end of 1970. Third platoon returned to the company by late October and not long afterwards Mike Kline became the company XO. In late December 1970, a new platoon leader was leading the platoon on a patrol when it came to a clearing previously occupied by another US unit. Foxholes were half filled in and there was a pile of discarded C-Ration cans. US units leaving a position sometimes booby trapped such piles, knowing that NVA and VC might search through them for food. The platoon leader ignored the established practice of skirting around such a spot and directed the platoon to cross the clearing.

SP4 William "Stony" Johnson hit a trip wire and a grenade, likely set by a US soldier, exploded, taking off both of his legs. Johnson was treated and medevaced and at first it looked like he would survive the wound. Mike Kline visited him in the hospital a few days afterwards and he seemed to be doing well. But sepsis set in and Johnson died in a hospital in Japan on January 10, 1971. He was 19 and from Atlantic City, NJ. Not long afterwards, the lieutenant was relieved and Kline returned to the field to again lead the 3rd platoon.

As Johnson was dying, the Senate voted to repeal the Tonkin Gulf Resolution, the legal authorization for the Vietnam War, and to ban further funding for US ground and air operations in Cambodia and Laos. President Nixon ignored the change in law, arguing that he had constitutional authority as commander-in-chief to continue the war. Bombing in Cambodia and Laos went on for another year and a half.

Early in 1971, the battalions and companies of the 1st Cavalry began pulling back in anticipation of their return to the States. By then it appeared that Charlie Company eliminated its mortar platoon and operated with four understrength rifle platoons, with squads usually having five or six men. The platoons were split up and based near Vietnamese villages and spent less and less time actually humping in the field. The battalion headquarters relocated to the large rear base at Bien Hoa and platoons began going there for short standdowns after time in the field.

Bien Hoa offered amenities to the men that they hadn't seen since their tours began. It was a joint Army-Air Force base and the Air Force had air-conditioned clubs with Korean or Filipino go-go bands almost every night, a swimming pool, and a well-stocked and air-conditioned PX. It was also close to Saigon and men headed there whenever they got the chance. But it seemed that the Military Police in Saigon took special pleasure in stopping anyone wearing a 1st Cav patch or looking like they had been in the field.

After months in the field, Jim McKeever had been reassigned as the company clerk, probably because the first sergeant found out he could type. As platoons came back, he took it upon himself to issue phony travel orders to men wanting to go to Saigon for a few days. He never bothered to tell either Captains Laughlin or Parrish, figuring they were better off not knowing. As for the threat of consequences if he got caught issuing fake orders, he had the attitude, pretty common at that point, "What can they do, send me to Vietnam?"

McKeever and many other men in Charlie Company had never gotten their R & R, the seven day 'rest and recreation' break in another country promised to each soldier in Vietnam during their tour. Squads and platoons were understrength in 1970 and early 1971 and the company was required to keep ninety percent of its men in the field. As the battalion moved back to Bien Hoa, the ninety percent requirement was no longer strictly enforced and McKeever submitted an R & R request for himself and about twenty other company troopers. To his surprise it was approved and the men voted to go to Bangkok, Thailand as a group in early February 1971. He remembers it well: "There's no doubt that no Charley Company member ever had a better R&R. Imagine that many rowdy grunt brothers together in one rocking city during their final time together. It was wild and unbelievable that nobody wound up in jail."

Being in the rear brought problems as well. Drug and alcohol use were widespread, especially in the rear where men had time on their hands and weren't in immediate danger. Officers in combat units usually overlooked marijuana use in the rear as long as troops didn't smoke it in the field—and it appears that few in Charlie Company did—but heroin was a growing problem among support troops. Racial animosity and conflicts were also on the rise. By late 1970, the Army routinely required infantry companies coming in from the field to turn in all weapons and ammo when arriving at a base in the rear.

Before leaving Vietnam, Charlie Company had one more combat mission. LTC Richard Kattar became the 1/5th's last battalion commander of the war in early 1971 and energized the battalion for its last months in-country. He visited each company, bringing the men ice cream and telling them:

Now I have a beautiful wife, three lovely children, and a great life ahead of me. I want to get this done and get back to that. The things I can guarantee you are that I will die for you, if it's necessary, and that I will never experiment with you, and that if you listen to what I tell you and do as I say and am prepared to do with you, then your opportunity to fight and win will be the greatest, will be maximized. Because it makes no sense to me at all for someone to draw the conclusion that they are giving themselves an opportunity to get back home by walking around the jungle in a stupor, either because of dope or preoccupation of mind. The best way to get home is to be a superb infantryman. When you walk through that jungle, you'll walk through there sharp and intent upon insuring that if that sonofabitch raises his goddam ugly head to blow you away, you're going to blow him away first.

And then we're going home.

— *South Vietnam on Trial, Volume 11 of the Time Life series The Vietnam Experience,* **Boston Publishing Company (1984).**

Kattar took a number of steps to keep the battalion effective and disciplined. He improved firebase security and required his men to change the positions of 105mm howitzers after dark. He ordered more patrolling and forbade the wearing of bandannas by men in the field, making them wear their steel pots. He also put a stop to one of the characteristic "grunt" symbols of the war — the wearing of belts of M-60 machine gun ammo crossed over the shoulders. Only the gunner could carry belts of ammo that way. The rest had to be carried in metal ammunition boxes.

Not surprisingly, men grumbled and complained. In some units, such measures might have made him a candidate for 'fragging' by disgruntled troops. But he also came out to the field and talked to the troops on a regular basis and even went with them on sweeps on the ground, something no battalion commander did, showing them that he shared the same risks they endured.

In February 1971, the men of the 1/5th were notified that the battalion would be leaving Vietnam in late March and that they would be standing down within a month. A few days before the battalion was due to leave the field, intelligence revealed that part of the 33rd NVA regiment was on the move and Kattar ordered the battalion into action, getting permission for the operation from the somewhat reluctant division commander, MG George Putnam.

Charlie Company made a night march and linked up with an attached troop of the 11th Armored Cavalry Regiment and at daybreak they swung off the road and headed into the jungle toward the suspected NVA camp, covering the sound of the tanks and armored cavalry vehicles with artillery fire. At dusk, Alpha and Delta companies air-assaulted from the other direction, hoping to catch the NVA fleeing from the ground assault. There were a few small firefights and some NVA tripped an automatic ambush, but for the most part they got away.

Still, while other units were refusing to go into the field, the 1/5th carried on until almost their last day. The end of the operation was described in *South Vietnam on Trial*:

> As the battalion came off the helicopter pad at Bien Hoa to stand down prior to leaving Vietnam, the troops were enthusiastic, shouting "All the way!" and "Airborne!" as they left the war behind them. General Putnam, who had come out to the airfield, was clearly moved by the sight, remarking that it was the picture he wished people would remember of the US soldier in Vietnam. "They were aggressive right up to the day they stood down," said Putnam. A writer from the division historical office asked operations officer Lt. Stube how the battalion commander [Kattar] had managed to get these troops to act as they did. "He is the finest leader I have ever known," Stube answered. "He motivated soldiers and officers to do the right thing."

On March 26, 1971, the 1st Cavalry Division stood down in Vietnam. A formal ceremony was held at Bien Hoa with speeches and the division band playing military marches. 1Lt Mike Kline was the last acting CO of Charlie Company in Vietnam, having taken command when Captain Parrish had to return to the States for surgery. Battalions began flying home and the men of Charlie Company returned to the US sometime in early April 1971. Most of them anyway—men with more than 90 days left to go in Vietnam were reassigned to units still there.

Most of these men went to a newly created 3rd Brigade Task Force, also called "The Garryowen Brigade", consisting of four infantry battalions and aviation, artillery, and support units. The battalions were the 2/5th, 1/7th, 2/8th and 1/12th and their mission was to continue to interdict trails in War Zone D, train Vietnamese units, guard the US large bases at Bien Hoa and Long Binh, and act as a reserve and continency force as other units departed.

The 1st Marine Division also left Vietnam in 1971, followed by the 25th Infantry Division, the 1st Brigade of the 5th Infantry Division, the 101st Airborne Division (Airmobile), and two brigades of the Americal Division. The 11th Armored Cavalry Regiment left in early 1972.

The 3rd Brigade left Vietnam in June 1972, although a battalion sized task force built around the 1/7th Cav remained for two more months. With this, the 1st Cavalry was the first full division to arrive in Vietnam and the last to leave. Leaving around the same time was the 3/21st Infantry, a battalion of the 196th Light Infantry Brigade, that had also stayed. Both battalions claim to have run the last US combat patrol in the war. Some men stayed and were reassigned to static security companies, but there were no more American combat units in South Vietnam for the first time in more than seven years.

While in Vietnam, the 1st Cavalry lost 5,444 troopers killed and another 26,592 wounded, more than the division's casualty totals for World War II and the Korean War combined. Not counted as a KIA in this number is John Nacy, who died in his home in Detroit, MI, in November 1975 of the effects of wounds he received on December 29, 1968, in the same firefight where Lt Rathmann was killed.

Photographs

Captain John Pope, First Sergeant Ralph Caveto and Sgt. Bob Parrish
(L to R) near An Khe, 1965. Photograph by Bob Parrish.

Charlie Company on search and destroy mission. Bong Son 1966. Photograph by Rick Roy.

Bong Son 1966. Photograph by Dean Shultis.

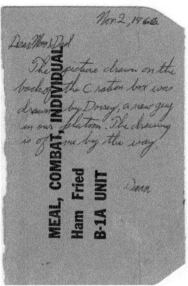

Drawing of Dean Shultis by Carlito Dorsey. November 1966.

PFC John Dalton. Fall 1966. Source unknown.

*1/5th Memorial service, December 1966. Captain Robert
Lowry and Charlie Company. Source unknown.*

LZ Bird the morning after the attack. December 27, 1966. Photograph by Dean Shultis.

SP4 William Fells checking a bunker in the coastal village.
December 1966. Photograph by Dean Shultis.

SP4 John Stumpf cleaning his M-60. Early 1967. Photograph by Jack Hanger.

Charlie's Hole, early 1967. Tyrone Moon on left, others unknown. Photograph by Jack Hanger.

Members of the third platoon eating sugar cane by a Viet Minh monument. SSgt Henry Brown on the left. Bong Son Plains. Early 1967. Photograph by Dean Shultis.

Village sweep on the Bong Son plains. February 1967. Photograph by Steve Hassett.

Medic Pete VanTil in a Bong Son village. Spring 1967. Photograph by Sonny Cowan.

Men of Charlie Company waiting for choppers. Fall 1967. Photograph by Gary Navratil.

Troopers Harry Wixon, Jack Sandin, Doc Rogers, Barry League,
and M.C. Kirby returning to the field after the last standdown
in An Khe. December 1968. Photograph by Neal Wolf.

First platoon setting up its blocking position at An Tinh. George Macias with his M-60. January 2, 1968. Photograph by Charlie Brown.

Charlie Company at LZ Pedro, waiting for choppers for assault on Quang Tri. January 31, 1968. Photograph by Charlie Brown.

*LZ Wharton in the morning. April 4, 1968. Medic Marv
Anklam on the left without helmet. Associated Press.*

*Captain Joe Lyttle, WIA 4 April, Top Robert Fowler, KIA 4 May, and Captain Dan
Terry, WIA 9 May, at LZ Stud. April 3 1968. Photograph by Charlie Brown.*

Patrick Manijo and Leonard Silva at LZ Stud. Early May 1968. Source unknown.

Night ambush leaving the perimeter. June 1968. Photograph by Don Heth.

David Keene and Dennis Rondorf on a perimeter bunker.
Fall 1968. Photograph by Gerald Ruesler.

C-rations in the field. 1969. Photograph by Dave Hart.

John Grose on patrol. 1970. Photograph by Dave Hart.

Charlie Company troopers boarding a Chinook. 1970. Photograph by Dave Hart.

Captain Bill Vowell. 1970. Source unknown.

Steve Branham in 1970. Photograph by R Dean Sharp.

Third brigade commander Col. Robert Kingston addressing Charlie Company on a firebase.
Early 1970. Captain Kevin Corcoran standing at left. Photograph by Fred Escalante.

Captain Kevin Corcoran on two radios at "the City" in Cambodia.
Early May 1970. Photograph by R Dean Sharp.

Charlie Company troopers and a Kit Carson scout at "The City". Michael
Tuff fourth from left. Early May 1970. Photograph by R Dean Sharp.

Charlie Company leaving Cambodia. June 1970. Photograph by Fred Escalante.

Jim Stein on patrol. 1970. Photograph by Dave Hart.

Part 5: Charlie Company — A Day in The Life

Claude Newby was a battalion chaplain who did two tours in Vietnam with the 1st Cavalry, the first in Bong Son with the 2/8th Cav in 1966-1967 and the second with the 1/5th and 1/9th Cavs in 1969. He later wrote about his experiences in *It Took Heroes: A Cavalry Chaplain's Memoirs of Vietnam*, where he included this description of life for an infantryman in Vietnam:

The regular infantryman's combat tour was a year—if he made it all the way—of near-total misery. He was always wet and muddy or hot and soaked with sweat, engulfed in the stench of unwashed clothing and bodies. Often he drank water that was "fortified" with dead polli-wogs and leeches; and he was accustomed to finding leeches in unpleasant places on his person.

Several factors rendered the regular field troopers' existence incomparable to that of anyone else. These factors included carrying everything they needed on their backs; constant vigilance around the clock; unending danger; spirit-draining, backbreaking, and exhausting labor; and an existence almost devoid of such creature comforts as frequent baths, clean clothes, beds, and uninterrupted nights. They humped and dug every day. They pulled perimeter guard, OP duty, or ambush every night, no matter what else occurred. All this was interspersed with intentional dashes into combat and those totally unexpected times of terror during firefights and ambushes by the enemy. And with all this, the regular infantrymen got few breaks, even during occasional stints providing firebase security or palace guard. Exhaustion and sleepiness were the grunts' constant companions.

The infantryman came to the war alone, committed to a one-year tour. If he survived the first battle, he was accepted as a veteran. He lived in unrelenting stress and endured unimaginable horrors. Often, he would carry the bodies of killed or terribly wounded buddies, sometimes for hours until they could be flown from the field; there was no escape from close companionship with death and maiming. Nothing compares to the regular infantryman's existence in combat, not in the Army and not in life.

I don't hardly know how to explain what Vietnam is like. It is hot, humid, trashy, smelly, swampy, and overpopulated, that about sums it up. It is not the kind of place you would want to visit every day. So far all I have done is pull guard duty. I pull guard duty for four hours, then I'm off for eight. About the only bad time to pull it is at night, but I guess that beats filling sandbags or pulling K.P. I don't know how long I'll be here at the 90th Replacement. As soon as I get to my permanent company, I'll write and give you the address.

— Sonny Cowan (letter) 1966

The next day I was flown to An Khe for I had been assigned to C Company, 1st Battalion, 5th Cavalry, an infantry unit. The chicken house looking barracks were in rows and there was a lot of smoke. Here, the restrooms were not in barracks — they were outhouses with oil barrels cut in half to catch the waste. Each morning the new guys got the privilege of latrine detail: pulling those half barrels out into the open, pouring diesel fuel into them, and then setting fire to them. About midway through the process, you had to stir each of them with a 2 by 4 several times until it was completely burned up. That's when I realized where all the smoke was coming from. Not to mention the smell.

— **Minor Chaney 1967**

Early in the morning the rain and lightning hit and it was a terrible storm. The water literally ran up hill. I was sharing the tent with my platoon sergeant and the weapons squad leader. We would take two ponchos and snap them together using tree limbs to hold it up. We literally held the tent down to keep if from blowing away. When the storm passed, I was soaking wet, as well as everyone else. My air mattress had sprung a leak and was flat; and the runoff from the rain was down my back. I thought, well it is almost time to get up anyway and looked at my watch. It was 1:30 in the morning

— **Jim Wolfe 1966**

While in the field, we usually woke up between 5:00 — 6:00 am. Breakfast was c-rations. If you wanted to heat part of the meal, we sometimes had heat tabs but more often it was done with a piece of C-4 plastic explosive. Ignited with a blasting cap, C-4 is a high explosive, but lit with a match it burns but does not explode. There would be time to shave, wash up, and brush our teeth. Water for this was a small amount in the "steel pot," the outer part of the helmet. We would take up our nighttime defensive measures and clean up the camp. Any unused food would be opened and burned or buried so as not fit to be salvaged by the enemy. With few exceptions, we moved every day, typically walking 3-6 miles but sometimes longer distances. We carried everything needed on a belt and in or on a rucksack. On my belt I typically carried a 2-quart canteen, 2 or 3 hand grenades, and an ammo pack with about 20 magazines for the M-16 or machine gun ammo when I carried the machine gun. I carried smoke grenades, empty sandbags, and except during the monsoon season another 2 or 3 quarts of water attached to the rucksack. In the rucksack, I typically carried 2 or 3 additional grenades, toiletries, a couple of pairs of socks, air mattress, poncho, poncho liner, C-4 plastic explosives, C-rations, and sometimes additional ammo. When I was the machine gunner or assistant, I also carried at least 2 belts of machine gun ammo angled across my shoulders. A squad also carried several claymore anti-personnel mines with wire and detonator and trip flares which everyone shared in carrying.

— Don Phillips 1969

One night in the rainy season we set up camp for the night and I lay down to rest and covered up with my poncho. I had to get up twice in the night for guard duty. After going back after the second time, I got about another hour of sleep. The next morning as I was folding my poncho, a bamboo viper comes out of my bed. These snakes are very poisonous. He must have slept with me to stay dry. We jokingly referred to the two different kinds of snake we saw the most as a one-step or a two-step. That was about how far you could make it and live after being bitten by one.

— Larry Touchstone 1970

At the Battalion outdoor movie, they have television night. This night they showed the TV show "Combat". Boy whoever made that decision sure has a warped sense of humor.

— Jim Wolfe (letter) 1966

Nights in the jungle. They were dark, wet, and cold, but perhaps most disturbing of all, eerily quiet. The jungle treetops were so high that they blocked out not only available light but sometimes obliterated the entire sky as well. There were no stars out there to reach out to or attempt to hold on to. When we lay down on the ground at night on our chosen lonely spot, our thoughts came ricocheting back at us loudly. Hearing ourselves think was the only conversation available at times. So, we got used to it. We talked to ourselves, and then rolled over and got some rest until it was our turn at radio watch.

— Roger Allan Byer 1970

I remember as we moved off of the LZ, one of the machine gunners was carrying his M-60 machine gun on his shoulder. He went under a low hanging tree limb and hit it with the gun. Well, there was a large ant mound on that limb which then landed on his back. Never saw a man strip completely nude so quickly.

— Jim Wolfe 1966

After being in the field about four days, I began to feel pretty chafed and raw from all the walking and sweating in the heat and humidity. I asked Neil if there was any baby powder available. He looked at me in disbelief and said, "Man, are you still wearing those underwear? You need to throw those things away!" Now, I was not about to go without underwear, but as time wore on, so did my drawers. I kept getting more and more chafed and raw until I nearly couldn't walk, So I thought I would try his advice. Sometimes, it pays off to listen to someone with some experience.

— Minor Chaney 1967

Yesterday evening we had a total of eight Viet Cong captured. About ten minutes before a chopper came in to pick them up, one of our prisoners took off running. The bad thing about it was we didn't catch him. Later when the interpreter was questioning the other prisoners, we found out that the one that got away was a VC company commander. I guess that's the breaks of the game…Today we captured six more VC. It really gets scary going down in those tunnels and pulling them out. Needless to say, just as soon as we got our prisoners today we tied them up, nobody got away.

— Sonny Cowan (letter) 1967

I arrived at An Khe just before Christmas of Dec 1966. I thought it was a tank unit, but when I was issued all my equipment and they told me I was going to an infantry company, I told them right away that I was a tanker. I was told to go next door and talk to Colonel Siegrist. I reported to the Colonel and he wanted to know how he could help me. I told him that I was a tanker and they were sending me to an infantry unit. He told me to pick up my boots and look at the bottom. Then he asked me what they looked like, and I told him the tread on a tank. He then told me to "put them on and to truck your ass on over to the infantry company." They had just lost almost the whole company in a battle. I said, "Sir, I am drawing pro pay as a tanker" and he said he would make a deal with me that I would draw pro pay for the whole time I was in Vietnam until I got back to the States, plus one year, if I did get back to the States. So, I saluted him and went to the infantry company.

— **Bill Sharp 1966**

When I first joined the squad in the field, I had been warned about a guy in the squad named Baker who had the bad habit of turning the time forward on the wristwatch being used to keep track of the guard. By doing so, he made his turn on guard come to an end that much quicker. Mysteriously that night on LZ John, the wristwatch we were using gained quite a bit of time. Baker had been up to his old tricks. I do not know why Baker was so against taking his turn on watch, since he probably slept on duty anyway.

— **John Nowling 1967**

Charlie Company is still in Pleiku. Several of us officers from the Battalion went up to the MACV compound and ate at their mess hall. They had tables, tablecloths, plates, and real silverware. Our normal meal is c-rations that come in a cardboard box with a plastic spoon wrapped in plastic. We were all muddy and dirty and tracked mud in their nice, clean eating area, not to say what we did to their showers. The next day the Compound was placed off limits to us combat troopers.

— **Jim Wolfe (letter) 1966**

We've been out on another long Range Patrol for the last 6 days. From where we were at, we flew to LZ Ollie and joined up with the rest of the company. Then we started walking. The first day out, we walked over the top of a mountain range and down in another valley. We set up ambushes that night. The next day, we went on patrols up in the hills and set up ambushes down in the valley that night. Then the next day, we went back up in the draws. That night we set up with the rest of the company and went patrolling the next day. That night we got up at 2 o'clock and surrounded a village on the other side of the valley. After we checked it out, we went up in the hills for the rest of the day and then we went on a night patrol that night. The next day we slept and tried to keep dry because it was raining. We went on a night patrol again that night. Is sure is fun stumbling and falling down in rice paddies and streams. It's bad enough trying to walk in the daytime.

— Gary Clayton (letter) 1967

One day the villagers brought a small boy and his brother into our compound. They had found a "DUD" M79 grenade and had been kicking it around when it went off. The older brother did not have serious wounds, but the younger one, who looked about five years old, had chest and stomach wounds. He lay there with his eyes wide open and did not cry while our Medic got him ready to transport. After they took him, we never heard what happened to him. Thirty-five years later at a reunion I met a man who had been at Quan Loi when the dust-off bird arrived. The little boy had died on the trip.

— Larry Touchstone 1970

One of the men in the platoon got a letter from his wife and she wants a divorce. They have a two-month-old son. He has only four months left in Vietnam but she will not wait and wants the divorce now.

— Jim Wolfe (letter) 1966

We had some fantastic Medevac pilots flying choppers. One guy had four helicopters shot out from under him in one day and came back again. I had to threaten another Medevac pilot because he wouldn't come down and pick up our wounded. That gives you the range of how good and how bad some of these helicopter pilots were.

— John Zajdlik 1969

Medic Dick "Doc" Boutileir, from Great Falls, Montana, exemplified bravery. When I carried an M-79 grenade launcher I also had a .45 automatic pistol. During an engagement, Doc GAVE AWAY HIS RIFLE (!) to somebody whose weapon had jammed and used my .45, which would have worked best by throwing it.

— Richard Levenson 1968

The other squad had already gone into the bunker complex, just out of our sight…Before we could get up and start moving in to help, our platoon leader came back out. I was the first one he saw, and he said, "Touchstone swap rifles with me"…We were trained to follow orders instantly without question or I never would have done it, so I handed him my rifle. The platoon leader grabbed my M-16 and dropped his CAR-15 into my hands…At first,

I couldn't understand why he did this, but as soon as I tried to clear and check his weapon, I found he was a sorry Officer. The rifle was rusty and dirty and when he fired the first round it has frozen in the chamber. I immediately tried to get it out with a cleaning rod, but it was stuck so tight that I couldn't move it. So, I find myself in a bunker complex without a working rifle because of a sloppy officer.

The only weapons I had was a bayonet and 6 hand grenades ... I remember getting a rifle later that afternoon from one of the wounded men that was sent back on the dust-off ... I never saw the platoon leader that took my rifle again, because I was wounded that night and spent two weeks back in the rear. By the time I got back that platoon leader had been transferred.

— **Larry Touchstone 1969**

Nothing really exciting has happened today. Another of our lieutenants came back with me the other day. He came in to see the doctor for he hasn't been able to keep anything in his stomach. But I think that I know what's wrong with him, he's lost his nerve. The kid hadn't been here but two weeks when his platoon got in a firefight and he got shot through the leg. He has been here about two months and he got out of the hospital about a week ago. When I get back off R&R I am going to take him back to the field with me if I have to throw him on the airplane. It's his only chance or he will go off his rocker.

— **Jim Wolfe (letter) 1966**

One day Top (Fowler) and I had a M79 shooting contest. I won and Top gave me a smack on the back and walked away without saying a word. That was enough for me ... a few days later he had me covering his back when he went out on one of his far flank afternoons.

— Bill Pelton 1967

Our descent down the Cay Giep mountains was accompanied by a tremendous display of firepower that day. Artillery from land batteries and even from a ship at sea was walked down the mountain ahead of us, When the artillery would let up, tactical jet air strikes were dropping fragmentation bombs and even napalm. Large pieces of metal from napalm canisters were falling into the treetops near us. If that were not enough, a huge thunderstorm moved in on us and drenched us with heavy rain accompanied by wind and lightning. We kept moving until nightfall. It was impossible to establish a defensive perimeter on a steep mountain trail at night so we just stopped in place and teamed up two men to a position along the trail, so one man at a time could sleep. There was an eerie illumination in the near distance that was kept up all night for the company that had had the heaviest contact. Puff the Magic Dragon kept a stream of tracer rounds from its Gatling guns pouring into the mountainside most of the night.

— John Nowling 1967

Exiting a helicopter hovering six feet above the ground when you were carrying a rucksack with all your food, supplies, and clothes, M-16 rifle in one hand, your medical aid kit in the other; two twelve clip bandoliers of ammo and four full water bottles strapped around your torso; wearing a heavy steel pot helmet, dealing with a swaying platform and the backwash of other choppers flying nearby; along with the possibility you are already taking hostile fire, and scared shitless as was routine on those occasions—well, it always struck me that there had to be a better way.

— Roger Allan Byer 1970

Around this time a man named Ernie was at the end of his tour. He had a very "hot" girlfriend and had been showing pictures of her to everyone. Ernie had a cassette tape player and his girlfriend must have been one of the first to record sex messages on one. We were not aware Ernie had these tapes, as he kept them hidden. When he left for home, he forgot and left one of the tapes in his bunker. Our CO found it and late one night he played the tape on the Battalion radio network. This was totally unexpected; no one knew he had it.

The girl friend did not leave out any details. She would say, "I'm doing this to you Ernie and you are doing that to me." She was making sound effects with the headboard and bed springs. Then it was, "OH Ernie, OH Ernie." If that girl only knew what effect she had on all of those guys. We never heard from Ernie again, so we always wondered what happened to them. For many months after that tape was broadcast, every now and then you could hear one of the men say, as he was throwing sandbags on his bunker, "OOOH Ernie." Things like this were sometimes all that kept us going.

— Larry Touchstone 1969

You said you were going to go exploring in the mountains around there. That's about all I see around here—mountains. If we aren't walking straight up or straight down the side of one of them, we're walking ankle deep in rice paddies' mud. I haven't decided which is worse. We're supposed to be completely air mobile. Sure, they fly us out to where we start walking and believe me, they make Basic & AIT seem like Sunday picnics.

Vietnam is a beautiful country, although most of the time I'm too tired to notice. It's beautiful to look at, but it's really Hell to try to walk through. It is pretty well torn-up in places but when you get way out in the boonies, it's pretty much intact. When you get up in the air, it looks pretty bad with all the artillery, ARA, and bomb holes, but down on the ground you don't notice it. That's because it's so dense you usually can't see more than 10 or 15 meters. The monsoons are starting and it rains every day.

— **Gary Clayton (letter) 1967**

Back in the States, when we were boarding the plane to go to Vietnam, a group of men were there, and they were passing out Bibles, each one a small New Testament along with Psalms and Proverbs. I carried mine with me all over Vietnam and it became a great source of comfort and security for me … A day or so after Bernie Poblock was killed, we had a little time, and I was going to read a little from my Bible. I'd always carried it in my left shirt pocket, but I didn't button the flap down and when I reached for it, it wasn't there. I looked all through my gear and where I'd slept that night, but it was nowhere to be found … I was devastated that my Bible was gone. I was feeling like I was going into battle with no ammo, or at least no security …

A day or two later, we were preparing to make an air assault. The choppers were headed for our position, and we were ready to board as soon as they landed. I was the first troop on the first bird, and when I jumped into the aircraft, there was a little New

Testament just like mine, lying on the floor of the chopper. I picked it up and looked inside and there was no name or any kind of ID in it anywhere...There was no way for me to know who it belonged to, so my next thought was that God wanted me to have it. In fact, I believe He placed it there for me to find. I put it in my pocket and this time, I buttoned the flap. I carried that Bible with me the rest of my time. All the way from the Bong Son area to Hue, Quang Tri, Phu Bai, Khe Sanh, and the DMZ.

— Minor Chaney 1968

One night in Vietnam, our unit was up the Northern Mountains. It was Monsoon Season and there had been a lot of rain. Day and night, nothing but rain. The wind and rain were so hard one night, I had the men strapped to trees so we wouldn't get blown off of the mountain! Anyway, it was nightfall and I was sleeping through a very pleasant dream. Now that doesn't happen over there very often. But I was very warm and comfortable in my dreams. I don't remember the dreams, but I certainly didn't want to wake up. When I finally woke up, I found out why I felt so warm and cozy. I was completely under water, except for my face!!

— Ron Pape 1967

Marijuana was seldom used in the field but occasionally, not often, I could smell marijuana after dark from a nearby foxhole. Each squad had a location on the perimeter of our nighttime encampment. Not a single time was I aware of any drug used at my squad's foxhole location in the 9 months I was with them.

There was more use of marijuana when we were back at the safer conditions at the battalion landing zone. Marijuana was frequently being smoked after dark when things were quiet at the LZ. This included some, but not all, of my squad. Even then, I never saw anything out of the ordinary committed by troops high on drugs.

— Don Phillips 1969

On one occasion the platoon was online, and we were crossing a large open area. Possibly it was an old dried-up rice paddy. In any case, we had just moved out of the tree line, when across from the other tree line a large, fully grown water buffalo emerged. This one was big and not happy. He immediately took one look at us and began to snort and paw the ground in front of him. I looked at SFC Burchfield, my platoon sergeant. He took one glance at me and immediately stepped in front of the platoon. Without any hesitation, he immediately removed his steel pot, waved it in the air like a cowboy hat, and hollered "eeyie". The water buffalo took one look at Burchfield and immediately retreated back into the wood line it had come from. Yep, Burchfield was from Texas.

— Jim Wolfe 1967

I once confided to a brother soldier that I wanted to be sure my girlfriend would be faithful to me while I was in Nam. He suggested that I tell her that it would be okay to date while I was gone just in case I was killed here. He said that would make her love me more and promise to be faithful. Guess what! She said that she agreed and would start dating again and to thank your friend for his advice. I told him to watch his back on the next firefight!

— Larry Walsh 1970

One night early in our stay at LZ Hammond, Larry Bowling and I and one or two others were sitting on top of our bunker, talking quietly. Suddenly we were startled by a loud noise, followed suddenly by the anguished cry of a man in pain. We hastily took cover with our weapons at the ready and strained to make out details in the moonlight—there was the possibility that the shot had come from a sniper. After a few minutes our squad leader approached the bunker and told us what happened.

Woods had received a 'Dear John' letter earlier that day and had somehow managed to buy enough beer from the locals outside the wire to get drunk. In his drunkenness, he became despondent and wildly threatened to take his own life. He ran out of his bunker, claymore detonator in hand, and threw himself down near a claymore intending to blow himself up. John "Hardcore" Thomas was in the same bunker and rushed out after him to prevent the suicide. He did not grapple with Woods for the detonator but instead made a dive for the claymore in order to yank the blasting cap out of it. He had just removed it when Woods squeezed the detonator and the cap exploded in his right hand, shards of metal cutting through the muscles at the base of his thumb.

The wound was serious and Thomas was evacuated immediately and would miss about six weeks before coming back to the company. He had risked his life to save a drunken buddy from suicide and came within a fraction of a second of losing his own life. Woods was removed from the field for a few days, probably for psychiatric testing, and was soon back with us, to me a very disturbing presence.

— **John Nowling 1967**

Well, this is your stupid son who survived 10 months and 11 days of combat and got put in the hospital by an exploding garbage sump. I saw a box get blown out of the sump and walked over to see what it had in it to cause it to explode. While I was kneeling next to the sump it blew up again and I caught some fragments in my side and forehead. All I can figure is some yo-yo threw a grenade in there. I'm not really hurt but I am sore, the doc tried to get the frags out but he couldn't find them so he sewed me up and left them. I'm in the 85th Evac Hospital in Qui Nhon right now and I don't know how long I'll be here.

— **Jim Wolfe (letter) 1967**

My battalion went on a two-day raid into the An Lao Valley which turned out to last four days. So far on one mountain we have found and destroyed over seventy tons of rice … Yesterday we got into a firefight just as we were heading up the mountain … After about thirty minutes of fighting, we withdrew and called in artillery and jets. When we headed back up the mountain, we found all kinds of blood trails. We were checking out one of the caves and heard a baby crying. When the man came out of the cave he had three women, four, five children and a VC with half his arm blown off.

— **Sonny Cowan (letter) 1967**

Willie Harris, a man in third platoon, was in a fire fight in Cambodia. We carried our M16 magazines in bandoliers around our chest. Harris had an AK-47 round pass between his chest and the bandolier, cutting the side of a magazine open. There is less than ½ inch space there. It did not cut him or set off a round in the magazine. This is as close as it gets. He carried this magazine the rest of his time in Vietnam. He wanted to take it home with him. When he was processing out to go home, they told him it was government property. Even though it was totally useless to the army, he couldn't keep it.

— Larry Touchstone 1970

I was awarded the Bronze Star by General Tolson today. Do you think I should tell Mom about it, or do you think it would worry her more? I'm very proud of it, but I'd give it and a lot more to have the buddies back who died that day.

— Gary Clayton (letter) 1967

One of the boy's mother wrote and wanted to know exactly how her son was killed. He was killed in action about 3 months ago and he had been here about 30 days when he died. So, what am I supposed to do…write and say, "Look lady, your son was blown apart by a hand grenade because he didn't listen to his squad leader?" Of course, this isn't what I will say, although this is what happened. But why does she want to know? Good God, he's dead, he's dead. I'll tell her something but I don't know what. Mary, if these young kids would just listen to what we tell them and use their heads, they would walk off that airplane in Frisco instead of going off in a box. They've all seen the war movies and read the

384

war books and they all want to be heroes. They're anxious to get in a firefight. I guess that's the hell of it, they're all so young and I look at them and wonder how many will not make it back.

— Jim Wolfe (letter) 1966

My tour ended in mid-August with Charlie Company still in Bong Son. After processing out in An Khe, I flew out of Cam Ranh Bay on an Air Force cargo jet with a few hundred other men. Instead of stewardesses and hot meals, we had airmen in flight suits passing out box lunches, but no big deal—we were just glad to out of Vietnam.

We landed in California late the day before we left and were bussed to Oakland Army Terminal, getting there around midnight. In the next seven hours, we were fitted for new dress uniforms, fed steak and eggs, and had our orders reviewed for our next assignments. At about 8 AM I caught a cab to San Francisco International with two other sergeants I had met while processing. They were lifers and weren't infantry, but I was and had the props to prove it: blue infantry rope and the Combat Infantryman's Badge; airborne wings, ribbons, and the 1st Cav patch; and a gaunt look and deep tan from my neck to halfway up my forehead.

We had time and went to the airport bar and ordered beers. The bartender served the other two men but asked for my ID. He looked at it and said he couldn't serve me—I wasn't 21 yet. It had never occurred to me that would be an issue. He was matter of fact and the two lifers shrugged their shoulders and looked at their beers. I ordered a coke and sat there, wondering why I should be the one to feel embarrassed.

— Steve Hassett 1967

Afterword

The war ended for Charlie Company when it returned to the States in the spring of 1971, but it dragged on in Vietnam for another four years. Many of the key battles in those years took place in the areas previously fought over and guarded by Charlie Company and other units of the 1st Cavalry Division. In late March 1972, the NVA launched their Easter offensive across the DMZ, a conventional attack with hundreds of tanks and many of its best divisions, the largest such military operation since the Korean War. They followed it a week later with attacks against Kontum in the Central Highlands and Loc Ninh, An Loc, and Quan Loi on the approaches to Saigon.

Quang Tri City and the rest of Quang Tri Province fell to the NVA in less than a month and they got almost to Hue. No US ground forces were involved—the few remaining infantry battalions left South Vietnam as the offensive ground on—but the US responded with massive air support for the hard-pressed ARVN units. Tactical Air Force squadrons were sent back to Vietnam from South Korea and the US and five aircraft carriers sailed back into the Tonkin Gulf to conduct operations.

During July alone, American aircraft flew 5,461 tactical sorties and 2,054 B-52 strikes as the NVA attacks faltered and

ARVN units went on the offensive. The Nixon Administration also resumed widespread bombing of North Vietnam for the first time since late 1968, including B-52 strikes against Hanoi and the main North Vietnamese port of Haiphong for the first time in the war.

Ultimately, the NVA offensive failed and ARVN forces recaptured the ruins of Quang Tri City in September 1972, although the NVA continued to hold most of the rest of Quang Tri Province, including Dong Ha and Khe Sanh, as well as much of the border areas in the Central Highlands and the provinces north of Saigon. Peace talks resumed in Paris and in early October 1972, Henry Kissinger and his North Vietnamese counterpart Le Duc Tho reached a tentative peace agreement, which President Nixon hoped to have finalized and signed prior to the presidential election in early November 1972.

But the agreement had been negotiated without the involvement or consent of the South Vietnamese and contained provisions they would not agree to, even though Kissinger was aware of their stance as he negotiated with their enemy. When the South Vietnamese demanded additional provisions, the North Vietnamese also balked and the tentative agreement fell apart. In response, Nixon ordered additional bombing of Hanoi over the 1972 Christmas holiday. Many historians feel the purpose of the bombing was as much to convince the Saigon regime of US support as it was to punish the North Vietnamese.

Talks resumed in early January 1973 and the South Vietnamese fell into line when Nixon and Kissinger simultaneously threatened to unilaterally end all support to South Vietnam and made a secret commitment to South Vietnamese leader Nguyen Van Thieu to provide air support and military supplies if North Vietnam resumed offensive operations. This was a hollow promise as they knew there was no support for further operations in Congress or among the American people.

The "Agreement Ending the War and Restoring Peace in Vietnam" was signed by all parties on January 27, 1973 and was basically the same agreement that had been reached the previous October. The U.S. agreed to withdraw its remaining military personnel from South Vietnam within 60 days. North Vietnam agreed to a ceasefire and to return all American prisoners of war. North Vietnam was permitted to leave 150,000 soldiers and to retain the territory it controlled in South Vietnam. In addition, an International Commission of Control and Supervision was created to supervise the Peace Accords. According to US estimates, when the agreement was signed, the South Vietnamese military totaled about 920,000, with 210,000 being combat regulars and the rest regional and popular forces militia units and support troops. North Vietnamese forces in the south totaled about 219,000, 123,000 being NVA regulars and the rest Viet Cong and support troops.

By the end of March 1973, American POW's had been repatriated and almost all American troops had exited South Vietnam. MACV ceased to exist and most US equipment was turned over to the South Vietnamese. Only 250 military personnel remained as part of a new Defense Attache Office, along with a small contingent of Marines assigned to guard the US embassy in Saigon. By then, the International Commission of Control and Supervision was reporting that both the North and South Vietnamese were violating the terms of the Peace Agreement on a regular basis.

On April 2, 1973, South Vietnamese President Thieu concluded a two-day visit to the United States. Nixon promised continued economic aid to South Vietnam, dependent upon congressional approval, and Thieu pledged to never ask the United States to reintroduce American troops into South Vietnam. In mid-June, both houses of Congress passed a bipartisan bill that prohibited further US military activity in Vietnam, Laos Cambodia Vietnam War, although the U.S. continued to provide military equipment and economic support to the South Vietnamese. Nixon opposed the bill but it passed by veto proof margins and he was forced to sign it. Two weeks later, the last American to be inducted into the US military as a draftee began his term of service. He had been drafted in 1972, but his entry was delayed.

For the next year and a half, both North and South Vietnam routinely violated the terms of the Peace Agreement and jockeyed for position in anticipation of a resumption of the war. Richard Nixon resigned as President on August 9, 1974, avoiding impeachment for the Watergate scandal, and making any secret commitments he had made to South Vietnam effectively meaningless. In mid-December 1974, the North went on the offensive, attacking the provincial capital of Phuoc Long Province, northeast of Saigon. The axis of their attack came through Bo Duc, passing what had once been LZ Jerri. In a few weeks, they overran much of the province, destroying some ARVN units and taking over 2,400 prisoners.

The US did not respond to the NVA's offensive. Efforts by President Gerald Ford to get funding for new military aid for South Vietnam were defeated in Congress by wide bipartisan margins. With both the lack of a response by America and the poor performance of some of the ARVN units in Phuoc Long, the North Vietnamese decided to launch a general offensive in early 1975.

It began on March 4, 1975 in the Central Highlands with the goal of cutting South Vietnam in half, the same strategy feared by General Westmoreland and the Pentagon ten years earlier when they deployed the 1st Cavalry Division there. Soon after, additional attacks were made against Quang Tri, Hue, and Da Nang to the north. Some ARVN units initially fought well, but others collapsed, with thousands of soldiers deserting and throwing away their weapons and uniforms. The Saigon regime panicked and ordered what was left of their best units south to defend Saigon, abandoning the northern two-thirds of the country. Within a month, the NVA had taken Kontum, Pleiku, An Khe, Qui Nhon, and Quang Tri, as well as all the villages, valleys, and mountains members of Charlie Company had fought and died in from 1965 through the end of 1968.

Battles for the approaches to Saigon continued for another month. Charlie Company's Area of Operation in the last years of its deployment was quickly overrun by the NVA. On April 23, 1975, President Ford gave a speech at Tulane University and stated: "Today America can regain the sense of pride that existed before Vietnam, But it cannot be achieved by refighting a war that is finished as far as America is concerned." Saigon fell and the South Vietnamese government surrendered on April 30, 1975.

But for many of the men of Charlie Company who made it home, the war never finished and is refought in their minds and memories on a regular basis. And in those memories, the men of Charlie Company who died in Vietnam remain young and present.

About one hundred forty-four men assigned or attached to Charlie Company died in its sixty-seven months of combat operations in Vietnam. The exact number may never be known. There are discrepancies in the accounts of the company's larger battles in the war, as well as with people's memories of events and the toll they took throughout the war. Names have still been added to the list of known dead from the company five decades after their deaths.

The term 'combat operations' covers a lot of ground, both literally and as a way of labeling a man's death. Charlie Company did cover a lot of ground in South Vietnam, operating in three different parts of the country, each with its own distinct terrain, on missions reflecting the changing goals and circumstances of the war. And the category of combat operations is as vast as each man's death was both 'typical' for the time and place of the war and unique to that man, the men with him when and as he died, and those left behind 'back in the world.'

If the pace of death was steady through the war, Charlie Company would have had slightly more than two men killed in each of its sixty-seven months in-country. But the numbers ebbed and flowed. One man was killed in 1965 and then fifty-nine died in 1966, the worse year for Charlie Company. More than half of them died in the Ia Drang Valley on November 21, 1966, the deadliest day for the company. In the three months prior to that, another seventeen men died on search and destroy missions in the Chu Pong and Soui Ca Mountains. Those three months and one week account for over a third of the combat deaths for the company.

The death toll dropped in 1967, with eighteen men killed, most in firefights in March and October. For most of the year, the company was involved in the Binh Dinh Pacification campaign and operated in and around villages. While firefights were less common, it was likely the worst year for the company for men seriously wounded by booby-traps.

1968 brought a new mission and environment and casualties doubled, with thirty-seven men killed that year, seventeen of them in the first week of May. The combined total of over fifty dead and wounded from the battle in the dunes on May 9th is the highest for Charlie Company for any one day or battle in the war. The end of the year brought another change of mission and environment as the 1st Cavalry moved south to screen the Cambodian border. Twenty-seven men died there in 1969 and ten died in 1970, five of them in the Cambodian incursion in May and June. One man died in January 1971 of a wound he received in a firefight the previous month.

Of these deaths, twelve were by friendly fire, over half by misfired artillery or mortar rounds and the others shot by mistake by another man in the company. One more man was intentionally killed by a South Vietnamese scout he shared a position with. Four men drowned, two swept away trying to cross a river in a monsoon storm and two swimming in the South China Sea on a sunny day during a twenty-four-hour truce with the Viet Cong. As least five of the men killed in action were medics attached to the company from battalion headquarters.

At the time of their deaths, eighty-one men were PFCs and thirty-six were SP4s. Another twelve were Sergeants E-5, or 'Buck' Sergeants, most of them squad leaders. During the first year of the war, they were mostly men with three to five years in the Army. From 1967 on, they were men who had been promoted to sergeant in the field. Another nine men were Staff Sergeants and Sergeants First Class. The highest-ranking enlisted man killed in Vietnam in Charlie Company was Master Sergeant Robert Fowler, the company's First Sergeant from late 1966 to May 1968.

Five of the dead were First or Second Lieutenants, all platoon leaders. Charlie Company had fifteen Captains as company commanders, plus two or three lieutenants as acting commanders, during its sixty-seven months in Vietnam. At least six of the company commanders were wounded while leading Charlie Company, but none were killed, making the company luckier that way than the other companies of the 1/5th Cav.

Six men were eighteen years old when they were killed and another twenty-nine were nineteen. There were twenty-nine men aged twenty, thirty-two men aged twenty-one and eleven men aged twenty-two. Another thirty-six men were age twenty-three or older, mostly career soldiers. At least thirty of the casualties were African American, and twelve more were Hispanic. Of the one hundred and twenty-nine men who were E-5 or under when they died, seventy-seven of them had been drafted and fifty-two were enlistees. The dead came from thirty-seven states and Puerto Rico.

In addition to the combat deaths, two men are known to have died from malaria and encephalitis while in Vietnam. Another man died of malaria about a month after getting out of the Army. He was discharged directly from Vietnam in late 1965 and did not show symptoms until he was five days home. The last man counted as a Charlie Company casualty died at home from his wound in 1975, five years after he received it. Others may have died of the effects of their wounds or of a disease contracted in Vietnam in the months or years after they left the country without anyone they served with ever learning of their deaths. More may have died in the ensuing decades of the effects of exposure to Agent Orange, which was heavily used in many of the areas where Charlie Company operated.

For the rest of us, maybe our experience is best summed up by a line from one of Bob Dylan's songs: "You can always come back, but you can't come back all the way."

Acknowledgements

My thanks and deepest appreciation to everyone who has helped and contributed to this history. While my name may be on the cover, it is really a collective effort and could not have been done without the input of all of the veterans of Charlie Company who are quoted or mentioned in these pages, as well as other individuals who provided resources or allowed me to quote from their works. Special thanks to Kevin Corcoran, Dan Barlow, John McGuire, Charlie Brown, Mike Kline and John Nowling for proofreading, editorial suggestions, providing me with copies of military records they possessed, and their general support for this project. Thanks also to Jim Wolfe, Roger Byers, Larry and Barbara Touchstone, Bob Parrish, Patrick Manijo, Minor Chaney, Don Phillips, Mary Moore, Claude Newby, Sharon Clayton, Kevin Knudsen, Dean Shultis, Dean Sharp, Dave Hart, Fred Escalante, and Amy Cowan Sanchez for providing and allowing use of their previously written material, letters, and photos. And a special thanks to my wife Marie for her support of this project, even as it seemed to take on a life of its own, her proofreading and editorial assistance, and for having my back on the days I delved deeper into my and others' memories of Vietnam.

Bibliography and Map References:

Byers, Roger Allan, *Tattooed Memories: Under the Canopy of the Vietnam War*, Clunis Publishing (2014)

Clayton, Sharon, *Remembering Gary*, Presto PhotoBook (2011)

Coleman, Maj. J. D., *The 1st Air Cavalry Division: Vietnam August 1965 — December 1969*, Editor in Chief, HQ, First Cavalry Division (Airmobile) (1970)

Coleman, J.D., *Incursion*, St. Martin's Press (1991)

Coleman, J.D., *Pleiku: The Dawn of Helicopter Warfare in Vietnam*, St. Martin's Press (1988)

Garland, John M., *Stemming the Tide: Combat Operations in Vietnam*, May 1965 to October 1966, Center of Military History, U.S. Army (2000)

Marshall, S. L. A., *West to Cambodia* (Chapter: "Ordeal By Ambush"), Battery Press (1968)

Miller, Sergio, *No Wider War: A History of the Vietnam War*, Vol. 2: 1965-75, Osprey Publishing (2021)

Karnow, Sidney, *Vietnam: A History*, Viking (1983)

MacGarrigle, George L., *Taking the Offensive: Combat Operations in Vietnam*, October 1966 to October 1967, Center of Military History, U.S. Army (1998)

Maitland, Terrence, *South Vietnam on Trial*, Volume 11 of the Time Life series The Vietnam Experience, Boston Publishing Company (1984)

Newby, Claude, *It Took Heroes: A Cavalry Chaplin's Memoirs of Vietnam*, Presidio Press (2003)

Shawcross, William, *Sideshow: Kissinger, Nixon, and the Destruction of Cambodia*, Revised edition, Cooper Square Press (2002)

Stanton, Shelby L., *Anatomy of a Division: The 1st Cav in Vietnam*, Presidio Press (1987)

Stanton, Shelby L., *The Rise and Fall of an American Army: U.S. Ground Forces in Vietnam*, 1965-1975, Presidio Press (1985)

Starry, Gen. Donn A., *Vietnam Studies: Mounted Combat in Vietnam*, Department of the Army, 2002

Touchstone, Barbara, *Silent Heroes*, (Self-published 2020)

Villard, Eric, *The 1968 Tet Offensive Battles of Quang Tri City and Hue*, Center of Military History, U.S. Army (2008).

Villard, Eric, S*taying the Course: Combat Operations in Vietnam, October 1967 to September 1968*, Center of Military History, U.S. Army (2017).

Wilkins, Warren, *Grad Their Belts to Fight Them: The Viet Cong's Big Unit War Against the U.S., 1965-1966*, Naval Institute Press (2011)

"Vietnam Combat Operations 1965: A chronology of Allied combat operations in Vietnam", Stephane Moutin-Luyat, (2009).

"Vietnam Combat Operations 1966: A chronology of Allied combat operations in Vietnam", Stephane Moutin-Luyat, (2009)

"Vietnam Combat Operations 1967: A chronology of Allied combat operations in Vietnam", Stephane Moutin-Luyat, (2011)

"History of the First Battalion, Fifth Cavalry Regiment "Black Knights": 1 July 1965—31 December 1965", Captain Harold B. Aldrich III, Adjutant, HQ, First Battalion, Fifth Cavalry (1966)

"History of the First Battalion, Fifth Cavalry Regiment "Black Knights": 1 January 1966—31 December 1966", 1Lt. Clayton Knowles, Liaison Officer, HQ, First Battalion, Fifth Cavalry (1967)

"History of the First Battalion, Fifth Cavalry Regiment "Black Knights": 1 January 1967—31 December 1967", 1Lt. Richard E. Paelen Jr., Liaison Officer, HQ, First Battalion, Fifth Cavalry (1968)

"Operation Irving: 2—24 October 1966", Captain Charles S. Sykes, Jr., Unit Historical Report No. 5, First Air Cavalry Division Office of Information and History (1967)

"The Battle of Charlie 1st of the 5th on the Cambodian Border: 21 November 1966", 1Lt William E. Kail, Unit Historical Report No. 7, First Air Cavalry Division Office of Information and History (1967)

"The Attack on LZ Bird: 21 December 1966", 1LT William B. Fisher, Unit Historical Report No. 8, First Air Cavalry Division Office of Information and History (1967)

"Hill 534: 14-15 August 1966", 1Lt William E. Kail, Unit Historical Report No. 12, First Air Cavalry Division Office of Information and History (1967)

"Combat After Action Report, Operation Eagles Claw", HQ, Second Brigade, First Cavalry Division (Airmobile), 16 March 1966

"Combat Operations After Action Report (Mosby II)", 1Lt

James Long, Adjutant, HQ, 1st Battalion (Airmobile), 5th Cavalry, 1st Cavalry Division (Airmobile).

"Operations Report for 1 Feb to 30 Apr 70", 1Lt Dennis K. Macvittie, HQ, 1st Battalion (Airmobile), 5th Cavalry, 1st Cavalry Division (Airmobile).

"Operations Report—Lessons Learned: 1 May—31 July 1970", HQ, 1st Cavalry Division (AM)

"After Action Report: Battle of An Tinh", Captain John A. Topper, 1st Battalion (Mech), 50th Infantry

"The Battle of Binh An", Major Ralph B. Garrison Jr., Armor Magazine, July-August 1969

"The 11 Armored Cavalry Regiment in Vietnam, January 1969 through June 1970", Major Edward Chesney, Master's Thesis, US Army Command and General Staff College, Ft. Leavenworth

"Bombs Over Cambodia", Taylor Owen and Ben Kiernan, The Walrus, October 2006

"Saber", 1st Cavalry Division Association, Volume 50, Number 5, September/October 2001

Don Moore article on John Zajdlik, Charlotte Sun, Port Charlotte, FL, 6 June 2011. Donmooreswartales.com/2011

Vietnam Magazine, December 2012, "'Sugarbear' and the Mod Squad", Bennie R. Atkins

Vietnam Magazine, August 2021, "1st Cav's Return to Ia Drang: Another Ambush and High Casualties", Steve Hassett

The First Team Magazine, Spring 1970, "The Pacification Company", SP4 Dennis Thornton

Map References

The University of Texas Tech maintains a large library of documents related to the war in Vietnam, including most of the topographical maps used by US units on day-to-day operations. These can be found at https://maps.lib.utexas.edu/maps/topo/vietnam/. The names of the maps and the specific grid coordinates of locations and incidents mentioned or described in this history are listed below. For large geographical features (such as the An Loa Valley), only the map name is listed. For smaller features or events (firebases, firefights, etc), coordinates are also listed when available, but they are only as accurate as the records they are taken from. For larger bases or features (such as Camp Radcliffe, Utah Beach, the Razorback) or events, the coordinates are for the approximate center of the base or event.

Location/Incident	Map Name	Coordinates
Battle in Iron Triangle, 2/16-20/66	Tien Thuan	775758
Battle for Hill 534, 8/14-16/66	Pl Ya Bo	861958

Location/Incident	Map Name	Coordinates
Battle at Hoa Hoi, 10/2-3/66	Phu My	032699
Battle in Ia Drang Valley, 11/21/66	Pl Ya Bo	759175
Battle for LZ Bird, 12/27/66	Hoai An	730805
Battle on Bong Son Plains, 3/20-21/67	Tam Quan	853093
Battle at Dam Tra-O Lake, 1/2/68	Bong Son	998832
Battle of Quang Tri, 1/31/68	Ba Long	362490
Battle for Old French Fort, 4/5-7/68	Huang Hoa	865375
Battle at Dong Ha, 5/9/68	Quang Tri	236678
Battle at Binh An, 6/27/68	Thon Ngo Xa Dong	400635
Battle in Rubber Plantation, 2/28-3/2/69	Tri Tam	N/A
Battle for LZ Dolly, 3/26/69	Tri Tam	523587
Battle for LZ Jerri, 11/7-11/69	Phuoc Binh	960225

Location/Incident	Map Name	Coordinates
Firefight, 9/29/66	Phu My	871730
Firefight, 10/15-16/66	Tien Thuan	757748
Firefight, 12/20/66	Kan Nak	382559
Firefight, 2/7/67	An Lao	747042
Firefight, 4/13/67	Mo Duc	827420
Firefight, 4/22/67		
Firefight, 10/7/67	Hoai An	823784
Firefight, 2/16/68	Ba Long	287483
Firefight, 4/14/68	Huang Hoa	828321
Firefight, 5/4/68	Huang Hoa	788375
Firefight, 8/2/68	Ba Long	72316
Firefight, 8/28/68	Ba Long	290330
Firefight, 9/18/68	Ba Long	325345/333344
Firefight, 11/1/68		
Firefight, 12/29/68	Dong Xoai	984781
Firefight, 1/9/69	Dong Xoai	983860
Firefight, 4/7-8/69		
Firefight, 5/25/69		
Firefight, 6/1/69		
Firefight, 11/29/69	Phuoc Binh	097162
Firefight, 1/8/70	Loc Ninh	810087
Firefight, 5/23/70	O Rang	361597
Firefight, 6/19-21/70	O Rang	289561
Firefight, 9/18/70	Xa Tram Da Mi	130431

Location/Incident	Map Name	Coordinates
LZ Albany	Pl Ya Bo	943043
LZ Columbus	Pl Ya Bo	975035
LZ Crystal	Phu My	893661
LZ Dog	Bong Son	882996
LZ Dolly	Tri Tam	523588
LZ Eagle 1	An Loc	700925
LZ Eleanor	Dong Xoai	918732
LZ English	Bong Son	878007
LZ Falcon	Xuong Kuang	025035
LZ Fort Granite	Phuoc Binh	929082
LZ Golf	Pl Ya Bo	847077
LZ Hammond	Phu My	884536
LZ Hawk	Pl Ya Bo	765190
LZ Hereford	Tien Thuan	652625
LZ Jane	Ba Long	377428
LZ Jerri	Phuoc Binh	960225
LZ Lori	Tri Tam	607621
LZ Montezuma	Mo Duc	814385
LZ Peanuts	Huang Hoa	809390
LZ Pedro	Ba Long	249485
LZ Pony	Hoai An	801829
LZ Shirley	An Loc	773897
LZ Stud	Thon Doc Kinh	000485
LZ Two Bits	Bong Son	845945
LZ Uplift	Phu My	928755
LZ Wharton	Thon Doc Kinh	879364
LZ X-Ray	Pl Ya Bo	934010
FSB David	O Rang	346653

Location/Incident	Map Name	Coordinates
An Khe/Camp Radcliffe	An Tuc	465480
An Loc	An Loc	758885
An Lao River and Valley	An Lao, Hoai An	
Bo Duc	Phuoc Binh	968252
"The City"	Map not available	
Deo Nang Pass	Binh Khe	581445
Black Virgin Mountain	Tay Ninh	280580
Bong Son Bridge	Bong Son	872959
Camp Evans	Hai Lang	535312
Coastal village (1/1/67)	Bong Son	979897
Co Roc Mountains	Huong Hoa	745315
Crescent Mountains	Bong Son	880780
Crow's Foot	Hoai An	735805
Dak To	Dak To	004217
Dong Ha	Quang Tri2	45613
Duc Co SF Camp	Thanh An	840255
Gay Giap Mountains	Bong Son9	32904
Gio Linh	Quang Tri	215732
Happy Valley	Tien Thuan & Binh Khe	
Ho Son Mountains/ Iron Triangle	Hoai An	815770
Kan Nak SF Camp	Kan Nak	420648
Khe Sanh Combat Base	Huong Hoa	845417

Location/Incident	Map Name	Coordinates
Kim Son River and Valley	Hoai An	
Kontum	Kontum	780890
Lai Giang River	Bong Son	
Lang Vei SF Camp	Huong Hoa	794363
Loc Ninh	Loc Ninh	738098
Mang Buk	Mang Buk	983417
Mang Yang Pass	Plei Troeh	229510
Michellin Rubber Plantation	Tri Tam	
O Rang	O Rang	366640
Phu Bai	Hue	885149
Phuoc Vinh	Phuoc Vinh	960495
Plateau Gi	Chuong Nghia	083146
Plei Djerang SF Camp	Polei Yome	857535
Pleiku	Pleiku	770470
Plei Me SF Camp	Xuong Kuang	163059
Plei Trap Valley	Polei Jar Sieng	785915
Quan Loi	An Loc	820908
The Razorback	Tri Tam	500560
Suoi Ca Mountains	Hoai An, Tien Thuan	
Utah/Wunder Beach	Thon Ngo Xa Dong	499560
Vinh Thanh SF Camp	Tien Thuan	615605

About the Author

 Steve Hassett grew up in upstate New York and enlisted in the Army and volunteered for Vietnam when he was 19 years old. Steve served twelve months with Charlie Company in 1966-1967 as a machine gunner, rifleman and squad leader and then spent most of 1968 in South Korea as an intelligence analyst with the 8th Army. After his discharge, he attended college on the GI Bill and became active with Vietnam Veterans Against the War. Steve eventually went into law and spent most of his career with the Washington State Attorney General's Office, working in child protection, child welfare and juvenile law. He currently lives in Buffalo NY with his wife Marie.

CPSIA information can be obtained
at www.ICGtesting.com
Printed in the USA
LVHW040814160623
749954LV00044B/285